Linux® Routing

D0890283

Contents At a Glance

Linux® Routing

Joe Brockmeier
Dee-Ann LeBlanc
Ron McCarty

New Riders

www.newriders.com

201 West 103rd Street, Indianapolis, Indiana 46290
An Imprint of Pearson Education
Boston • Indianapolis • London • Munich • New York • San Francisco

Linux® Routing

Trademarks

Warning and Disclaimer

Publisher
David Dwyer

Associate Publisher
Stephanie Wall

Managing Editor
Kristy Knoop

Acquisitions Editor
Ann Quinn

Development Editor
Chris Zahn

Product Marketing Manager
Stephanie Layton

Publicity Manager
Susan Nixon

Copy Editor
Chrissy Andry

Indexer
Joy Dean Lee

Manufacturing Coordinator
Jim Conway

Book Designer
Louisa Klucznik

Cover Designer
Aren Howell
Brainstorm Design, Inc.

Proofreader
Stacia Mellinger

Composition
Ron Wise

From Joe:
This book is dedicated to all the developers and people who develop and use GNU/Linux and Free Software because they believe in working towards something that benefits everyone— not just their own bank account.

From Dee-Ann:
To my mom, who told me that one can never dedicate too many books to one's mother!

From Ron:
I would like to dedicate Linux Routing *to my wife, Claudia.*

Table of Contents

About the Authors

Joe "Zonker" Brockmeier has been using Linux since 1996 and writing nearly as long. A refugee from radio broadcasting, Zonker writes regularly for *Linux Magazine* and *UnixReview.com* and has written for a number of other online and print publications. His home computer collection is completely out of control, and he spends too much time watching gangster movies and *The Sopranos*.

Dee-Ann LeBlanc is the author and co-author of ten computer books, with more on the way. She specializes in Linux and has written such books as *Linux Install, Configuration Little Black Book*, *General Linux I Exam Prep*, *Linux System Administration Black Book* for The Coriolis Group, and *Linux for Dummies* Third Edition for IDG/Hungry Minds. She was also one of the first to attain her RedHat Certified Engineer certificate, and has written a growing number of technical articles for clients such as ElementK Journals and IBM.

On the education front, Dee-Ann teaches Linux, UNIX, and other computer-related topics both online and in person. She also presents at conferences and develops online course materials for institutions such as DigitalThink—specifically, part of their popular RedHat series. The combination of these three different occupations (writer, teacher, and course developer) helps Dee-Ann stay in touch with what people really want and need to know when learning Linux and its associated tools.

In her copious spare time, Dee-Ann works on a medieval fantasy novel, is walked by her dog Zorro, and squeezes in a few minutes to spend time with her husband Rob and see the beautiful scenery in BC, Canada. She also is involved in the Society for Technical Communications and the Vancouver Linux Users Group, when time permits.

You can contact Dee-Ann through email at `dee@renaissoft.com`, and surf her web site at `http://www.Dee-AnnLeBlanc.com/`.

Ronald W. McCarty, Jr. is a Senior System Engineer for Sonus Networks, an industry leader in next-generation networking. His current responsibilities include presale design and support of carrier class network products. Ronald has published articles on the RADIUS protocol, IP security including intrusion detection, and other networking subjects. He currently writes the monthly column "Net Admin" for *Sys Admin* magazine.

About the Technical Reviewers

These reviewers contributed their considerable hands-on expertise to the entire development process for *Linux Routing*. As the book was being written, these dedicated professionals reviewed all the material for technical content, organization, and flow. Their feedback was critical to ensuring that *Linux Routing* fits our reader's need for the highest-quality technical information.

Brad Harris has been involved in the IT industry for six years, beginning with his work with the Department of Defense developing biometrics models. He continued his work with DODD penetrating and attacking medium and high assurance networks. He has an extensive background in networking protocols, operating system internals, and various programming languages. His strengths include security analysis, vulnerability and exploit discovery and creation, reverse engineering, and securing systems and networks. He is currently a senior software engineer for ACS, Inc., where he specializes in vulnerability development and system/network penetration.

Joseph Hamm is a freelance technology consultant with experience in engineering and deploying IP-based communications solutions. The past year Joseph has focused on design and deployment of Cisco VoIP solutions including network and cable plant implementation, gateway configuration, dial plan construction, and call processing system implementation. At this time, Joseph is spending the majority of his time researching and writing about the evolution of computing platforms and operating systems.

Acknowledgments

From Joe:

Being an author has many advantages, not the least of which is being able to publicly thank the important people in your life when you finish a book.

I'd like to thank my family for being...well, my family. A big thanks also to Denise Bay and her family for being a great "second family."

Thanks to all of my friends who listen to me talk about Linux and computers without obvious signs of boredom. It's greatly appreciated! Bonnie, Suzanne, Jason, Pete, Bevin, Barb, you're all great.

A huge thanks to the *Linux Magazine* folks, Adam, Lara and Bob the "Big Beer Guy." (You thought I'd forgotten?) It's huge fun working with you all. Also a big thanks to the folks at *UnixReview.com*, for being great to work with.

I've met a lot of people in the GNU/Linux Community in the last three years who are very important to me. Even though I don't get to see or talk to you regularly, I'm glad that I've been lucky enough to be involved with GNU/Linux over the last several years.

From Dee-Ann:

I would first like to thank the members of the IP Multicast mailing list available from www.stardust.com/multicast for their great help as I was trying to familiarize myself with IP Multicasting. It's thanks to them that I was able to cover some of the subtleties of what protocols are used when, and so on. I'd also like to thank the folks who peer-reviewed what I intended to cover before the writing started. Their comments helped to shape much of what you find in this book.

Additional thanks go to the technical reviewers who helped keep me on my toes throughout the project. It's their job not only to keep me from looking silly with putting large mistakes in print, but also to make sure that you, the reader, get the most benefit possible from the pages within.

Last but not least, I would like to thank my co-authors, Joe and Ron. I was ill through a good part of this project, and after a long search we brought these two fine gentlemen in to ensure that not only was the book finished in a timely manner, but that it remained the best possible quality and usefulness to the readers. This book is far greater than the sum total of its parts thanks in part to their hard work.

From Ron:

Special thanks to the technical reviewers, Brad Harris and Joseph Hamm.

From Dee-Ann, Ron, and Joe:

We would like to thank Chris Zahn, the Development Editor, and Ann Quinn, the Acquisitions Editor, for the professional insight and diligence that they showed in working to create the book you are reading. Thanks to rest of the team at New Riders who also helped make this book possible—Stephanie Wall, Kristy Knoop, Chrissy Andry, Joy Dean Lee, and Ron Wise.

Tell Us What You Think

As the reader of this book, you are the most important critic and commentator. We value your opinion and want to know what we're doing right, what we could do better, what areas you'd like to see us publish in, and any other words of wisdom you're willing to pass our way.

As Associate Publisher at New Riders Publishing, I welcome your comments. You can fax, email, or write me directly to let me know what you did or didn't like about this book—as well as what we can do to make our books stronger.

Please note that I cannot help you with technical problems related to the topic of this book, and that due to the high volume of mail I receive, I might not be able to reply to every message.

When you write, please be sure to include this book's title and author as well as your name and phone or fax number. I will carefully review your comments and share them with the author and editors who worked on the book.

Fax: 317-581-4663

Email: stephanie.wall@newriders.com

Mail: Stephanie Wall
          Associate Publisher
          New Riders Publishing
          201 West 103rd Street
          Indianapolis, IN 46290 USA

Introduction

In the Linux world, when we talk about routing we're usually just referring to utilizing the route command to set up some nice, simple data delivery information. A Linux box is capable of so much more. With the proper setup and tuning, you can build a stable and efficient router for your network and its subnets. *Linux Routing* gives you the background and techniques you need to choose the appropriate routing protocol(s), configure the routing daemon(s), add security and obfuscation to protect your data and machines, fine tune the kernel for this very task-specific setup, and even monitor your traffic and adjust it to make it more efficient.

What's Inside?

Because so many Linux administrators haven't had to tackle the ins and outs of routing protocols, multicasting, IPv4's classless addressing possibilities, and more, this book begins with a thorough discussion of much background information that you must understand before you can easily proceed with the rest. To this end, we've broken this book into Parts for simpler navigation:

- Part I, "Routing Basics," contains Chapters 1 through 4.
- Part II, "Linux Routing Issues and Technologies," contains Chapters 5 through 15.
- Part III, "Appendixes," contains Appendix A and B.

From there, it's the individual chapters that are of interest, so let's take a look.

Chapter 1, "Unicast Protocols"

As the saying goes, it's usually best to begin at the beginning. The unicast routing protocols contain some of the oldest Internet protocols that are still in use. This chapter introduces an example network used throughout Part I to give you a consistent framework to compare and contrast how these protocols work—and how they work is covered in detail. Specifically, it covers static routing and the protocols: RIP version 1 (RIP-1), RIP version 2 (RIP-2), and OSPF version 2.

Chapter 2, "Multicast Protocols"

Not everyone is content to stick with unicast. This chapter covers the most popular multicast routing protocols. Once again, we use the example network to discuss how each of these works so that you have a solid framework from which to decide which of these you want to implement. Specifically, this chapter covers the multicasting features of RIP-2, plus the following multicast protocols: DVMRP, MOSPF, PIM-DM, and PIM-SM.

Chapter 3, "Introduction to Border Routing Protocols"

While the previous two chapters focus on what you're doing in your own little part of the world, there has to be a way as well for your networks to talk to others. Without such a method there would be no Internet. This chapter focuses on both unicast and multicast protocols where implementations are available for Linux use. These protocols are: EGP, BGP, BGMP, and MSDP.

Chapter 4, "IPv4 and IPv6 Addressing"

Many Linux aficionados know the standard ins and outs of IPv4 addressing. This chapter begins with a thorough look at IPv4 subnetting for those who have never had to learn the math behind it and have just used certain set solutions in the past. Then, we move into new territory. The next item is IPv4 Classless InterDomain Routing (CIDR), which allows you to break up your addressing space without sticking to class A, B, and C boundaries.

Finally, it's time to get familiar with IPv6 before the transition takes you by surprise. We take a look at the basics of working with this addressing system so you'll know how to recognize types of addresses, break IPv6 addresses down into their hexadecimal components, and more.

Chapter 5, "Inside the Unicast Kernel 2.2.x Daemons"

There are a fair number of daemons available for routing in Linux. If we were to have covered them all in depth, then that would have filled the entire book. So in this chapter, we take a look in great detail at good old `routed` and the public version of `gated`. Here you'll learn not only about these daemons, but everything there is to know about configuring them. When it comes to `gated`, this means you'll learn how to set it up for all of the unicast protocols that you've learned about so far. Pointers to the other potential routing daemons are included.

Chapter 6, "Inside the Multicast Kernel 2.2.x Daemons"

Multicasting data is a growing movement, but it has not yet reached the mainstream proportion that its proponents would like. This chapter covers two different multicasting daemons available for Linux. One of these is `mrouted`, which is typically used to connect to the MBONE—the multicast backbone—because it implements the DVMRP protocol; and the other is `pimd`, which is used for most other multicast applications because it supports the PIM-SM protocol.

Chapter 7, "Kernel Support Tools"

Not all networks and individual machines are connected to one another through Ethernet cabling. Some our WANs and other solutions require dial-up networking, and this more often than not requires making use of our old friend PPP. In this chapter, you learn the ins and outs of this protocol and what it's capable of, as well as how to utilize the pppd daemon for Linux PPP connections. After that, you learn about rip2ad, the daemon that lets you add some basic RIP-2 routing functionality to your PPP connection.

Chapter 8, "Kernel 2.4.x Routing Daemons"

There are far too many tools to cover in just this one book. In this chapter, we take a look at additional items such as zebra and iproute2, and also take a look at the differences between the kernel 2.2.x series and 2.4.x series from the point of view of routing.

Chapter 9, "Inside the Commands"

Linux has a suite of commands that most of us have used already to handle our networking needs. However, most of these tools are actually far more complex than many people realize. This chapter covers the detailed innards of arp, ifconfig, netstat, ping, route, tcpdump, and traceroute. These tools will all serve you well in your networking and routing needs.

Chapter 10, "Planning Basic Router Layout and Function"

Here's where we really get into the *how* of routing. Before you get into the actual implementation, you need to have put some serious thought into how you intend to keep your own routing tables manageable and how you plan to help not contribute to the overall Internet's tables. By the time you finish this chapter you should be just about ready to start setting up your router.

Chapter 11, "Linux Routing Basics"

If you picked up this book, you probably don't have a simple network setup. You've got some complicated LAN, a WAN, or even a VPN that you're trying to get working as a single routing unit. This chapter tackles the ins and outs of getting the various popular network types to route seamlessly, which helps with your security because people don't realize that the machines aren't all in the same building.

Chapter 12, "Network Hardware Components, Technology, and Solutions"

Networks—especially ones that connect to the Internet—don't work without telecommunications hardware. Not only does this chapter cover the various methods of making connections, such as over cable modems and DSL, it also discusses the various kinds of setups you might use to allow remote administration of networks. In addition, there is discussion of the types of router interfaces that exist for digital data transfer.

Chapter 13, "Building a Routing Kernel"

Whenever you intend to use a machine for a single purpose, or even just a few specific tasks, it's important to remove as much extraneous functionality as possible. This concern applies not just to programs, but to the kernel as well. Once you've pulled out everything you know you don't need, there's more to do—namely, enabling any number of esoteric features that you otherwise wouldn't need. This chapter covers building a custom kernel for your Linux router.

Chapter 14, "Security and NAT Issues"

Routing just by itself doesn't have anything to do with helping to secure your network. A router just ensures that your data gets where it needs to go. This chapter covers many of the tools you have available to turn your routing machine into your network's first line of defense, including packet filtering and mangling, IP masquerading, and NAT.

Chapter 15, "Monitoring, Analyzing, and Controlling Network Traffic"

In this chapter, we take a step back from the actual routing of data and look at the tools available for Linux that allow us to gather information on how efficient our network is and make corrections to any problems we find. Tools such as SNMP, MRTG, and IPtraf are included, as well as information on how to set quality of service (QoS) rules.

Appendix A, "Linux Routing Resources"

This appendix is dedicated to helping you quickly locate the many programs mentioned in this book, as well as others we didn't get to. There are also pointers to the central documents used to define how various Internet and networking protocols work and mentions of various additional resources that might be of use to you in your networking pursuits.

Because things change so rapidly in the networking world, consider these items a jumping-off point to start from.

Appendix B, "Linux Hardware Routing Solutions"

This appendix is dedicated to routing appliances with Linux under the hood and network cards that you can utilize with Linux to build a router. As the Linux market matures, we expect that this list will grow significantly.

Who Is This Book For?

This book is for experienced Linux users and administrators who are interested in utilizing Linux to implement routing solutions that go beyond very simple static networking and subnetting. If you want to go beyond routing into heavier firewalling tactics, then check out the New Riders book *Linux Firewalls*, by Robert Ziegler.

Who Is This Book Not For?

This book is not for Linux or networking novices. There are few if any instructions about how to compile and install the packages mentioned because you are expected to know how to do this already. There is coverage of IP addressing and subnetting but simple IPv4 class addressing is not the focus. If you are interested in this field but find that by looking through this book you feel unsure, consider beginning with the following New Riders titles: *Networking Linux: A Practical Guide to TCP/IP* by Pat Eyler, *Inside Linux* by Michael Tobler, *Vi IMproved—Vim* by Steven Oualline, and *Linux System Administration* by M. Carling, Stephen Degler, and Jim Dennis.

Conventions

The following typographical conventions are used in this book:

- Monospaced font indicates code, output, filenames, web sites, command prompts, commands, and options.
- Italicized font indicates a variable where you should substitute a value of your own choosing.
- Code continuation characters ➥ appear where the line would not ordinarily break but had to be broken to fit on the printed page.

I

Routing Basics

Unicast Protocols

MANY PEOPLE HAVE ONLY A VAGUE IDEA of what routing is and how it works. When the knowledgeable Linux user or novice system administrator thinks of routing, he or she thinks of it in terms of a black box that takes chunks of data, looks at where the data is trying to go, and sends the data happily skipping along in the right direction. This in some ways is not far from the truth.

A router is basically a traffic director. When data travels throughout IP networks, as well as in many other kinds of networks, many different paths are usually available for it to take. Data is bundled in *packets*—the individual units of data that are sent over an IP network. In general, a router's job is to choose the current best path for the packet to follow to get to its destination.

Exactly how the router makes this decision is determined by the routing protocol used. Each protocol has its own way of keeping track of what paths are available and which are the most efficient. A unicast routing protocol, in particular, sends information directly to the other routers it is configured to talk to. This class of protocols is a solid choice for networks where bandwidth is at a premium. You must, however, be very careful to ensure that all routing protocols know what routers they are supposed to talk to.

If you want to get right into how to set things up, you can proceed to Chapter 10, "Planning Basic Router Layout and Function" and go from there. However, it's important that you understand the protocols enough to make an educated choice that best suits your networking needs.

The Example Network

It's easier to follow a theoretical discussion if there is a real world example thrown into the mix. For this purpose, I have added a sample network that you can refer back to throughout *Linux Routing*.

The Internet is one huge IP network. As you probably already know, every machine on such a network has its own IP address in the format, xxx.xxx.xxx.xxx, except in cases where private addressing schemes are used, such as 192.168.xxx.xxx and 10.xxx.xxx.xxx. However, the entire Internet is a bit large to use in the discussion here. Instead, I'll define a smaller network set to work with while learning how specific routing protocols work. I will then use this same example network in the chapters where things are actually set up. The starting point will be the Linux machine, "Red," which has the private range IP address, 192.168.15.10.

A lone machine, of course, is not in and of itself a useful or interesting network. Perhaps this Linux box is on the mixed-operating system LAN presented in Figure 1.1, having the private class C address space 192.168.15.0 all to itself. Which operating systems these machines are running doesn't matter at this point. Many people don't realize that any operating system that natively speaks TCP/IP (most modern operating systems) can share a TCP/IP Ethernet connection with any other operating system without a problem. It's sharing data and files that causes the headache.

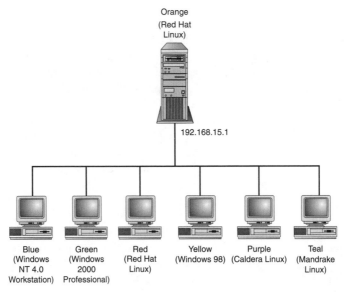

Figure 1.1   The Linux box, Red, within the network 192.168.15.0.

When an application tries to send or retrieve data within the network, for example when sending data from our starting point at Red to Teal (both Linux machines), a routing protocol is unnecessary. Machines within the same subnetwork or unsubnetted network use other techniques to find each other. It's when you pass outside of that subnet or unsubnetted network that routing becomes an issue.

Now, to connect this network to a larger set of networks you add a new network card with the address 192.168.15.1 to the machine, Orange, as shown in Figure 1.2. These two separate network interfaces are absolutely necessary when you start spanning from one subnet or unsubnetted network to another, whether the interfaces are physical or virtual. In this case, one (192.168.15.1) connects to the Internet. The other (192.168.15.2) connects to the internal network.

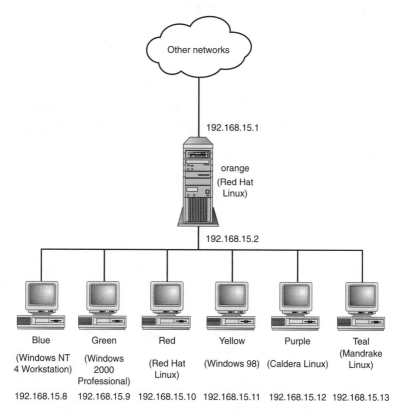

Figure 1.2   The network 192.168.15.0 connected to the other networks in the office.

These simpler structures will be needed later for setup discussions, but this book is about routing with Linux, therefore a larger example is required—something that actually requires routers. Next, this LAN will be connected to the machine, Emerald, in another part of the building as shown in Figure 1.3.

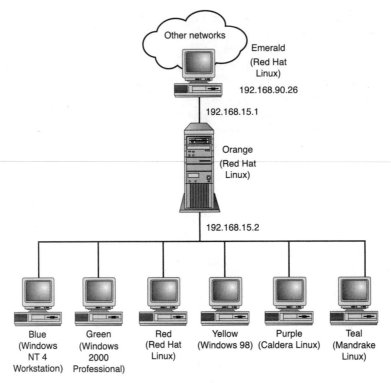

Figure 1.3   The main LAN connecting to Emerald elsewhere.

Now we're starting to get somewhere! Emerald is on an entirely different network than Red—192.168.90.x instead of 192.168.15.x. Routers become necessary as you start crossing network boundaries. The data has to know how to get to each network and subnetwork.

An overall network at any location may consist of a single LAN with an internal class C, such as our 192.168.90, or it may be a collection of smaller networks and subnetworks. If the network is connected to the Internet, as most seem to be these days, it connects somewhere along the way to an Internet Service Provider (ISP). An ISP may have tens, dozens, hundreds, or even thousands of networks and machines directly attached to it. Many of these networks also might have their own subnetworks and lead to yet more networks, perhaps even through a backup link to another ISP with its own collection of thousands of networks.

Imagine that you have a packet that needs to get from "here" to "there." How fast or slow this data travels does not matter. How geographically far it needs to go does not matter. The only thing that matters is network boundaries. At the moment that a packet must cross from one subnetwork or unsubnetted network to another, it needs help knowing where to go.

Let's take a look at how this works. One day you send data from Red to a machine named Abacus out on another of your networks. A name lookup tells TCP/IP that the packets need to go from 192.168.15.10 (Red) to 192.169.13.9 (Abacus). Your packet reaches 192.168.90.26 (Emerald), and the only information this packet has associated with it is that it needs to go to 192.168.13.9. The packet itself has no idea whether the network 192.168.13 is in your collection of networks, attached to someone else on the same ISP, on another ISP, where it is physically in the world, or where it is in the overall structure of all of the networks in the world. That is not a packet's job in TCP/IP. Other machines, protocols, and tools handle how to make the trip.

Fortunately, Emerald is one of these special tools—a router. The routing protocol(s) it uses are not important at the moment and will change throughout the discussion of routing protocols in this chapter and the next. Regardless of the protocol used, each one decides how to give this packet a customized roadmap. Figure 1.4 rounds out the structure needed for the examples, adding a few routers in the middle along with the end destination. This example is set on a fictitious campus with Emerald as a department router within the Chem building and Abacus as a departmental router in the Math building.

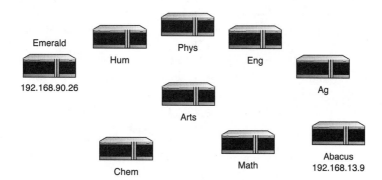

Figure 1.4   The path from Emerald to Abacus, with the main building routers in between.

The physical connections between each of these routers, as outlined in Table 1.1, are going to become important as we discuss how the protocols work.

Table 1.1   **Hardware Between Each Point in the Example Network**

Start	End	Connection Type	Speed
Emerald	Hum	ISDN dual channel	128Kbps
Hum	Phys	T1/DS1 full 24 channels	1.54Mbps
Hum	Chem	T1/DS1 full 24 channels	1.54Mbps
Hum	Arts	DSL	3Mbps
Chem	Math	ISDN single channel	64Kbps

continues

Table 1.1 **Continued**

Start	End	Connection Type	Speed
Phys	Arts	T3/DS3	44.736Mbps
Arts	Math	T3/DS3	44.736Mbps
Arts	Eng	T3/DS3	44.736Mbps
Eng	Ag	T1/DS1 full 24 channels	1.54Mbps
Math	Ag	T1/DS1 full 24 channels	1.54Mbps
Ag	Abacus	ISDN dual channel	128Kbps
Math	Abacus	modem	56Kbps

Static Routing

The simplest form of data routing is *static routing*. You've probably used it, even though you may not recognize the term. In static routing, you create a routing table that simply stays as it is until you tell it to change. There is no attempt by the software to ensure that the routers listed remain valid or to watch for any changes in the network topology. You have to do it all by hand.

Static routing, however, is only useful in limited situations. Because you have to maintain a separate static table on each machine involved manually, you can probably imagine how much work it requires to make any form of changes in a large network. This problem is made worse when you are pressed for time, for example when you are trying to alter the tables to route around connectivity problems.

Static routing under Linux involves assigning route information with the `route` command and is covered in almost all Linux books that include networking skills. This command is covered more in depth in Chapter 6, "Inside the Multicast Kernel 2.2.x Daemons," and the `routed` daemon that goes with it in Chapter 5, "Inside the Unuicast Kernel 2.2.x Daemons."

Routing Information Protocol Version 1 (RIP-1)

The Routing Information Protocol (RIP) was the first of the TCP/IP routing protocols used on what is now the Internet. There are two versions of this protocol available today: RIP-1 and RIP-2. Both of these versions are still important in today's routing schemes—the first for backward compatibility and the second because of its broader range of capabilities.

The Algorithm

Let's separate out the algorithm behind RIP-1 from the protocol itself for a moment. RIP-1 uses a *distance vector algorithm* to determine where to send packets, and a number of newer routing protocols have followed suit. To be specific, RIP-1 uses the Bellman-Ford algorithm to make its computations. This algorithm begins with the source location, which is a single point when we ignore the routing aspect. It assigns the distance from the source point to itself as zero. The distance to all other points is assumed to be infinite.

The major assumption applied is that there is at least one way to get from any point in the system to the source point; no points are completely isolated from the source. Furthermore, the path to the source point ends when it reaches the source point. It does not travel through it, around some more, and then back. It also cannot travel the same path twice.

The goal of this algorithm is to find the shortest total travel distance from any single point to the source point. Bellman-Ford works in iterations. To start, take a look at the graph points in Figure 1.5 (you should recognize these from Figure 1.4).

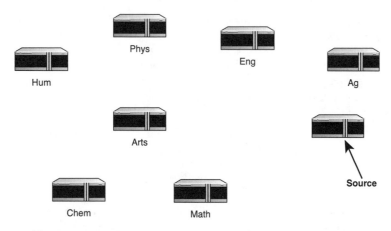

Figure 1.5   Graph points for Bellman-Ford algorithm demonstration.

The algorithm maps the path from the remote points to the source points for each iteration using a specific number of jumps and the distance for each jump. Iteration one results in Figure 1.6.

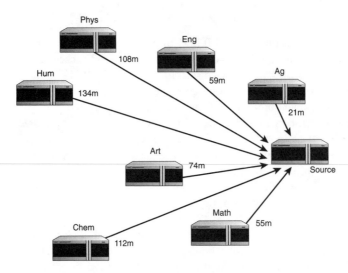

Figure 1.6   First Bellman-Ford iteration for the specified graph.

The moment you get past just one jump, you have to start looking for more than just the correct number of iterations. In each case, the total distance must be as short as possible from the destination point to the source point. As you get into two jumps (Figure 1.7), three jumps (Figure 1.8), and more, you refine the determination of what exactly is the fastest way to get from any point to the source point.

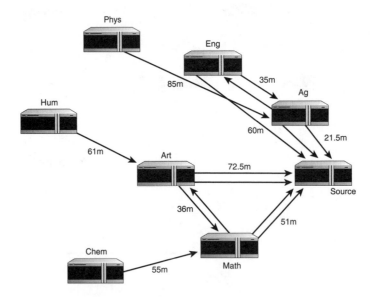

Figure 1.7   Second Bellman-Ford iteration for the specified graph.

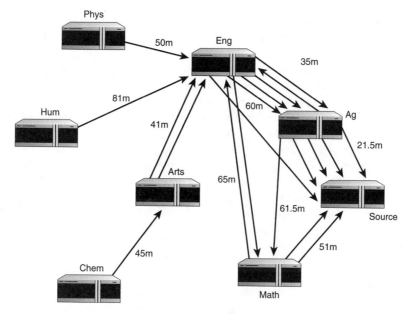

Figure 1.8   Third Bellman-Ford iteration for the specified graph.

Examine these first three iterations only for now. Table 1.2 outlines the total distance it takes to get from each point to the source per iteration, using the point labels shown in Figure 1.5.

Table 1.2   **Breakdown of Travel Distances for Three Bellman-Ford Iterations**

Point	Iteration 1 (m)	Iteration 2 (m)	Iteration 3 (m)
Ag	21	95	147.5
Eng	59	56.5	147.5
Phys	108	106.5	106.5
Hum	134	133.5	137.5
Arts	74	87	97.5
Chem	112	106	146
Math	55	108.5	121.5

Notice the wildly varying results in this table. In some cases, the shortest distance is one jump. In others, it's two. None in this example benefit from three iterations, although Phys comes close. This is not always the case, however. It really depends on the spread of the points. Completing the example would require four more iterations, a total of seven, just as there are seven points not counting the source point.

Of course, RIP-1 uses this algorithm from the perspective of TCP/IP routing. When you are trying to find the fastest way to get from "here" to "there" from a routing point of view, distance is not the only factor to consider. Another important issue is that of how long it takes the data to travel from connection to connection. The shortest physical distance is not always the fastest route.

Rather than referring to a purely physical distance between points A and B, the distance in RIP-1 is a weight value defining how long it will take information to travel if it jumps between the two points in question. Originally, all distances were listed as one. This is meant as a *hop count*—with each router the data must pass through being one "hop." Distances used today are more varied, with the number being slightly higher for cases where data has to travel along a very slow connection to get to the next point or other reasons that might cause delays.

Let's return to Figure 1.8 from the example network and the data in Table 1.1. The first thing you might do is go through this table and assign the distance or cost of traveling between each of the points. One example of what you might end up with is shown in Figure 1.9.

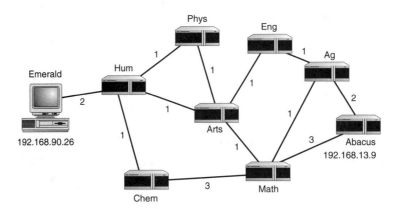

Figure 1.9   RIP-1 speed factors applied to the example network.

There are two things to notice here. First, there is not a path from every point to every point as there would be in the raw Bellman-Ford algorithm. The only valid paths are the ones where there are physical connections in place. Second, notice that distances are not assigned exactly according to speed. Anything at least the speed of a T1 line received a one, and from there down the costs increased. A number of approaches can be taken when assigning distances. This is just one of them.

You are in charge of Emerald. For each destination in your routing table—in this case, Abacus and the main campus routers—you must enter the information regarding where to send data to get to that destination. Let's start with the longest piece of travel, from Emerald to Abacus. Using the Bellman-Ford algorithm, iterate using the number of jumps. There is no single-jump direct route available. Neither is there a two-jump route, nor a three, but there are four-jump paths:

A) Emerald → Hum → Chem → Math → Abacus

B) Emerald → Hum → Arts → Math → Abacus

There are also five-jump paths:

C) Emerald → Hum → Phys → Arts → Math → Abacus

D) Emerald → Hum → Chem → Math → Ag → Abacus

Six-jumps paths:

E) Emerald → Hum → Phys → Arts → Eng → Ag → Abacus

F) Emerald → Hum → Phys → Arts → Math → Ag → Abacus

G) Emerald → Hum → Arts → Eng → Ag → Math → Abacus

Seven-jump paths:

H) Emerald → Hum → Chem → Math → Arts → Eng → Ag → Abacus

I) Emerald → Hum → Phys → Arts → Eng → Ag → Math → Abacus

And, finally, the eight-jump path:

J) Emerald → Hum → Chem → Math → Arts → Eng → Ag → Math → Abacus

Table 1.3 lays out the cost of each of these paths. As you can see, the quickest path for this packet to follow is B—with C, E, and F all good second choices. Notice what a difference the weighted values make. If every hop were worth one, as they were originally, you would always go with either A or B, while A is among the third longest "distances" the data can travel.

Table 1.3 **Travel Cost for Example Network Using Bellman-Ford**

Jump	Values	Total
A	2+1+3+3	9
B	2+1+1+3	7
C	2+1+1+1+3	8
D	2+1+3+1+2	9
E	2+1+1+1+1+2	8
F	2+1+1+1+1+2	8
G	2+1+1+1+1+3	9
H	2+1+3+1+1+1+2	11
I	2+1+1+1+1+1+3	10
J	2+1+3+1+1+1+1+3	13

One thing to be aware of with RIP-1 is that you cannot have more than fifteen jumps if you use the value of one per jump rule. This protocol is not designed to carry data for longer distances than that. We hit the limit just in this one small example. With some of the jumps weighted higher than one, the largest total we get here is 13.

You might wonder then what use this protocol is if it cannot handle more than 15 jumps or a value of 15 total cost. RIP-1 is not used to handle the majority of Internet traffic. Its purpose is to work within network groups, such as an office building or campus with complex network structures, where RIP-1 is there only at the most local levels.

RIP-1 is also often the least common denominator protocol. While you may have no specific reason to use this protocol for your own needs, you may need your routers to be able to communicate with outside routers that do not use your primary choice of routing protocols. RIP-1 is often considered a kind of insurance policy in these situations.

A router running RIP-1 keeps its data in a *routing table*. This table stores information on:

- **Network gateways**. Machines containing more than one network interface (such as an Ethernet card or using an IP with an alias under Linux), with each interface leading to a different subnet or network.
- **Routers**. The traffic directors on the Information Superhighway.
- **Hosts**. Individual machines that require special mention, such as remote machines in a WAN or VPN.

The router then occasionally sends copies of its routing tables to its direct neighbors, and it receives updates from them as well. Whenever a router receives an updated table from one of its neighbors, it calculates whether there have been any changes in the cost metrics applied downstream. For example, say that Emerald received an update from the router at Hum. Our router knows that the cost of the trip from itself to Hum is two. The Emerald RIP-1 tool then adds two to all of the items in the table it just received and compares them against its own. The following list describes the actual values contained within the RIP-1 routing table:

- The TCP/IP network address or host IP address referred to
- The gateway that must be traveled through to get to this address
- The hardware interface that must be traveled through to get to the gateway
- The route cost
- The time since this entry was last updated

If one or more of the results from Emerald and Hum's tables do not add up, there has been a change in the metrics. Any new values received from Hum are copied, have two added to them, and then are placed in Emerald's routing table as a new metric value.

There Can Be Only One

Notice that there is only one entry for each destination in the RIP-1 routing table. RIP-1 stores only the current best path of travel; it does not store the entire results of the algorithm calculation.

The Bellman-Ford algorithm does not have to deal with the fact that some of the points may become permanently or temporarily unavailable. RIP-1 does, however, avoid the risk of sending packets on a road to nowhere if a particular connection or machine goes down or is removed.

The update message discussed previously is sent every 30 seconds in RIP-1. Whenever an update is received from a particular machine, the time since update is changed in the routing table for that single machine. After 180 seconds of silence from that particular machine, it is assumed that there is a problem, and the router is marked in the table as unavailable by setting the distance to this destination as 16, one higher than the maximum cost.

How It Works

Now, let me set up an example. As I mentioned before, Emerald needs to send data through Abacus. All Emerald knows is that to get data to the appropriate network (192.168.13.x), it needs to send that data through the interface that leads to router Hum. Hum knows that the fastest way for it to send data to network 192.168.13 is through Arts. Arts knows to send the data through Math, and Math knows it can send directly to Abacus.

This data path works great until Hum does not hear from the router at Arts for 180 seconds, which is a series of six check-in times. Router Hum then marks Arts as unreachable and passes this information to Emerald. As a result Emerald doesn't know how to send any data to Abacus! Remember, there is only one method of getting from here to there kept in the RIP-1 routing tables.

Several different things could be going on here:

- Router Arts was intentionally removed. It had a critical failure, and there is no backup router available to take its place for a week.

  Because it can take a long time for news to travel from router to router in RIP-1, the administrator in Emerald's section explicitly tells router Phys that the new cost for router Arts is 16, which means that it is not available. After the usual 30 seconds, router Phys sends out its updates. These updates include all of the routes that are available through Phys.

  Phys's only neighbor now is Hum. Phys sends Hum its list of networks to which it knows how to send information, as well as the costs to get to those networks. Included in this list is the fact that it now costs 16 units to get to Arts through Phys. Router Hum knows that it costs one to get from Hum to Phys, so it adds the two costs together and updates the cost for data to go to from Hum to Arts to a total of 17. Hum doesn't know that it is talking about Arts; it only looks at the networks it can get to fastest through Phys. Phys is not part of the path to get to 192.168.13.x, so Hum still does not know it has a problem. Hum does know, however, that it cannot reach anything that requires it to go through Phys and then Arts.

After 180 seconds of not hearing from Arts, Hum realizes for itself that Arts is unreachable. It now updates its own cost to get data to Arts to 16. The problem now is that this is the only way Hum knew to get data to 192.168.13.x. Any data that comes from Emerald with the destination 192.168.13.x is going to get bounced back or simply lost in the great void of networking problems. The same happens with all of the other routers, eventually, when they need to send data through Arts.

- Router Arts was intentionally removed. It is not going to be replaced with anything else. The administrator has access to router Chem and updates its tables to advertise routes through Math that replace the invalid routes through Arts.

The administrator for router Chem removes Arts from its routing tables and recalculates the distance vector. In its usual 30-second update after the change, Chem tells its neighbors—Math and Hum—that they can get to the networks that became unreachable through it. The cost from Chem to Abacus through Math is six (3+3), so this is the cost that Chem advertises in the routing table to get to 192.168.13.x. Hum knows that its cost to get to Chem is one, so it now tells Emerald and Phys about the cool new path to 192.168.13.x at a cost of seven (3+3+1). This change spreads through the network as well until everything is fully operational once again.

- The connection Arts uses to access the network went down temporarily, isolating this router, the machines on its own network, and any networks that it is supposed to pass data to from everyone else. This connection stays down for three hours.

By the time the connection comes back up, all of the neighbor routers have long since noticed that Arts was unavailable and have passed the information along to all of the other routers in the example network. When router Arts's connection comes back up, it will have decided that all of the other routers are unavailable as well.

The details regarding this scenario are discussed later in this section.

At least one problem might become obvious from the scenarios listed above. Routers send updates to all of their neighbors, even the ones from which they just received an update. If a router blindly trusts what its neighbor tells it, this problem can wreak all kinds of havoc. Routers that have marked another router as unreachable might be told by neighbors that it, in fact, is working fine—when it's not. In the meantime, packets of data are being sent all over the place and are getting lost while the routers continue to disagree.

A technique often used to solve this dilemma in routing protocols is *split horizon*. This addition simply uses a common sense rule: Do not send updates about a route to the router from which you just heard the news. For example, consider the problem of

Arts going down again. In Scenario 1, an administrator tells router Phys that Arts is no longer accessible. Thirty seconds later router Phys has incorporated this data into its tables, marking certain networks as unreachable through it, and shares this information with its neighbors, which now turn out to be just Hum.

Thirty seconds later, Hum has incorporated the data into its tables and has marked certain networks as unreachable through it, and Hum now informs its neighbors. This would now be Phys, Emerald, and Chem. However, it received the news from Phys. Due to split horizon, Hum sends an update to all of the machines but only sends information involving data that has to go through Phys to Emerald and Chem. After all, Hum has other information that does not pass through Phys, and Phys has to be kept up to date about that.

Then, Chem tells Math about the updates but does not send Hum the items relating to it. From there, Math shares the new information with Ag and Abacus. Abacus gives the new information to Ag because it got the news from Math and not from Ag, and Ag tells Eng. Figure 1.10 illustrates this progression.

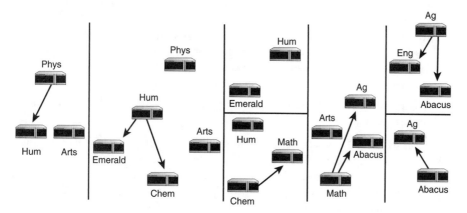

Figure 1.10   Routing tables sharing information through the split horizon method.

This is not a perfect method, but it's more efficient than letting conflicting information bounce back and forth between the same machines. There is still another concern, however. Loops can be formed where a series of routers end up trapping packets accidentally. Because it only prevents updates of routers from which it just received the update, split horizon is not enough to take care of this fact.

RIP-1 uses a combination of split horizon with *poisoned reverse*. In a way, this takes us back to what we were doing originally. Routers send updates about all routes to all neighbors, even the one they just received a particular route from. The difference is that if Phys tells Hum that Arts is back up and the distance is one, Hum then tells

Emerald and Chem that Arts is available and that the cost is two, but Hum tells Phys that
the cost to get to Arts from Hum through Phys is 16. Got that? Let me break it down:

1. Router Arts's network connection comes back up.

2. All machines have given up on router Arts, and router Arts has given up on all
   of the other machines. Therefore, router Arts is not going to send any updates to
   anyone else, and no one is going to send data to Arts.

3. The administrator of router Phys knows Arts is back up. The administrator manually resets Phys's routing table with what the cost to Arts was before it went
   down (one).

4. Thirty seconds later, router Phys sends updates to Hum and Arts. Suddenly Arts
   sees that it is not alone in the world, and Hum finds out that Arts is back up.

5. To simplify things, I am going to ignore Arts for the moment and only follow
   the path from Hum. When using a combination of split horizon with poisoned
   reverse, Hum sends its next 30-second update to Emerald, Phys, Arts, and Chem
   to tell them where it can send data. However, the information sent to Phys is
   different than what is sent to the others. Hum tells Phys about all of the networks it can send data to, including those that pass through Phys. Any items that
   pass through Phys are marked as having a cost of 16. The purpose of this is to
   prevent Phys and Hum from ending up in a perpetual loop, sending data to one
   another that never arrives at its destination.

6. The propagation continues in this manner until all routers are updated and can
   see Arts once again.

As you can see, RIP-1 is a relatively basic routing protocol. It has rudimentary features
for keeping track of which machines are available but would not be reliable in a network where things change often. The program used to implement RIP-1 under Linux
is `routed`. You can also use the multi-protocol daemons `gated` or `zebra`. See Chapter 5
for more information on where to find these programs and how they work.

Routing Information Protocol Version 2 (RIP-2)

RIP version 2 (RIP-2) is an updated version of the original Routing Information
Protocol. There are a few additional features in RIP-2 that make it a far more appropriate routing choice for many network administrators, especially as we continue with
the problem of the IP addressing shortage. The first of these new features is the ability
to add information gleaned from an *Exterior Gateway Protocol* (EGP). See the section,
"Exterior Gateway Protocol," in Chapter 3, "Introduction to Border Routing
Protocols," for more information regarding the data carried from one router to
another.

Essentially, RIP-2 packets contain a backpack into which data from an EGP can be
dropped and carried from router to router. Take another look at the example network
in Figure 1.10. In this image it's shown isolated, yet somewhere along the way this
network talks to the outside world through the Internet.

Let's say that there is a straight line going up from router Phys that leads to the Internet Service Provider (ISP) for this campus's entire network, as shown in Figure 1.11. The example network now magically uses RIP-2 instead of RIP-1.

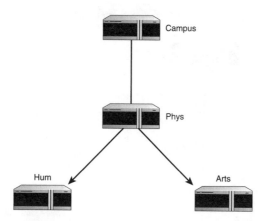

Figure 1.11   The example network's connection to the outside world.

This line leads to a router running a different protocol from your network, which I'll call router zero. Router zero is passed information from another router and includes that information as a little add-on, as shown in Figure 1.12. Much more detail about what might be carried by EGP is provided in Chapter 3.

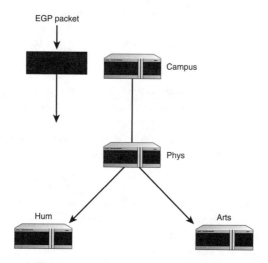

Figure 1.12   Incoming EGP information.

As this data reaches router Phys, RIP-2 is able to accept it and incorporate it into its next 30-second update, as shown in Figure 1.13.

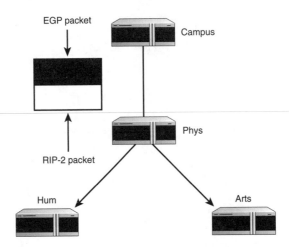

Figure 1.13 RIP-2 carries EGP data piggyback with its own data.

This combined data is then sent to Hum and Arts, and so on. The nice thing about this capability is that it decreases the need for direct administrator intervention; however, it also creates a new problem.

Introducing the ability to obtain and pass information gained from outside sources opens the door for someone to feed the routers false information. Having anticipated this dilemma, another addition to RIP-2 allows for a simple password authentication scheme. You can set your router to accept updates only from those to which you have given the password.

The administrators in our example network trust one another. Rather than agreeing upon one password for all of their routers, they each choose one and notify the administrator of their neighbor routers in writing. Please note that email is most definitely not a secure alternative unless you use encryption such as Pretty Good Privacy (PGP) or Gnome Pretty Good Privacy (GPGP). The administrators then add the American Standard Code for Information Interchange (ASCII) passwords to their configuration files for each of the neighbors. For example, router Phys would have passwords for Campus, Hum, and Arts. If there are neighbors that the administrators do not want to accept updated information from, then the administrator simply does not give out the password to that neighbor's administrator. Data can still pass from router to router; that function is not hampered. That particular neighbor just cannot input data into the routing tables.

Another interesting addition that makes up RIP-2 is the ability to advertise alternative routes that use other protocols to other RIP-2 routers. To utilize this feature, RIP-2 must be running on the same router with the other protocol. Let's look at the sample network again. Routers Chem and Math are heavily subnetworked not only for their individual departments, but for groups inside the departments as well. Therefore, we decide that their networking needs require a different routing protocol than RIP-2. Which protocol we choose specifically doesn't matter for the moment.

If RIP-1 were being used, then Chem and Math wouldn't be able to talk to the others anymore. Sure, data could pass from their neighbors through them, but Chem and Math could not send updates to the other routers about the networks past them. RIP-2 allows for these updates to happen regardless of protocol. Math's administrator then adds a new network behind this router. The administrator adds the information about the new network to Math's routing tables.

Math has no problem informing Chem about the change. Fortunately, even though Chem and Math are using some unknown, as yet not discussed, protocol, Arts, Abacus, and Ag are all using RIP-2. The updates pass through just fine, and eventually all of the routers in the network and beyond find out how to get to this new network.

Finally, the new capability that brings RIP-2 into the next Internet age is its ability to carry subnet mask information. In fact this was the primary reason for building a new version of RIP-1 in the first place. One solution to the IP addressing shortage is the use of variable subnet masks rather than using a single mask for an entire network. The original RIP-1 was unable to comprehend this type of setup.

As you can see, RIP-2 is a more sophisticated version of RIP-1 that handles updating information slightly better and also speaks the language of the modern Internet. However, this is still not a protocol for a huge set of networks. It really is meant for more limited use.

The program used to implement RIP-2 under Linux is `gated` or `zebra`. Both of these daemons can handle more than one protocol at once. See Chapter 5 for more information on where to find these programs and how they work.

Open Shortest Path First (OSPF)

The Open Shortest Path First (OSPF) routing protocol is a *link-state* protocol. This term refers to the reduced amount of information that OSPF keeps track of compared to a protocol such as RIP-2. A link-state protocol uses an entirely different method of choosing routes than a distance-vector protocol.

The Algorithm

Link-state protocols use one of a collection of Shortest Path First (SPF) algorithms. Once again, these algorithms are based on solving graphing problems and then were applied to networking. In the case of OSFP, the algorithm behind the method is the Dijkstra algorithm. Here again, we start with a collection of points. We'll use the same set shown previously in Figure 1.5.

You must define which points are reachable from which right up front in this case. We don't start with a theoretical graph where everything can reach everything. You cannot set this data in one direction, either. Some points may only be accessible one way, and others may have a different cost in one direction than in another. So again, let's use the physical connections laid out in Figure 1.9, adding a new weighting scheme as in Figure 1.14—this time representing both directions of traffic.

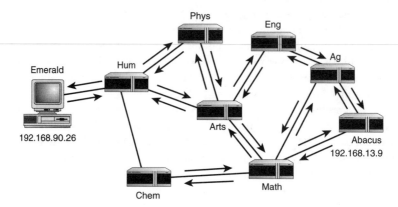

Figure 1.14   The example network with bi-directional data paths.

Look back at Table 1.1. The places where data travels over T1, T3, or Integrated Services Digital Network (ISDN) are going to have equal bandwidth traveling in both directions. However, where DSL or 56Kbps modems are used, it might be a different story. Three of the most popular DSL line types consist of two different data pipes and the fourth has four, as shown in Figure 1.15.

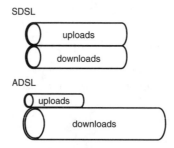

Figure 1.15   Data in two types of DSL connections.

The Asynchronous Digital Subscriber Line (ADSL) DSL type has two differently sized pipes for data travel. These bandwidth pipes do not mix. Even if you have completely filled your download bandwidth, it will not start using room allocated for uploading. For the High Density Digital Subscriber Line (HDSL), however, the pipes are equally sized though there are four instead of two. The ISDN Digital Subscriber Line (IDSL) type is a hybrid between ISDN and DSL. While the other DSL types listed here do not keep a connection open on a constant basis (they make the connection when it is needed), IDSL keeps the connection constantly open. This DSL type also has the longest transmission range of the DSLs available today. The fourth popular DSL type is the Synchronous Digital Subscriber Line (SDSL). This line type has equal-sized pipes in both directions.

So, for the sake of making the example network an effective one, let's say that the DSL item listed in Table 1.1 is ADSL.

The second issue is the 56Kbps modem. Once again, this hardware has different download and upload speeds. You only get 56Kbps for downloads—if you are able to get this speed at all. Uploads are limited to 33.6Kbps in many brands, and while some are able to achieve higher speeds, they typically do not have identical upload and download speeds. The costs to travel from point to point in each direction, taking this information into account, are shown in Figure 1.16.

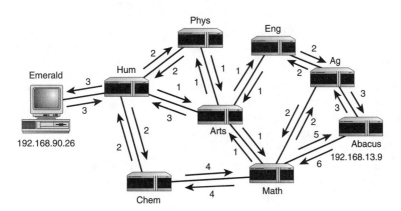

Figure 1.16   Cost values for our example network using OSPF.

Now that the routers and travel costs are in place, it's time to actually find the initial best paths. Again, we need a place to start, so let's use Emerald for consistency. The only place to go from Emerald is Hum, so the algorithm first finds Emerald to Hum, as shown in Figure 1.17.

Figure 1.17   OSPF algorithm in first iteration.

There are three different places you can go from Hum, not counting Emerald (you never travel through the same point twice): Phys, Arts, and Chem. The distances in this direction for each of these are two, one, and two. One is the shortest distance; therefore, the shortest path through these routers, so far, is Emerald to Hum and then to Arts. The paths as they are now are shown in Figure 1.18.

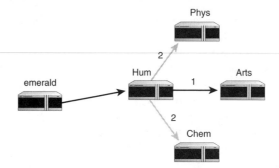

Figure 1.18 OSPF algorithm in second iteration. The heavier line shows the fastest path.

Now we move to the next iteration. This iteration starts at Phys, Arts, and Chem. We cannot pass through a point we've already used, so Phys is out of the running for the fastest, shortest path and will not be used in further iterations. However, one key to this algorithm is that we're not just looking for one path—we're looking for the fastest way to get from Emerald to *everywhere*. So, the paths shown in the lighter lines in Figure 1.18 still are useful.

We can still go places from both Arts and Chem. Router Arts reaches to the not yet used nodes of Eng and Math. Chem all of a sudden also has nowhere to go (see Figure 1.19).

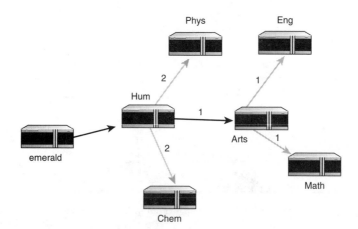

Figure 1.19 OSPF algorithm in partial third iteration. The heavier line shows the fastest path up to where it stalls.

Notice that you're in a dead heat in the costs for going from Arts to Eng and Arts to Math. While this doesn't affect issues such as where the data's going, it does cause the problem of determining the central fastest path. This central path is used to determine which router gets the priority as the algorithm goes through its motions. Items on the fastest path get to go through their iterations first, which is why certain points result in dead ends.

How do we then resolve this dead heat? OSPF uses a technique called *load balancing* to handle such an issue. It literally decides to use both paths alternatively in order to attempt to get the fastest possible data flow. This, however, does not help us with the algorithm itself. To get to the fastest, shortest path and to break the tie, we choose the point with the least number of routers to pass through to get to the rest of the world, which is seven (shown in Figure 1.20).

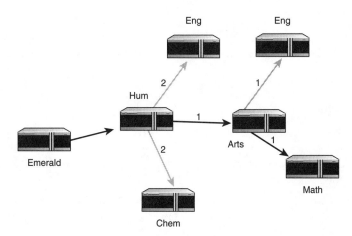

Figure 1.20   OSPF algorithm with third iteration complete. The heavier line
shows the fastest path.

Now that we have this issue handled, we can move to the fourth iteration. The only remaining place to go to from Eng is Ag, and from Math there's Ag and Abacus. Once again we have to take the fastest central path into account to determine what happens. Because Math is part of the fastest path, we follow that one first. This means that Math leads to both Ag and Abacus, and Eng is another dead end. The algorithm has now finished its job, as shown in Figure 1.21.

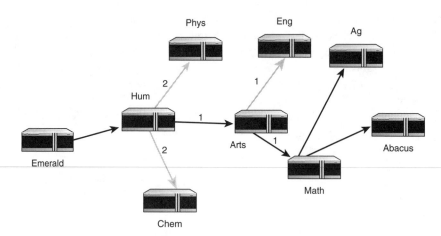

Figure 1.21   OSPF algorithm with fourth iteration complete. The heavier lines shows the fastest path. The lighter lines are all paths as well but are dead ends.

How It Works

Now that you understand how the algorithm works, let's apply OSPF with the same examples used earlier. This protocol is far more complex than RIP-2, so expect this to be a fun ride. Once again, we want to send data from Emerald to Abacus. Emerald knows the following:

- What interfaces lead to what routers in its *area*. An area in OSPF is an independent unit. The example network is a single area in this case. Router three, as it turns out, is the area's *designated router*.

- A designated router is in charge of talking to the outside world. Within an area, every machine knows how to send data to every address in that area. However, once you get outside of the current area, the routers there see only the designated router and none of the others. As a result, when traffic goes to one of the networks within the area, any router outside sends to the designated router, which then uses its own routing tables to send the traffic to its destination.

- If you have an area at all, then you have at least two. Otherwise, there is no need to create one. The sum total of your areas adds up to a full *autonomous system* (AS). Figure 1.22 shows conceptually how these components all come together. Notice that router Phys has a boundary (and interface) in both of the areas. Remember that the routers have to be able to talk across boundaries! There also will be a router that talks to the outside world from the AS.

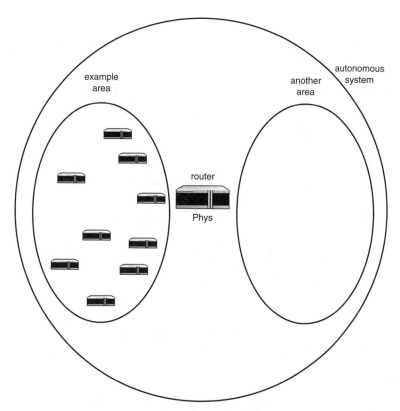

Figure 1.22   The example network in its own area, sharing
an autonomous system with other areas.

Routing Table Size

The size of routing tables is a very important issue, regardless of what protocol you are using. The Internet initially did not have to be concerned with how large the tables were because back in the late 1960s and early 1970s (the days of ARPANET), there were very few machines connected. Today, of course, is a different story.

One reason that older routing protocols, such as RIP-1 and RIP-2, are not sufficient for large-scale use is that each router must contain individual instructions for every single network and subnetwork in existence. The larger the tables get, the longer it takes to look up where data needs to go. Transit times slow until the network is virtually useless.

Entering the newer routing protocols and segmentation tools such as areas, ASs, and more allow administrators to greatly shrink their routing tables for various network parts. More knowledgeable and powerful routers can then handle passing the information between the smaller sections so that it eventually gets where it needs to go.

- The cost of sending data through each interface. OSPF does not see these costs as any kind of distance measure. They are used simply as a method of weighting which interfaces are going to produce the fastest traffic and which will slow things down.

- The *shortest paths tree* we calculated earlier. Emerald specifically has the tree shown in Figure 1.21. Remember, each machine has its own tree with OSPF.

- The cost and path for sending data to the backbone.

Emerald has already used the algorithm we covered earlier to calculate the shortest, fastest paths to all of the other routers. Emerald then knows not only what the next hop will be, but also knows every step of the journey that it would like the data to take. What Emerald does with the data is simply forward it to router Hum, which takes over from there.

Router Hum also has the entire map of the network with costs and both directions. However, it does not use Emerald's fastest, shortest path calculations. Hum does its own. I'll leave the algorithm part as an exercise for you, but what Hum comes up with in the end is shown in Figure 1.23.

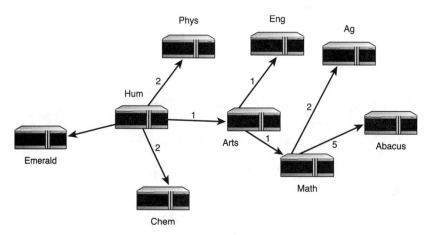

Figure 1.23 OSPF algorithm results from Hum's point of view.

Hum sees Arts as its fastest way to get to Abacus, so it forwards the packet there. Arts then checks its own routing table and fastest, shortest path calculations, as shown in Figure 1.24.

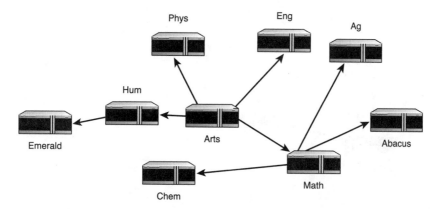

Figure 1.24   OSPF algorithm results from Arts's point of view.

From Arts, the data goes to Math, and then to Abacus. This time, however, Abacus isn't on the fastest path. This path gets fairly skewed as each machine builds its own tree.

Now that things are working so nicely, let's throw the usual wrench in the works. What if our infamous router Arts goes down as it did in the RIP-1 discussion? We'll use the same three scenarios as we did before to bring home the differences in robustness between RIP-1 and OSPF:

- Scenario 1: Router Arts was intentionally removed. It had a critical failure, and there is no backup router available to take its place for a week.

  All routers running OSPF regularly—once per *HelloInterval* setting—make use of the HELLO protocol. This separate communications protocol is used exclusively to connect to the *neighbor* OSPF routers (those directly connected to the router in question) and to keep that connection going in both directions. The HELLO protocol accomplishes this by using *HELLO packets*. These special data packets contain introduction information about this router and the costs for traveling through its interfaces, as well as the names of the neighbors of which it is aware.

  Arts's neighbors (Hum, Eng, and Math) are all happily sending out their HELLO packets and receiving them in turn. However, they begin to notice that they are not getting anything from Arts within the set HelloInterval time, which is advertised within the HELLO packets. If they do not hear from Arts within the *RouterDeadInterval* time after the first missed HELLO packet, the neighbors declare that router unavailable. It won't be long, then, before all of Arts's neighbors give up on Arts.

  When Hum, Phys, and Math give up on router Arts, they each calculate brand new fastest, shortest path trees with this gaping hole taken into account. No one needs to tell them anything. They can do this all themselves. Thus, where Hum previously had the tree shown in Figure 1.23, it now has the one shown in Figure 1.25. The other two also calculate new trees.

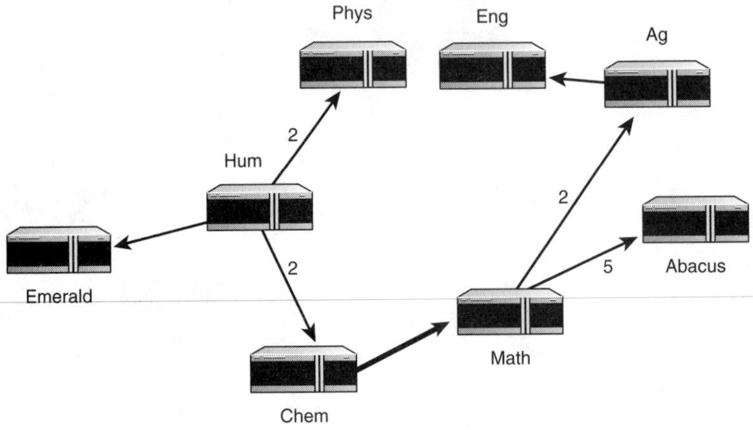

Figure 1.25   Hum's new path tree when Arts goes down.

As Hum, Phys, and Math send HELLO packets to their neighbors, those neighbors are going to notice the absence of Arts in those packets. They write off Arts as well, and each rebuilds its own tree.

- Scenario 2: Router Arts was intentionally removed. It is not going to be replaced with anything else.

  While this example was a significantly different issue in the RIP-1 section, it is not here. There is no need for administrators to tell the other routers that Arts is gone. They will all figure this out pretty quickly on their own and build new routing tables, as discussed in Scenario 1.

- Scenario 3: The connection Arts uses to access the network went down temporarily, isolating this router, the machines on its own network, and any networks that it is supposed to pass data to from everyone else. This connection stays down for three hours.

  At first, this situation behaves as it did in Scenario 1. The fact that there is no router Arts ripples through the network just fine on its own. When the router comes back up, however, you'll see another big difference in how RIP-1 handled the scenario.

  The moment router Arts comes back up, it sends out a broadcast of HELLO packets. All of the neighbors (Phys, Hum, Eng, and Math) get this broadcast and respond to Arts. Then, when these neighbors send out their HELLO packets to others with a list of their neighbors, more of the network sees Arts, and so on. No human intervention necessary.

OSPF and Authentication

One thing to keep in mind here is that all the routers in the area use the same authentication scheme. Every area has to use the same scheme throughout, though from area to area different levels can be used within the same AS. This is a handy way to break up the network into more and less secure areas, something that works especially well in conjunction with other security methods.

OSPF IP packets also have to pass a *checksum* test, meaning that the packet contains a count of how many bits were included when it was sent, and the router that receives the packet makes sure it has this same number of bits. Consequently, if the packet were either damaged or altered, it would not be accepted.

One problem with OSPF's implementation is that if someone can get access to a connection to one of the lines between your routers, they can set up a *packet sniffer*—a program that is used to take a look at the data traveling through a network—to listen for anything meant for a specific address and actually grab a copy of your password. Even with the checksum test, OSPF's authentication is not sophisticated enough to protect against this kind of intrusion.

If you take a glance back at Figure 1.23, you'll see that this overall system consists of two areas within an AS. This changes the dynamics of the area we've been talking about, so let's discuss that first before we get into the bigger picture. Router Phys is the designated router, also called the border router because it has interfaces in both this area and another. This means that router Phys is considered adjacent, or a neighbor, to every router in the area. Every router sends HELLO packets to Phys, and Phys answers them all. This ensures that Phys always has the big picture of what's going on in its area.

Now, consider the bigger picture. Figure 1.26 lays out the second area (the dormitories [names abbreviated], which are also networked in the overall campus structure) that router Phys is attached to, and Figure 1.27 shows the fastest, shortest path tree that router East comes up with. First, I need to adjust my vocabulary here. The term router Phys so far has referred to a single machine because you didn't know it had additional area interfaces. Phys actually refers to the Ethernet card that directly connects to the campus Area. East refers to the Ethernet card that directly connects to the dorm Area.

The tree for each area is stored separately, and router Phys/East actually runs two copies of the OSPF software for each area. OSPF packets are all marked with an area ID of area they came from, so they don't leak across a border by accident.

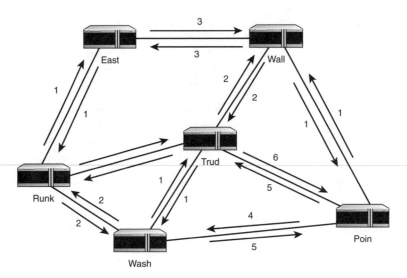

Figure 1.26 The other area in the AS, where router East is the other interface on router Phys.

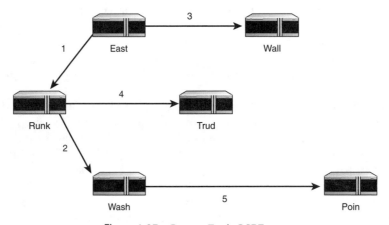

Figure 1.27 Router East's OSPF tree.

Stepping back even farther, there must be a way available for data to move in and out of the AS. This requires at least one—preferably more than one—AS boundary router. I'll be a bad network administrator here and add a single AS boundary router to our image, shown in Figure 1.28.

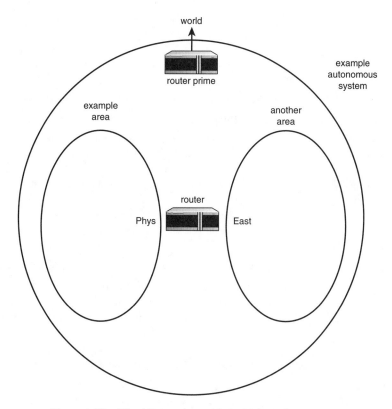

Figure 1.28   The AS complete with its AS boundary router.

This AS boundary router is actually going to receive route advertisements from the outside world as well as send route advertisements to the outside world. These are referred to as *external link advertisements*. External routing information is shared with all of the routers in the AS with one of two different types of costs:

- **Type 1**. An extension of the path algorithm outside of the AS. Costs for each leg of the path are taken into account exactly.

- **Type 2**. Another type of path extension, except that additional costs are added such that an external path always costs more than any internal path.

The thing to realize is that Phys and East are not designated routers for their Areas because they were somehow born or destined to be designated routers. The HELLO protocol actually elects both a designated and backup designated router. You can stuff the ballot box, though, by giving the specific interface connecting the router to that area a higher priority than the others. If you have two routers connected to the out-side world—as you should—then you weight the other one high enough to make it the backup designated router automatically.

Each area in your AS must be internally consistent in its behavior. While I have mentioned some of these values before, a full list of all of the settings that must be identical among all routers in an area—or in the case of an area border router, among all router interfaces in an area—are shown in Table 1.4.

Table 1.4 **OSPF Router Settings that Must Be Identical with an Area**

Setting	Purpose
Area ID	The identification value set for the particular area
Backup Designated Router	The IP address for the interface leading to the backup designated router
Designated Router	The IP address for the interface leading to the designated router
Type	The kind of network the interface points to: broadcast, non-broadcast, point-to-point, or virtual link

Now let's drill down a bit farther. You also need to be internally consistent for your networks. If you have more than one router attached to a network, which can be a good idea for redundancy reasons, there are certain settings that must be identical for each of the routers attached to that network. The settings I'm talking about here are listed in Table 1.5.

Table 1.5 **OSPF Router Settings that Must Be Identical for Networks**

Setting	Purpose
HelloInterval	The number of seconds an OSPF router waits before it sends out its next HELLO packet
Network Mask	The netmask for this network, or 0 for an unnumbered point-to-point network or a virtual link
RouterDeadInterval	The number of seconds an OSPF router waits since the last HELLO packet before it declares a router dead

HELLO Packets and Network Type

The infamous OSPF HELLO packet behaves differently depending on the kind of network you place it on. If you choose a non-broadcast network, then all of the OSPF routers on that network need a list of their neighbors and their ranking in case of a designated router election. On other network types, this is not necessary.

Drilling down farther still, we get to the OSPF router's routing table. This table contains:

- The IP networks, subnets, and hosts that this destination can forward information to.
- The netmask when the destination points to a network or subnet or 0xffffffff if the destination is a host.
- The Type of Service (TOS) that should be sent along this route. OSPF is capable of routing data differently depending on its TOS setting.
- One of four path types used to send data to this destination: intra-area (within the same area), inter-area (to another area within the same AS), type 1 external, or type 2 external.
- The full cost to send data to this destination, as determined by adding the interface costs along the way.
- If the path is type 2 external, the routing table also contains the cost for sending the data outside of the AS.
- If there are two paths to the same destination with equal costs, the table actually stores the information for both paths in a single entry. In addition to the standard information, there is also the interface to send data out for the next router that can pass the data on to the destination and the IP address of that neighbor. If the destination is in another area or AS, the router ID of the router that data must pass through to get to the destination is included as well.

Finally, the question arises of how all of this data travels between the areas, making the AS a unit unto itself. Just as the Internet is said to have a backbone, an AS has one of its own. The *AS backbone* consists of area border routers, AS border routers, and networks and routers that don't exist in an area at all. It is essentially an area of its own, even though it passes through others.

Like a spinal cord, an OSPF AS backbone must be all in one piece to function properly. When two backbone routers are not connected directly by cables, you can connect them using a *virtual link* in the area border routers. You must create this link in both routers, which will then pretend to have a point-to-point connection between them. The cost for traveling through this connection is the sum of the costs for the real path that the data must take.

As you can see, OSPF is a much more advanced routing protocol than that of the RIP-1 family. It deals with changes in routing structure quickly and efficiently and increases network reliability. The programs used to implement OSPF under Linux are the multi-protocol daemons `gated` or `zebra`.

Summary

The unicast routing protocols you're most likely to use in large, subnetted or multi-network networks in Linux are RIP-1, RIP-2, and OSPF. RIP-1 is the oldest of TCP/IP routing protocols still used on the Internet. As such, it is also the least flexible and only really good for small networks. RIP-2 is a bit newer and more secure, and while it is really not any better for larger networks, is a wiser choice than RIP-1 in many situations. Finally there is OSPF, which is more robust. If your network tends to change or you have problems with machines going down, you're better off to choose this option.

Don't forget static routing either! For really small LANs (10 machines or so) or subnets, this might be sufficient. Table 1.6 lists pertinent data for each of the protocols that might be of interest to you.

Table 1.6   **The Programs Used to Implement Unicast Routing Protocols in Linux, and the RFC Documents that Contain Vital Background Information**

Protocol	Program	RFC
RIP-1	routed, gated, or zebra	1058
RIP-2	gated or zebra	1721
OSPF	gated or zebra	2328

One excellent place to read Request for Comments (RFCs) is http://www.faqs.org/. If you are a programmer and find that you have a hard time understanding how some things work until you can pour over some code, then go to http://www.packetfactory.net/ and examine their libnet project's code. There are features in there for handling RIP-1 and OSPF.

2

Multicast Protocols

A MULTICAST ROUTING PROTOCOL TAKES ADVANTAGE of multicast networking to broadcast information to an IP address (*channel* or *group*) to which any computer with multicast access can listen. When a router supports multicast protocols, it may or may not need to be aware of who is listening at any given time. It depends on how far your multicast channel reaches and which protocol you chose.

This chapter discusses background information for a number of commonly used multicast routing protocols. Use this information to make educated decisions about which protocols you want to use to manage your own networking needs.

Routing Information Protocol Version 2 (RIP-2)

No, your eyes don't deceive you. RIP-2 is in both the unicast and multicast sections. You can configure routers using this routing protocol to send out occasional updates to a multicast address—by default to 224.0.0.9. In fact, RIP-2 has four settings you can use to direct its behavior in the multicast and other realms:

- *None.* Disables all RIP-1 messaging.
- *RIP-1.* Tells RIP-2 to behave as though it were its predecessor.

- **RIP-1 Compatibility.** Tells RIP-2 to broadcast its updates directly to the other routers, taking into account those that need RIP-1 formatted data.
- **RIP-2.** Ignores RIP-1 issues and uses multicast to send updates.

None of these options, however, actually deals with multicast data aside from the protocol's own updates.

Multicast Open Shortest Path First (MOSPF)

The Multicast Open Shortest Path First (MOSPF) protocol is a version of OSPF that allows for efficient routing of multicast packets (as well as unicast packets) within an autonomous system. This implementation merges both OSPF and the Internet Group Management Protocol (IGMP), which handles multicast group memberships. Even better, it keeps the best capabilities of all, including using the OSPF authentication scheme.

MOSPF tracks who is currently a member of a multicast group using the same type of back and forth querying used by the HELLO protocol. Every MOSPF router calculates its own trees. Notice the plural on "trees." Each router calculates a separate tree for each source/destination pair. This tree reaches from the source, through the router, all the way out to the networks that contain members.

Stop and think for a second what this might mean. If MOSPF routers calculated trees for all existing multicast sources and groups in your autonomous system ahead of time, your MOSPF routers would be so busy calculating that they would be useless for directing traffic.

Instead, no tree is calculated until multicast data actually needs to travel from a source/destination pair that no tree exists for yet. Because multicasting is designed to deliver data to all group members, its packets (*datagrams*) drop off copies for each group member as they travel the shortest path. However, the tree is not unique to each router—as it is in OSPF. Instead, the tree's trunk is at the router from where the data came, and all of the routers receiving and passing on the data use that same starting point for their tree. So, all routers dealing with this data are using the same shortest path tree, even though they each calculate it themselves.

Handling Ties When Building Trees

If there is a tie between paths that have equal costs, load balancing is not used. Various MOSPF implementations have specific ways of choosing which branch to use for the fastest, shortest path tree.

Interestingly, you can mix OSPF and MOSPF routers within OSPF areas and even spread them throughout autonomous systems. To do this there just needs to be a contiguous set of routers capable of multicasting so the data can travel where it needs to go.

The program used to implement MOSPF is `mrouted`. There are also adjustments you need to make so the router is fully multicast-enabled. See Chapter 6, "Inside the Multicast Kernel 2.2.x Daemons," for coverage on how to accomplish this.

Distance Vector Multicast Routing Protocol (DVMRP)

The Distance Vector Multicast Routing Protocol is a child of the original RIP-1 and for use only within a single autonomous system. It does not actually handle unicast data. If you want to use DVMRP, you also will have to use another protocol to handle unicast information. All of the unicast protocols discussed earlier are viable.

This protocol is still considered experimental, so it is likely to change in some ways. Do the following to see if there is a newer version of this coming standard available:

1. Go to http://www.ietf.org/.

2. Follow the Internet-Drafts (I-D) link.

3. Follow the I-D Keyword Search link. This will allow you to do a search for the draft rather than having to wade through the hierarchal index.

4. Enter **dvmrp** in the text box and then click Search. One of the results has the title Distance Vector Multicast Routing Protocol. This is the document you're looking for. If the version is newer than draft-ietf-idmr-dvmrp-v3-10.txt, it is worth taking the time to look for differences within that document from what is discussed here.

The Algorithms: Introduction

DVMRP used to be made up entirely of the Truncated Reverse Path Broadcasting (TRPB) algorithm, which is a refinement of the Reverse Path Broadcasting (RPB) algorithm. Today, TRPB is only used for the first packet in a series of multicast data. Further packets are directed utilizing Reverse Path Multicasting (RPM), a more refined tree-building algorithm grown from both TRBP and RPB. This method should feel somewhat familiar because it includes the distance-vector style building of data paths used in RIP-1 (as you might have guessed from the protocol's name). In fact, the algorithm is similar to the Bellman-Ford algorithm you already know and love if you read Chapter 1, "Unicast Protocols." It is simply enhanced to take into account the unique requirements of transmitting multicast data as opposed to unicast data.

The Danger of Acronyms

If you're familiar with Red Hat Linux or its relatives, you probably immediately think of RPM as the Red Hat Package Manager. You might even think of RPM in terms of Rotations Per Minute or another representative value. In this chapter, whenever you see RPM, we are referring to Reverse Path Multicasting. Because this book is distribution neutral, you can generally assume that references to RPM throughout mean this as well. Where they do not, we will make it clear, though the context should be sufficient to clarify the usage in many cases.

The Algorithms: Truncated Reverse Path Broadcasting (TRPB)

No tree-building algorithms are used in DVMRP until a data transmission starts. In fact, if data has gone out to this multicast channel before, you skip this tree-building process completely. See the first "How It Works" section that follows for information on how DVMRP maintains an up-to-date tree after it's built.

When a multicast provider begins sending packets, the TRPB algorithm goes to work. Let's say that you are multicasting a radio show from a new machine that uses Emerald as its router. First, you need to know which of the routers in your autonomous system support multicast data. In the example network—now pulled together for your easy viewing in Figure 2.1—the following routers are multicast-capable: Prime, Emerald, Chem, Math, Arts, Phys/East, Runk, Trud, and Poin.

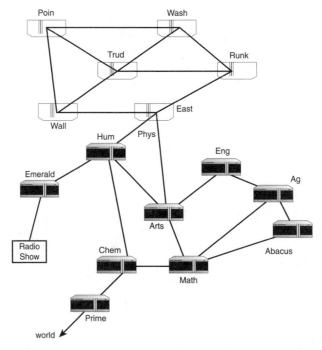

Figure 2.1   The autonomous system with the multicast routers identified.

The moment that Emerald receives the first packet from Radio Show meant for its new multicast channel, TRBP gets some help from IGMP, the multicast group management protocol discussed earlier. TRBP now delivers the first packet from this new machine to emerald. Emerald immediately passes the packet to East and Chem, and it continues from there to all of the multicast routers (I'll discuss how they get there without a direct connection in the "How It Works" section).

As this packet reaches each router, the machine goes to IGMP with the multicast channel address to find out which of its networks and subnetworks contain group members. The first packet is only forwarded to networks and subnetworks that contain group members. Let's say for example that router Math has the structure behind it shown in Figure 2.2.

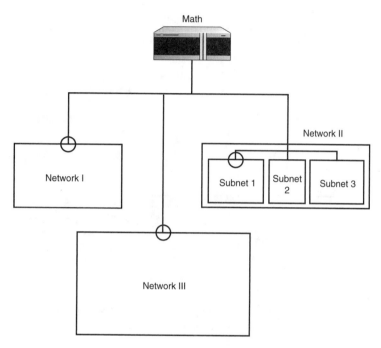

Figure 2.2   The networks served by router Math, with multicast group members circled.

IGMP fits in when this first packet of data from the new source arrives at router Math or one of its siblings. This router utilizes IGMP's group management data to find out which of the (sub)networks actually contains group members. In the example, networks I and III have at least one member, so the packet is sent to these networks. Network II is broken into subnets, however, not all of which contain group members. For III, the multicast packet is sent only to subnet 1.

The TRPB tree is built during this decision-making process. This tree might now look like what you see in Figure 2.3. Remember, this is a distance vector algorithm, so the path to each data point is predicated on how far it has to travel.

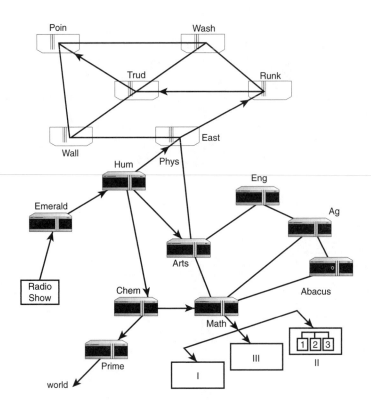

Figure 2.3   The delivery tree for packets broadcast to the
machine Radio Show's multicast channel.

The Algorithms: Reverse Path Multicasting (RPM)

After that first packet is delivered, RPM takes over. In fact, it takes over as the first
packet travels through the network. The major addition this algorithm brings to
DVMRP is the idea of *pruning*. RPM takes the initial tree built by TRPB and begins
pruning branches and twigs off of it to reduce the amount of multicast traffic using up
bandwidth throughout the autonomous system.

Each of the DVMRP routers circled in the previously mentioned figures already
used IGMP to see if it serves any group members for TRPB's benefit. Unlike router
seven, however, some are likely to find that they don't have any group members in
their networks and subnetworks. Let's say that routers Arts, Trud, Poin, and East have
no group members in the machines for which they provide routing. Each of these
sends a prune message to its upstream router:

1. Arts sends a prune to Hum.

2. Trud sends a prune to Runk.

3. Poin sends a prune to Trud.

4. East/Phys sends a prune to Hum.

DVMRP continuously examines the tree's prune messages, which actually have a specified life span. Whenever it finds a router that meets the two tests listed next, DVMRP then stops sending packets for this multicast channel to that router.

- Received prune messages from all of the routers downstream from it—as is the case for routers Trud and Runk

- Sent a prune message for itself to its own upstream—as is the case for router Trud

So, router Trud would no longer receive packets for this channel, along with Poin, until the prune's life span ended. The next packet coming from the specific source and to the specific channel that this prune message referred to would be broadcast using TRPB, and the pruning process would start all over again.

How It Works

Now let's take a closer look at how DVMRP works over the long haul. To start, all of the DVMRP routers specified in Figure 2.1 were just set up. They might have already been providing routing with OSPF or RIP-2, but DVMRP was installed at this time because you've decided you want to provide multicast services for your users.

All of the routers begin what should sound like a familiar neighbor discovery process. Each router sends a probing message through all of its multicast-capable interfaces as it comes up. As they begin receiving probe messages from each other, a list of all of the neighbors they have gotten probes from for that specific interface gets included in the probe. For example, look at Emerald. It sends out probe messages on its interfaces, and Hum receives one of these messages on a specific interface. Router Hum, in turn, sends out a probe message on each of its network interfaces. Now that it has heard from Emerald, it lists emerald as one of the neighbors it recognizes within any probe message sent through the interface that it learned of Emerald through. In fact, the first time a DVMRP router gets a probe from a neighboring router it's never heard of before, the router sends its entire routing table to the new neighbor.

When Emerald sees its name in Hum's list, it knows it has a two-way working connection with router Hum. From then on, every 60 seconds the routers send each other copies of their routing tables and make sure that they have all of the most up-to-date information. Emerald also now adds Hum to its own list of discovered neighbors, so that when Hum receives the next probe it knows it has a two-way connection. This process happens throughout the network until all of the multicast routers have discovered each other.

DVMRP essentially uses this process to keep a collective routing table for multicast traffic. Every 10 seconds, another probe goes out to each multicast-capable interface from each DVMRP router. The collective routing table shifts and changes as neighbors appear and disappear—if they are not heard from within 35 seconds.

Another issue that must be dealt with on an ongoing basis is making sure that routers connected to the same networks are not providing duplicate services. This is a waste of the additional router's processing time as well as bandwidth. This is where we return to the fact that the letters "DV" in the protocol name stand for Distance Vector. If multiple routers are capable of sending data from the transmission source to a specific network, then whichever router has the shorter path back to the source becomes the *designated forwarder*—or the router that sends data from this source to this point.

One concern that still exists at this point is data trying to loop around through routers it has already traveled. When a router chooses its designated forwarder, it uses the poison reverse technique discussed earlier. The DVMRP implementation of poison reverse involves sending a copy of the routing table with the metric number of hops the data has to make to go from point A to B—values from the router to its designated forwarder set to infinity (32) plus the real cost. This actually signals the designated forwarder to mark the router as *dependent*. The list of dependencies is used to help manage the pruning process.

Eventually, DVMRP builds a routing table for each interface on this router. The table contains the following information for each source that sends data to a particular multicast channel:

- **The IP address for the source and the interface through which it sends data.** A DVMRP routing table entry only contains data for one source.

- **The IP address for the multicast channel this source specified.** A DVMRP routing table entry only contains data for one source sending to one specific multicast channel.

- **The interface on which the packets for this source/destination pair arrives.** This would be the IP address assigned to the interface.

- **The total cost of data coming from the source to this interface.** Individual costs of hop-to-hop are not kept in the routing table.

- **The major and minor version of DVMRP running on the remote interface.** This ensures that newer versions will not overwhelm older ones with information they cannot utilize or manage.

- **The DVMRP capabilities available on the remote interface.** Most of these are used for backwards compatibility, but not all.

- **The *Generation ID* attached to the last probe message from the remote interface.** This identification number only changes when a router is restarted or its interface is taken down and then brought back up. It also is transmitted with every probe message. When the Generation ID changes, it signals neighbor routers to send a copy of their entire routing table to the remote interface. Doing this ensures that everyone always has up-to-date information.

As the table gets passed from router to router, the cost gets bigger as you go farther downstream, with a minimum of one being added for each interface. Thus, as each router pulls together routing tables from other routers, it makes its own choices of best paths back to the source using the metrics given.

Now let's turn to that notorious router Arts again and run through how DVMRP handles the usual scenarios:

- Scenario 1: Router Arts was intentionally removed. It has had a critical failure, and there is no backup router available to take its place for a week.

  After 35 seconds of not hearing any probe messages, Arts's only multicast neighbor, Hum, realizes that there is a problem. Hum now must make sure that it's not sending any data out into the great Net void by doing the following:

  - **Hum examines its routing tables.** Any routes it learned from Arts are deactivated—not deleted, just deactivated.

  - **In this example, there are no routers downstream from Arts.** If there were, however, Hum would delete all records of downstream dependants reliant on Arts.

  - **All data for which router Hum saw Arts as the designated forwarder must be recalculated.** If there were multiple routing paths to the networks behind Arts, the new best-cost interface would be marked as the designated forwarder.

  Any group members on the networks served by Arts now have a problem. They can't get any multicast data because they have been foolishly left without a backup multicast router. There is an alternative, however. Setting this up requires human intervention, but this solution could be left in place afterwards as a permanent backup.

  The first thing that needs to be done is to create another DVMRP router connected to the same networks that Arts serves. Eng is used, but none of Eng's neighbors run DVMRP. Fortunately, this protocol supports two types of *tunneling* (a virtual connection between machines), IP-IP and Generic Routing Encapsulation (GRE). After one of these is set up, Eng will think that it has neighbors, and everything will work just fine.

  At this point details of setting up a tunnel are not going to be discussed. See Chapter 11, "Linux Routing Basics," for more information on implementing this tool. Figure 2.4 shows the setup that could be used for the tunnel that is needed. Data would not reach the group members behind Arts until the administrator detected the initial failure and built the tunnel.

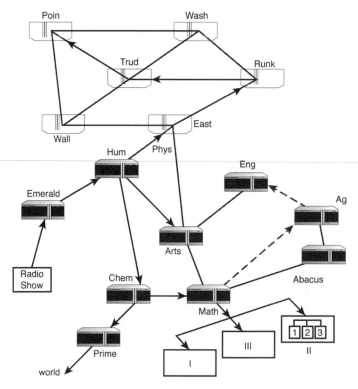

Figure 2.4   The new router tree, with the thick broken lines representing IP tunnels.

- Scenario 2: Router Arts was intentionally removed. It is not going to be replaced with anything else.

  This scenario is not appreciably different from the first. The major difference is that Eng could be set up for DVMRP, and the tunnel to Eng could be built before taking Arts down. Alternatively, both Ag and Eng could become DVMRP routers, or a new connection could be laid from elsewhere.

- Scenario 3: The connection that router Arts uses to access the network went down temporarily, isolating this router, the machines on its own network, and any networks that it is supposed to pass data to from everyone else. This connection stays down for three hours.

  Here is where things get interesting again. When Arts vanishes, the process is identical to when it was taken down in Scenario 1. The instructive part is when Arts finally comes back up, bringing its group members back out of isolation.

During its isolation, Arts deactivated all of its neighbors in its own routing table. As far as Arts is concerned it is the only DVMRP router in existence. However, a DVMRP router never gives up. It will continue sending probes out on each of its interfaces to the All-DVMRP-Routers multicast channel (224.0.0.4) and broadcast as well if there are machines that need to hear and cannot handle multicast, trying to find a neighbor to connect with. After Arts is back up, Hum will suddenly get a probe from it.

If all of the information Arts gives to Hum is identical to what it was before, then Hum just reactivates the routes that pass through Arts. Otherwise, routing tables are exchanged and edited.

There is one last thing to cover here. This chapter has talked about how DVMRP uses RPM to prune networks and routers off of its list of where to send data from a particular source. However, IGMP handles machines constantly joining and leaving multicast groups. We know how they get removed, but after they are gone, how do they get put back on?

The technique used here is *grafting*. Any pruned item can be grafted back onto the source/destination tree at any time. The DVMRP router monitors group membership. This router will cancel any prune messages that suddenly interfere with someone who just joined a group getting multicast data. These cancellation messages are Graft messages. When the DVMRP router receives the Graft, it sends back an acknowledgement (`graft ack`) to prevent repeats of the message and then adds the previously pruned branch back onto the tree. If this router also is pruned off of the tree, it sends a Graft request to its upstream for this particular source/destination pair—and so on.

The program used to implement DVMRP in Linux is `mrouted`, just as MOSPF is. There are also adjustments you need to make so the router is fully multicast-enabled. See Chapter 6 for coverage on how to accomplish this.

Protocol Independent Multicast

The Protocol Independent Multicast (PIM) tool is a routing protocol that is not beholden to any other existing protocols. This one actually works on top of existing unicast protocols so it doesn't have to handle any unicast packets. In contrast, DVMRP does occasionally deal with unicast transmissions, such as tunneling and sending individual router probes.

There are two different flavors of PIM available. Each of these is refined to deal with a specific spread of group members. Specifically, the question to ask in choosing between these two options is whether your group members are spread out in a *sparse* manner or packed together in a *dense* one.

Protocol Independent Multicast-Sparse Mode (PIM-SM)

A *sparse* multicast network has many more machines and/or networks that are not members of multicast groups than those that are. Group members can be spread out over a large geographical or network address span as well. The idea here is to not bog down the network structure with a lot of unnecessary multicast traffic.

The Rendezvous Point Tree (RP Tree)

PIM-SM uses two different sets of trees in its moment-to-moment operations. The first of these is the *Rendezvous Point* tree (RP tree), which is also known as the *Shared tree*. This tree is essentially the trunk of PIM-SM operation.

There is an RP router for each multicast group served in your routing domain. This router may host more than one group's traffic and, in fact, is typically configured to be the RP for a range of multicast addresses. For each group, there is a router tree that has the RP router as its trunk, and then all other routers that serve group members as the branches, including those who have to pass information from the RP to a downstream router but don't require it themselves. These routers simply tack themselves on as group members form in a location where they have the shortest path possible to the RP.

What algorithm is used in building this tree? Here's where things get interesting. Unlike what has been discussed so far, PIM-SM does not use algorithms to generate trees. It utilizes the underlying unicast routing protocol to generate the RP tree, saving some overhead.

The Shortest Path Tree (SPT)

The second of the PIM-SM trees is a shortest path tree (SPT) starting from the multicast source. This tree is only built and/or utilized if a heavy amount of traffic (you set the number of bits per second (bps), which defines "heavy") flows from this particular source, and each individual router can decide whether to join the SPT or stay with the RPT.

If a router decides it needs to belong to the SPT, it sends a Join message directly to the multicast group's source. This message must pass through other routers along the way. As it does so, these routers also add their own Join requests for the source's private SPT if they are not already members.

After the router is fully a member of the group's SPT, it sends a Prune message to the RP. As it passes through each of the intermediate routers, they check to see if this router is their only reason for being a member of the RPT. If this is the case, the intermediate router adds a Prune message as well, and some load is removed from the RP handling this multicast group.

Eventually, this burst of traffic will probably slow down. When this happens and the bps drop below what you defined as "heavy," this process reverses itself. The PIM-SM router sends a Join message to the RP to join the RPT, and when it and any necessary intermediates are solidly attached, it sends a Prune to the source to leave the SPT.

How It Works

Let's say that routers Phys and Arts are the most powerful of all of the routing machines in our domain. They also have fast connections to most of their neighbors. These would make good RP routers. Because we have many different multicast groups being served, we decide to split up the RP duties between these two.

After we have the unicast protocol and PIM-SM set up, the following happens when someone using a machine on one of your networks joins a multicast group:

1. IGMP notifies the closest *designated router* (DR) that there is a new member of this specific group. A DR is one of two things, depending on the situation:

   - If this is the only router that serves this part of the network, it is always the de-facto DR.

   - If multiple routers serve this part of the network, an election is held to determine which router is the DR for that network to avoid duplication of multicast packets. The router interface with the largest Ethernet MAC address wins this election.

2. The DR checks its listings for the rendezvous point (RP) router for this group.

3. The DR creates its own routing table entry for this group if it does not already have one.

4. The DR adds this group member to the group's table entry. If the router already has a group member, it does not follow through the rest of this process.

5. If the DR is not already handling traffic for this group—because this is the first member to join the group—it creates a Join packet.

6. The DR adds the interface address that leads ultimately toward the rendezvous point to the Join packet.

7. The DR sends the Join packet through the interface that ultimately leads to the RP router for the group.

8. Most likely, an intermediate router receives the packet. This router adds the interface on which the packet just arrived to the Join packet if it's not already part of the RP Tree.

9. The intermediate router passes the packet out on the interface that ultimately leads to the RP. If the Join packet ends up at another intermediate router, Step 8 is repeated.

10. All traffic from the group that the machine just joined was already being sent through the RP, on through the RP Tree, and eventually to the new group member.

I know some of this is repetitive, but I want to make sure that you have a chance to really let how this works sink in. The subtlety of the switch to the SPT was left out of this particular example. However, keep in mind that the end user does not choose which tree to be on—each router does. It's all transparent to the new group member.

By now, you've probably guessed what comes next. I made the mistake of making that nasty router Arts one of the RP routers. Let's see what happens when it gets unstable by going through our scenarios:

- Scenario 1: Router Arts was intentionally removed. It had a critical failure, and there is no backup router available to take its place for a week.

  Suddenly there is no rendezvous point router for about half of the multicast groups. Fortunately, I fibbed a bit when I said that you assign which RP handles what. You don't have to. PIM-SM routers also can elect which will be the RP. But first, the fact that Arts died without warning must be dealt with.

  The first thing that happens here is that the *bootstrap router* (sometimes shortened to BSR or BR) stops getting "I'm alive" notices from RP router 5. Routers continue trying to talk to Arts until the BSR sends out its next update, which suddenly has no pointers to Arts. The routers then all remove Arts from their own tables for multicast traffic.

  Now it's time to see another reason why there is more than one RP in our network. You not only can tell an RP to handle a specific range of multicast groups, but you also give it a priority value—the lower the number is, the higher the priority. This means that we did a clever thing when we set up our RPs. Router Arts handled half of the groups with the highest priority and had the lowest priority for the other half. Phys had the reverse.

  Now that the normal routers have nowhere to send data for some of the groups, they use the *hash* function (which is also referred to as an algorithm). This tool allows the routers to contact all of the available RPs and find out which ones support the groups on which they need to pass data. As the routers find themselves with no place to send data that need to pass through Arts, they send out a hash to Phys and find out that it can handle these groups. Tables are rebuilt, and life is good again.

- Scenario 2: Router Arts was intentionally removed. It is not going to be replaced with anything else.

  Perhaps you're beginning to notice a pattern—that for advanced protocols this scenario is no different than the first one. The same is true here.

- Scenario 3: The connection Arts uses to access the network went down temporarily, isolating this router, the machines on its own network, and any networks on which it is supposed to pass data to from everyone else. This connection stays down for three hours.

  The first part of this scenario works out identically to Scenario 1. The BSR notices that RP Arts no longer is sending its "I'm alive" messages and notifies all of the PIM-SM routers. These routers remove Arts from their tables, and when they need to send data to groups that were once served by Arts, they use hash to find out that Phys can take over these duties.

As usual, the more interesting issue is when router Arts comes back up. Here is where PIM-SM gets to show off its flexibility. Arts sends an "I'm alive" message to the BSR, which subsequently adds Arts, the groups it says it can handle, and the priorities for each group, to its PIM-SM tables. The BSR then sends its regular update to the general PIM-SM routers. All of them suddenly see that there is a router, Arts, that can handle some of the groups they are currently using Phys for and that Arts's priority is higher.

One by one, the routers send Join messages to Arts and Prune messages to Phys as necessary. Life is back to normal, and the administrator didn't have to do a thing.

The program used to implement PIM-SM in Linux is `gated`. Remember that you also have to have a unicast protocol installed, such as OSPF or RIP-2, for any of the PIM protocols to function properly.

Protocol Independent Multicast-Dense Mode (PIM-DM)

If your multicast network is *dense*, you would be wise to use this version of PIM. This term refers to having many multicast group members within the same geographical or network address area. The Protocol Independent Multicast-Dense Mode is in some ways an extension of PIM-SM. Later sections of the book will focus specifically on how it differs from its sparse-focused cousin.

PIM-DM is once again reliant on the mechanisms used by the unicast protocol with which it shares its routers. The trees are built from the source, through the routers, to the destinations, all using the unicast protocol's method. Consequently, there is nothing to discuss on the underlying tree-building front. The central question here is what happens when a group starts sending multicast traffic.

The machine named The Radio Show (refer to section "The Algorithms: Truncated Reverse Path Broadcasting (TRPB)") has been down for a few months, and now you want to run it again. In the meantime the system has been changed to a PIM-DM multicast network. When this source begins sending out its multicast traffic, each PIM-DM router automatically sends it to the other PIM-DM routers, as well as sending it out to all of the networks each router serves—this is a dense mode protocol. It assumes that there are many group members present. Once again, a separate table is created for each source/channel combination. But because this is a PIM protocol, all the information that is kept there is whether or not this interface is used.

This data comes from the fact that PIM-DM also uses graft and prune techniques. Routers that have no group members downstream can prune themselves off of the source tree, and if someone joins later can graft themselves back on. The algorithm used is Reverse Path Forwarding (RPF), which was introduced by Stephen E. Deering in his Ph.D. Thesis, "Multicast Routing in a Datagram Internetwork," for Stanford University in 1991.

One interesting fact is that Prune messages are sent to a specified multicast address, not to individual routers. The machine sending the request identifies itself and the router from which it is trying to Prune itself. Then there is about a three-second delay as routers downstream from the one trying to leave the tree have the chance to send a Prune-Override (if they have group members that would be left in the cold by this router's leaving the tree).

At regular intervals, all Prunes are flushed from the PIM-DM routing tables. Once again, routers can send Prune messages to be removed from the specific source/destination tree.

PIM-DM and Special Routers

The PIM-DM protocol usually does not use rendezvous point routers or DRs. However, IGMP Version 1 requires a DR in cases where there are multiple routers connected to the same network or network group. In these cases, the router with the highest IP address becomes the DR.

This doesn't mean, however, that PIM-DM allows packets to enter a network from two different routers. In these cases, the router with the best cost for data coming from the source—determined using the unicast protocol's costing mechanism—is chosen to forward the data.

So, let's run this protocol through our favorite three scenarios and see how it holds up:

- Scenario 1: Router Arts was intentionally removed. It had a critical failure, and there is no backup router available to take its place for a week.

  All PIM-DM routers send Hello messages out of each interface on a regular basis. Five's PIM-DM neighbors (refer to Figure 2.1), Phys and Math, notice that after a set number of seconds (set in the *Holdtime* Hello field) that Arts has not been checking in. They deactivate all references to Arts in their tables, and at least for a moment data that needed to head through this router has nowhere to go.

  Router Arts going down in this case is not just a change in the multicast routing, but in unicast routing as well. The underlying unicast protocol rebuilds the routing tables, and PIM-DM utilizes these to send traffic for the areas that were served by Arts.

- Scenario 2: Router Arts was intentionally removed. It is not going to be replaced with anything else.

  Once again, this is handled exactly as it was in Scenario 1.

- Scenario 3: The connection Arts uses to access the network went down temporarily, isolating this router, the machines on its own network, and any networks that it is supposed to pass data to from everyone else. This connection stays down for three hours.

The beginning of this scenario works exactly as it did in Scenario 1. However, when router Arts returns to life, its neighbors will suddenly notice Hello messages that it always sends out of its interfaces—even though Arts would have noticed its neighbors were gone as well.

After the neighboring routers add Arts back to the possible paths for source/group traffic, a series of DR elections might occur if Arts suddenly duplicates traffic that's being sent by another router to a certain collection of networks. It's not long before everything's back in order.

The program used to implement PIM-DM in Linux is `gated`. Once again, remember that you also have to have a unicast protocol installed, such as OSPF or RIP-2, for any of the PIM protocols to function properly.

Summary

The multicast routing protocols you're most likely to use in Linux are MOSPF, DVMRP, and either PIM-SM or PIM-DM. MOSPF is most useful in smaller multicast setups where you need a single protocol to handle both unicast and multicast, and RIP-2 doesn't really handle multicast data as much as it does multicast updates. DVMRP, PIM-SM, and PIM-DM all require an additional unicast protocol to work with. You would use PIM-SM if your multicast group members tend to be very spread out, and you'd use PIM-DM or DVMRP if they are more densely packed.

Table 2.1 outlines the multicast protocols available to you and the data you'll need to get started.

Table 2.1 **The Programs Used to Implement Multicast Routing Protocols in Linux, and the RFC Documents That Contain Vital Background Information**

Protocol	Program	RFC or Draft
MOSPF	mrouted	1585
DVMRP	mrouted	draft-ietf-idmr-dvmrp-v3-10.txt
PIM-SM	gated	2362
PIM-DM	gated	draft-ietf-pim-v2-dm-03.txt

See `http://www.multicasttech.com/multicast_faq.html` if you have questions about multicast in general.

3

Introduction to Border Routing Protocols

So far, this book has discussed routing protocols that are used within a specific autonomous system (AS). This isn't enough, however, if your AS is connected to the Internet or another AS. Along with the internal routing protocols you choose for your network(s), you also need to consider the *border routing protocol(s)* you are going to use to allow your intranets to talk to the wider world of the Internet. Border protocols take the information passed throughout your AS and determine what portions need to be shared with your neighbors, as well as bring in relevant data from the outside world.

We'll start with a look at the distinctions between interior and exterior TCP/IP gateway protocols and work our way up from the most simple of the offerings in the Unicast field through more modern solutions that streamline the routing process for both unicast and multicast.

Interior Gateway Protocol (IGP)

Let's start with a quick review of what's going on within the AS itself and introduce some terminology. Within this AS we have areas: at least one unicast routing protocol and perhaps one or more multicast protocols. All of the routing protocols used within the AS are *Interior Gateway Protocols* (IGPs).

Routing protocols fall under the class of gateway protocols because a *gateway* is something that connects two networks. This gateway can either be a special hardware device or a piece of software. Items that fall under the realm of gateways are computers that provide routing services, computers that connect various physical network types together (say, Token Ring and Ethernet), and computers that allow multiple network protocols to talk to one another (perhaps TCP/IP and IPX).

Now let's take a look at the collection of popular border routing protocols.

Exterior Gateway Protocol (EGP)

The *Exterior Gateway Protocol (EGP)* was the first inter-AS communications method used with TCP/IP and is still in use today in some circumstances. Rather than allowing your AS border router to locate neighbors on its own, you tell it up front the IP addresses or fully qualified domain names of other AS border routers with which it will exchange routing information. After you do this, EGP takes over to acquire those neighbors.

When an EGP-based AS border router comes alive, it is considered to be in an *Acquisition state* (EGP has a number of designations called "states" that describe the AS border router's status, where the terms often double as commands). The state can be different for each acquired neighbor at any given time. Available states in EGP are:

- **Acquisition**. Periodically attempts to acquire new EGP neighbors.
- **Cease**. Periodically lets neighbors know that this router is down, and when all acknowledge the message, transitions to Idle.
- **Down**. Responds only to a short list of commands.
- **Idle**. Stores no routing information and only responds to commands that request that it return to one of the more active states.
- **Up**. Fully participates with neighbors.

The router's state determines what commands it will accept and respond to. When this machine learns of a new neighbor, it sends a Request message—and continues to send them regularly. This message contains the following information:

- **The *sequence number* assigned to the Request.** All Request packets contain a sequence number, which is uniquely tracked only for a specific AS border router sending to another specific one.
- **How often *Hello messages* come.** We'll get to these in a moment. They are not the same HELLO's that OSPF uses. Default is 30 seconds.
- **How often *Poll messages* come.** We'll get to these in a moment as well. Default is 60 seconds.
- **How long to wait before giving up on the other machine.** If the AS border router does not hear from its neighbor within this time period, it declares it unavailable. Default is 120 seconds.

The neighbor sends a Confirm in response, verifying that it is up and running and accepts your AS border router as a neighbor. The AS border router then sets up a small data list including what was just discussed in the preceding list, plus the following:

- **The sequence number assigned to the Confirm.** All Confirm packets contain a sequence number, just as the Request packets do.

- **The *mode* this AS border router is in relative to the machine in question.** This router might either be in *active* or *passive* mode at any moment. The mode determines how the router responds to Hello and Poll messages. If the router is active, then whenever a Hello or Poll arrives it responds with one of the following message types: Confirm, I-Heard-You (*IHU*), or *Update*. A passive router might respond to one of these by entering the *Up* state, which returns the router to participating fully with its EGP neighbors.

- **The time the Confirm message arrived.** This is used to set the zero point for three different variables. The first counts how long until the next time this machine sends a Request to the AS border router in question. The second counts how long the machine waits before sending a Poll. The third maintains a countdown for how much time transpires since it last heard from the machine in question—in case it is silent too long.

Your router now changes to the *Down* state. This state allows for handling the commands *Cease*, *Hello*, and Request. The new ones here are Cease and Hello. An EGP router enters a Cease state in regard to a specific neighbor if it receives a *Stop command* from the administrator. In response to this command, the machine first enters the Cease state, and then sends a *Cease command* out to the specific neighbor it is ending its relationship with for the moment.

There are a couple of different things that can happen at this point:

- **The neighbor receives the Cease command.** If the neighbor is up and running just fine, it receives and understands the Cease command. In this case, the neighbor sends a *Cease-ack command* to your AS border router, and then changes to the *Idle state*, ignoring anything but a new Request command from the specific neighbor.

- **The Cease command does not reach the neighbor.** If there are network problems, or the neighbor is out of commission, the Cease command may be lost in the "great networking bit bucket." In this case, the EGP AS border router remains in the Cease state. The router will continue to occasionally send the Cease command until it gets a response. The administrator can issue a second manual Stop command to override waiting for a Cease-ack and immediately send the machine into Idle state relative to this neighbor.

Now, onto the Hello messages and Poll commands. When an EGP AS border router receives a Hello message, it sends back an I-Heard-you (IHU or I-H-U) message, verifying that it is up and running and received the Hello message. Then there's Poll. Remember that when an EGP AS border router receives a Request command it, sets how often Poll commands are sent to the requesting neighbor and then starts the timer that counts the number of seconds till the next time it needs to send the Poll command.

When the timer reaches the interval value, the machine sends a Poll command to the specified neighbor. When the neighbor receives the Poll command, the response depends on what state and mode this neighbor is in. An EGP AS border router ignores Poll commands if it is in the Down state or Passive mode. If it is not in this state or mode, the neighbor responds with an Update. It is this message that transmits actual information about the networks available in each autonomous system. The data contained in an Update consist of:

- **All gateways within the AS.** Remember that gateways are devices that connect two or more networks.

- **All gateways the router knows about outside of the AS.** This allows for a more complete routing table with less querying.

- **All networks available through each gateway.** The AS border router's neighbors need to know where to send information. Your router doesn't need to do as much "thinking" if the neighbors already know to send data directly to a specific gateway for a specific network.

- **How many routers and gateways data must pass through to reach each specific network from your AS border router.** This information allows for shortest path calculations internally within the AS.

- **Each neighbor's current state.** This information ensures that each of the routers know what kind of data each is expecting from the other.

As you can see, EGP has quite a job to do. Without some kind of method for AS border routers to share information, there would have to be a centralized list of where to send data for all specific networks. The program under Linux that implements this protocol is the unicast version of `gated`.

Border Gateway Protocol (BGP)

The child of EGP is the Border Gateway Protocol (BGP-4). This protocol has been through a number of versions, and the most current is BGP-4. All references to BGP in this chapter are to this fourth version. One of the primary issues that BGP-4 adds to the mix is that EGP was unable to handle some of IP version 6's capabilities, which are covered in depth in Chapter 4, "IPv4 and IPv6 Addressing."

BGP is another case in which you tell the AS border router who its neighbors are, and it has to get the information itself. In the BGP Active state, the AS border router opens a TCP connection with the new neighbor. After this connection is established, your machine does the following:

- **Sets the *ConnectRetry* timer to zero.** This timer typically counts from zero to 120 seconds. If it reaches this value, the AS border router assumes its TCP connection was lost and tries to reassert it.

- **Creates the framework within which BGP will store information about this new neighbor.** This framework includes creating all of the variables that need to be set.

- **Sets the *Hold Timer* to four minutes.** This timer sets how long the system waits between regularly exchanged messages before closing the connection with its neighbor.

After this, a sequence of messages passes between the two machines. First, your machine sends an *OPEN* message to the neighbor. This message contains:

- **The BGP version number.** We're talking about BGP-4 here.

- **The sender's AS number.** As mentioned earlier, every autonomous system has a unique identification number assigned by a central authority.

- **The setting to use for the Hold Timer.** If the two AS border routers have different settings, they agree upon the shorter time span of the two. If the Hold Timer value already set does not match the new choice, it is reset to match.

- **The IP address of the sender.** This also is referred to as the *BGP Identifier*.

When the neighbor receives this message, it stores the information given and returns a *KEEPALIVE* message back to your machine. When the KEEPALIVE message arrives, the Hold Timer is reset back to zero. From then on, KEEPALIVE messages pass back and forth at a rate of around one-third the length of the maximum Hold Timer time. It is the absence of these messages for the entire Hold Timer length that tells a machine that its neighbor is unavailable.

Finally, your AS border router changes to the *OpenSent* state relative to this neighbor. Here is where the machine waits for an OPEN message. It needs to receive one of these from its neighbor even though they have a connection because it's the only way to get the basic information about this neighbor. After the message arrives, the BGP AS border router ensures that the values it might already have for this neighbor are the same as given in the OPEN message. If not, they are updated.

After this is complete, the machine transitions to the *OpenConfirm* state. It remains there until it receives a KEEPALIVE message from the neighbor. After this arrives, the router now changes to the *Established* state. BGP AS border routers in this state regularly exchange *UPDATE* messages. These messages contain different information depending on their purpose. For example, an UPDATE message advertising a new route contains:

- **The *ORIGIN Type code*.** This code tells BGP whether the route it's dealing with is inside the AS that the UPDATE message came from or from outside of it. AS border routers do share information about paths outside of their control as well as internal paths.
- **The *AS_PATH segment type*.** This code specifies whether the list of autonomous systems the new route information passed through to get to this AS border router is in a specific order or unordered.
- **The ASs that this route information passed through.** The ordered or unordered list of AS numbers.
- **The IP address for the AS border router this one must send data to get packets to the specified new route.** This is called also the *Next Hop* attribute.
- **The number of bits in the following IP address portion.** Because routing is done for networks and subnetworks, not individual IP addresses, the information sent between AS border routers is a collection of IP address *prefixes* or the portion of the address that identifies the network or subnetwork in question.
- **The IP prefix that identifies the network or subnetwork to which this route applies.** This prefix has to end at one of the dots in the IP address. If the definition applies to 192.14.14.51, and it's a full unsubnetted class C network, the entry would be 192.14.14.

There can be only one new route per UPDATE message. However, BGP can withdraw as many existing routes as it likes in the same UPDATE message. Each of these route withdrawals includes all or part of the following information:

- **The total length of the *withdrawn routes* section.** This item ensures that there is no confusion from section to section, given that withdrawn routes can be any length. A zero means that there are no routes to remove.
- **The number of bits in the IP address portions.** Once again, the information sent between AS border routers is a collection of IP address prefixes, or the portion of the address that identifies the network or subnetwork in question.
- **The IP prefix that identifies the network or subnetwork to which this route applies.** Again, the prefix has to end at one of the dots in the IP address.
- **The total length of the *Path Attributes* section.** Once again, including this information avoids misread data.

How does the BGP AS border router decide about which routes to notify its neighbors? Each of these machines has a *Policy Information Base* (PIB) containing rules that the administrator sets by hand. Each machine also has a set of separate databases, each with a specific function. All of the routes this router is aware of are listed in its *Adj-RIB-In* database. Routing Information Base (RIB) is another term for the routing table. The BGP AS border router takes its PIB and applies the rules to every route in Adj-RIB-In. Anything that fits the rules is copied to the *Adj-RIB-Out* database.

One piece of data calculated using the PIB rules is the *preference* rating for each particular route. After this information is put together, the BGP AS border router looks at each destination it has routing information for and chooses the best route to each according to its PIB rules and preference ratings. The best routes are all stored in the *Loc-RIB* database.

There is still one more chunk of processing to do. Keep in mind that these databases are maintained from moment to moment. Each time new information goes into Adj-RIB-In or Loc-RIB, there's a trickle-down effect. Adj-RIB-Out relies on both of these databases and so must change whenever one or both of them does. Adj-RIB-Out is trimmed further than Loc-RIB in some BGP implementations. Duplicate routes are removed from this version of the database so that there is only one way for data to get from point A to B. This ensures that the databases don't get too large or redundant. Whenever there is a change to Adj-RIB-Out, that change is sent as an UPDATE message to the BGP neighbors.

Perhaps now you have an idea of why BGP is preferred over EGP in many situations. It is simply a smarter protocol with more internal checks and balances for route tuning. The programs under Linux that implement this protocol are `zebra` and the unicast version of `gated`. Once again, BGP is a unicast border protocol.

Border Gateway Multicast Protocol (BGMP)

Multicast protocols need AS border router attention too. This section deals with the Border Gateway Multicast Protocol, or BGMP. BGMP comes with the capability of building multicast group trees in the style of PIM-SM, where only group members belong to the tree at any given time. However, these trees don't consist of individual routers. Instead, each tree has only BGMP border routers as members. Once this tree is built, some domains build their own internal trees from there, depending on the protocol they are using.

The multicast domain advertising the availability of a specific range of multicast channels is considered the root for that range. Remember that multicast channels each consist of a single class D Internet address, which range from 224.0.0.0 through 239.255.255.255. So, perhaps our AS has the range of multicast channels from 231.15.19.120 through 231.15.19.140. BGMP would consider our AS the root domain for that range.

When a user joins a multicast group outside their domain or AS, their request is passed to the BGMP router. This router looks up the address for the router handling the root domain containing this particular channel. Once the BGMP router knows which domain to send the request to, it generates a BGMP UPDATE message containing the following information:

- **Address *prefix*.** This prefix tells BGMP the length of the included netmask.

- *Address family*, *protocol family*, or *protocol suite*—**these all refer to the same thing.** The type of networking protocol collection that this packet was meant to travel on. For the purposes of this discussion, let's assume that you're using an Internet-like network, and on it you're using TCP/IP.

- **Address.** The multicast address this UPDATE message refers to.

- **Netmask.** The netmask associated with the multicast address included in this UPDATE message.

- **JOIN message declaration.** This parameter specifies that this UPDATE message is in fact a JOIN message.

- **Additional declarations.** A BGMP UPDATE message can carry multiple message types. In this case the primary attribute is JOIN. So, this message also could serve the function of *GROUP*, *SOURCE*, or *POISON_REVERSE*. Inside these, you could nest even more JOINs, PRUNEs, and so on.

The BGMP router now looks in its tables and sends this UPDATE message to the router that will take it one step closer to the multicast root domain. The receiving router looks to see whether it already has an entry that tells it to forward data for this multicast group to the requesting router. If it doesn't, it creates this entry and sends the packet to the next closest BGMP router. This router looks to see whether it's already forwarding data from this group to the requesting domain. If not, it creates an entry to do so and continues. This process follows along the tree from router to router until the UPDATE message reaches the root domain.

Eventually, users leave. When a user disconnects from a multicast channel that is broadcast from outside its domain, the BGMP router is notified. This router first looks to see whether it has any other group members within its domain. If not, it generates an UPDATE message that is different from the JOIN message in one simple fact: Rather than having a bit set to tell the UPDATE it's carrying JOIN information, there's a bit set telling it that this UPDATE message carries PRUNE information.

The UPDATE message is sent along using the same pattern as a JOIN UPDATE message would use. It's sent hop by hop along the shortest path to the root domain. Each router along the way sees if it is serving any other members of this multicast group. If it is, the UPDATE message stops, and there is no need to send it along. However, if this was the only destination requesting data from that group, the UPDATE message advances further down the tree.

Along with changing multicast group memberships, BGMP routers also have to deal with changes in the overall multicast routing tables. Over time channels are added and removed as transmission content is retired and new players emerge.

BGMP is in many ways related to BGP but, as you can see, has features that allow it to work well in conjunction with multicast transmissions. The programs under Linux that implement this protocol are `zebra` and the multicast version of `gated`.

Multicast Source Discovery Protocol (MSDP)

Another multicast border router protocol is the Multicast Source Discovery Protocol (MSDP). This particular protocol can only be used to connect domains that also use PIM-SM internally. You might find it helpful to review the section, "Protocol Independent Multicast-Sparse Mode (PIM-SM)," in Chapter 2, "Multicast Protocols," before proceeding. This protocol also utilizes the BGP routing tables rather than building its own for unicast data.

MSDP routers keep a continuous connection open to their neighbors, or *peers*, using TCP. A KeepAlive timer is used to check whether KeepAlive messages arrive within specified intervals, though these messages are not sent unless no *Source-Active* (SA) messages have arrived within the KeepAlive requirements. If the interval is exceeded with no KeepAlive or SA messages having arrived, the peer tries to reset the TCP connection.

The developers of MSDP did not feel the need to reinvent the wheel. PIM-SM and MSDP utilize the already existing PIM-SM Rendezvous Point (RP) setup to speak to one another. Whenever a new source starts broadcasting and this information reaches an RP, the machine creates an *SA message* containing the following information:

- The IP address of the machine originating the broadcast
- The multicast channel address to where the data is being sent
- The IP address of the Rendezvous Point that handles this channel

This message is then sent to the MSDP border router. After the SA message is received, it is forwarded to all of the border router's MSDP neighbors except for the machine it received the message from—this is called *peer-RPF flooding*. When each peer receives the SA packet, it checks to see which of its neighbors is the *RPF peer* for this particular multicast channel. The RPF peer is the MSDP router closest to the MSDP router that sent the original SA message, which we'll call the *SA originator*.

The router double-checks any SA message against the RPF peer to avoid loop-back problems. If the SA message came from a machine that is closer to the SA originator than this router is, but is not the RPF peer, the SA message is ignored. Other than this, the MSDP router sends the SA message out to all of its peers—namely, those that are not closer to the SA originator than it is.

This process continues throughout the entire Internet, as long as there are more MSDP peers to talk to. Another thing that each MSDP peer has to examine is whether or not it's also a PIM-SM Rendezvous Point for its domain. If this machine serves both purposes, it checks to see if any of its own domain members have requested access to this new channel. Even one request causes this MSDP/PIM-SM RP to send a Join request to the channel's RP. Doing this creates the odd situation where the tree for this particular channel reaches out of its local domain.

As you can see, this protocol is fairly straightforward because it's able to rely on BGP for routing tables and PIM-SM for tracking group memberships. The Linux program that implements this protocol is the multicast version of `gated`.

Summary

Along with the IGPs that you must consider for use within your autonomous system or your portion of it, the overall network administrator also needs to look at the border protocols available and choose which best fits his or her particular situation. This chapter looked at the unicast border protocols, EGP and BGP, and the multicast protocols, BGMP and MSDP. Most administrators choose BGP over EGP today simply because BGP has more modern features and is more robust because of it. When it comes to choosing BGMP over MSDP, the right choice depends on whether you're using PIM-SM or not, as MSDP is optimized for PIM-SM.

Table 3.1 outlines the border protocols available to you and the data you'll need to get started.

Table 3.1   **The Programs Used to Implement Unicast and Multicast Border Routing Protocols in Linux, and the RFC Documents That Contain Vital Background Information**

Protocol	Program	RFC or Draft
EGP	gated	904
BGP	gated, zebra	1771
BGMP	gated, zebra	draft-ietf-bgmp-spec-01.txt
MDSP	gated	draft-ietf-msdp-spec-06.txt

4

IPv4 and IPv6 Addressing

LINUX NATIVELY USES TCP/IP AS ITS suite of networking protocols and tools. One aspect of this collection of rules and programs is that every machine on the network must have a unique value or address assigned to it according to the IP addressing scheme. Most of us are already aware of this and have experience assigning addresses in both the Internet and private network spaces. If this is the case for you, then feel free to either skip this chapter or jump straight down to the section titled "Classless IPv4 Addressing" and "IPv6 Addressing."

However, if you've never had to deal with more than just basic static TCP/IP networking with no subnetting, you're venturing into complex networking territory. Let's make sure that you have all of the knowledge you need at your disposal.

IPv4 Addressing

Over the years, we've all gotten comfortable with good old IP version 4. IPv4 is based on 32-bit host addresses. Addresses are first broken down into the classes A, B, and C, with D kept aside for multicast channels. The address class determines how many bits in the IP address apply to the network number and how many apply to the host number. All subnets made of these networks are of equal size and so on. Each new thing you learn about working with IP v4 lets you add more levels of complexity to your networking setups.

IPv4 Math Review

We're not going to dwell on IP basics too much here. Most introductory network and Linux books cover that kind of information. In case it's been a while since you really needed to deal with it, we'll start with a quick overview of the easy stuff, and then we'll dive into the math.

IP addresses are set in two different formats:

- The computer readable (binary) version is xxxxxxxx.xxxxxxxx.xxxxxxxx.xxxxxxxx, where every x (bit) is either a 0 or a 1. Every address is composed of four octets or four 8-bit binary numbers.

- The human readable (decimal) version is xxx.xxx.xxx.xxx, where xxx can range from 000 through 255. This is the decimal equivalent of each 8-bit binary number.

While the average user setting up his own box only needs to know the decimal IP values, sometimes it's useful or even required to understand how to go between decimal and binary when planning and setting up complex networks. At first, let's focus on reading just one of the 8-bit (byte) portions of a binary IP address. Each of the x's has a specific decimal value depending on its binary value (1 or 0) and its placement within the octet. The value is always 0 decimal if the x is a 0-bit. However, if the x bit has a value of 1, it is worth its location decimal value.

The eight bits in each byte are numbered 0 through 7. The x farthest to the right is at position 0, and each bit has an individual value of two to the power of its location. So, from right to left the positions are worth:

$2^0 = 1$
$2^1 = 2$
$2^2 = 4$
$2^3 = 8$
$2^4 = 16$
$2^5 = 32$
$2^6 = 64$
$2^7 = 128$

Figure 4.1 maps these values to their actual position in the byte.

| 128 | 64 | 32 | 16 | 8 | 4 | 2 | 1 |

Figure 4.1 Each bit in a single IP byte corresponds to a particular power of 2, counted from right to left starting from position 0.

So, let's take a look at an example. We'll return to the fact that an IP address has four bytes, not just one. So say that we have the binary IP address 01001101.00011101.10111001.10110110. What is this address in decimal? Each byte is calculated individually, and it really doesn't matter where we start. We'll start from the left, since it feels more natural for some. The first byte, 01001101, breaks down to the following, which is shown in two different ways:

$0x2^7 + 1x2^6 + 0x2^5 + 0x2^4 + 1x2^3 + 1x2^2 + 0x2^1 + 1x2^0 = 77$
$0x128 + 1x64 + 0x32 + 0x16 + 1x8 + 1x4 + 0x2 + 1x1 = 77$

The second byte, 00011101, breaks down into:

$0x128 + 0x64 + 0x32 + 1x16 + 1x8 + 1x4 + 0x2 + 1x1 = 29$

The third byte, 10111001:

$1x128 + 0x64 + 1x32 + 1x16 + 1x8 + 0x4 + 0x2 + 1x1 = 185$

And, finally, the fourth byte, 10110110:

$1x128 + 0x64 + 1x32 + 1x16 + 0x8 + 1x4 + 1x2 + 0x1 = 182$

So the decimal version of this IP address is 77.29.185.182. Now that we've got the address itself, we want to know things like which are the network bits and which are the host bits. To do that, we have to look at the standard IP address class table, as shown in Table 4.1.

Table 4.1 **IP Address Class Ranges, Without Special Addresses Removed and with Network Portions in Bold and Host Portions in Non-Bold**

Class	Start		End	
	BINARY	DECIMAL	BINARY	DECIMAL
A	**00000001**.00000000. 00000000.00000000	**1.**0.0.0	**01111111**.00000000. 00000000.00000000	**127.**0.0.0
B	**10000000.00000000.** 00000000.00000000	**128.0.**0.0	**10111111.11111111.** 00000000.00000000	**191.255.**0.0
C	**11000000.00000000.** **00000000.**00000000	**192.0.0.**0	**11011111.11111111.** **11111111.**00000000	**223.255.255.**0
D	11100000.00000000. 00000000.00000000	**224.0.0.0**	**11101111.11111111.** **11111111.11111111**	**239.255.255.255**

This isn't the whole story, though. Not all of these addresses are actually available. Let's weed out the network addresses first. For example, the entire network 127.0.0.0 is only used to loop back to the same machine you're working in. You can't use it to reach another machine. No one is assigned this network number. The very first network 0.0.0.0 isn't even listed. It's used to point to the default route.

We also can't use the very first and last address in each class. All addresses where all of the variable bits are either 0s or 1s are reserved for special use. This means that the following addresses also are unavailable:

- **Class A.** These have already been mentioned, but they are included here for easy reference. 0.0.0.0 and 127.0.0.0 are unavailable.
- **Class B.** 128.0.0.0 and 191.255.0.0 are unavailable.
- **Class C.** 192.0.0.0 and 223.255.255.0 are unavailable.

- **Class D.** 224.0.0.0 and 239.255.255.255 are unavailable. You might notice that the multicast class has no host addresses. None are needed. Multicast entirely consists of channels that machines with their own addresses join and leave.

Another set of network addresses that must be removed is the combined private IP networks. These addresses are specifically set aside for internal use and never point to a machine out on the Internet. Table 4.2 outlines these address ranges. Note that the table shows entire networks that have been reserved.

Table 4.2   **Reserved Private Networks, for Use in Intranets and Other Isolated Networks**

Class	Start	End
A	10.0.0.0	10.0.0.0
B	172.16.0.0	172.31.0.0
C	192.168.0.0	192.168.255.0
D	239.0.0.0	239.255.255.255

It's not just network addresses that get removed from the available-for-use pool. There are host addresses that cannot be used as well. While the host portions of the IP addresses were able to be left blank in the network discussions to isolate the network addresses, it's a bit trickier to do this but use real network numbers for a host discussion. So we will use x's for the network portion so we can refer only to the hosts, because what we're saying about the hosts applies to all networks. Each of the unavailable host addresses has a special purpose:

- The host address x.x.x.0 is reserved to refer to the network itself.

- The host address x.x.x.255 is the *broadcast* address or the "host" TCP/IP sends data to when it wants to send something to all network members.

- Believe it or not, that's it. Sort of. When we get into subnetting in the section "Applying IP v4 Addressing Across Subnets" in just a moment, we begin losing even more host addresses.

Let's not forget the issue of the network mask, or *netmask*, either. When you're dealing with one piece, intact networks, the netmask does not change. It is always as you see in Table 4.3.

Table 4.3   **Standard Netmasks for Each IP Address Class**

Class	Netmask
A	255.0.0.0
B	255.255.0.0
C	255.255.255.0
D	255.255.255.255

As you might notice, the netmask bits are set to all 1s in each byte that is used to determine the network number for the class. The 0 positions represent the positions that are available for hosts and subnets. As usual, you can see that multicast has no hosts, and you can't subnet a single IP address.

Applying IPv4 Addressing Across Subnets

Sometimes one network is not enough. You might have a full class C address, but there is an administrative, security, geographic, or other reason that you need to break your network into a set of subnets. Doing so causes more work. For one thing, you'll have to actually set up routing because you now have to tell each subnet how to send data to the other subnets and the outside world. You also have to calculate all of the IP bits and pieces, such as the new netmasks, new network addresses, new broadcast address, and so on.

You break an IP network into subnets by turning some of the host bits into network bits. No, this isn't a magic trick. You do this with the assistance of also changing the netmask. A netmask that is not standard for the address class tells TCP/IP that it is dealing with a subnetted network. So, let's take a look at how all of this is accomplished.

In the worlds of class A and B networking, subnetting is relatively simple. You can take a class A network such as 120.0.0.0—which has a netmask of 255.0.0.0—and divide it into subnets simply by using addresses 120.1.0.0 through 120.254.0.0 as network addresses and changing the netmask to 255.255.0.0. Look familiar? You've just turned your class A network into 254 class B network addresses or subnets. The same works for class B networks. Take 142.182.0.0, which falls in the class B range and so has the netmask 255.255.0.0. Give it a netmask of 255.255.255.0 and use 142.186.1.0 through 142.185.254.0 as network addresses, and you've just turned your class B network into 254 class C network addresses or subnets. However, how many of us really get our own class A or B to play with these days? Fat chance.

Things get more interesting when you want to subnet your class C network. You can't just break it down into class D networks; those are individual IP addresses. However, we can do it by changing the netmask and then breaking up the available hosts so each go into a different network. You then usurp some of the host addresses for network numbers and other reserved values.

IP v4 has certain limits on the subnets you can create for a class C address. Each subnet must be the same size, and the number of nets you divide your network into is determined by binary math. Because the first three bytes of the netmask for a class C address are fixed as 255.255.255., let's just look at the last byte. As usual, it is eight bits where x is either 0 or 1. Your first option for making subnets is to divide your network into two. Why? Because the first x can either be 0 or 1, you have only two options. So, suddenly your network bits (represented by n) are one bit larger, your host bits (represented by h) are one bit smaller, and your network bytes look like nnnnnnnn.nnnnnnnn.nnnnnnnn.nhhhhhhh.

The second chance for dividing your network is into four pieces because those first two x's can be 00, 01, 10, or 11. So now your network bytes are nnnnnnnn.nnnnnnnn.nnnnnnnn.nnhhhhhh. Once again, TCP/IP keeps track of this through your netmask. The last byte of your netmask is equal to the position values of the n's within it. So the netmask for a two-subnet network is 255.255.255.128. It follows that the netmask for four subnets is 255.255.255.192. Table 4.4 outlines the possible IP v4 subnets for a class C address and their pertinent values.

Table 4.4 **Pertinent Facts About the Possible IP v4 class C Subnets, Where n Stands for Network Bit, h Stands for Host Bit, and x Stands for Network Byte**

Number	Network Bits	Binary Netmask	Decimal Netmask
2	nhhhhhhh	.10000000	255.255.255.128
4	nnhhhhhh	.11000000	255.255.255.192
8	nnnhhhhh	.11100000	255.255.255.224
16	nnnnhhhh	.11110000	255.255.255.240
32	nnnnnhhh	.11111000	255.255.255.248
64	nnnnnnhh	.11111100	255.255.255.252
128	nnnnnnnh	.11111110	255.255.255.254

Now, some of these subnet sizes are pretty unrealistic. We'll illustrate why by getting into the internals of the subnetwork addresses, host address ranges, and more. Let's take the two-subnet case to start with. You can use the remaining host bits to help you determine the range of host numbers that goes toward each subnetwork. In the case of the two-subnet breakdown, the h's (host bits) in nhhhhhhh add up to 127. So subnet 1 is from x.x.x.0 through x.x.x.127, and subnet 2 is from x.x.x.128 through x.x.x.255.

It's not that simple though. The first and last host bits are always reserved, even in a subnetted network, so you really only get x.x.x.1 through x.x.x.127 and x.x.x.128 through x.x.x.254 for your subnets. Now we have to pull out the network addresses. For subnet 1 this is x.x.x.1 and for subnet 2 this is x.x.x.128—for the entire network it's x.x.x.0, and that's all the rest of the Internet sees. So your available host IP addresses are now x.x.x.2 through x.x.x.127 and x.x.x.129 through x.x.x.254. We now need the subnet broadcast addresses, as opposed to the x.x.x.255, which broadcasts to the entire network. Those would be the last address in each subnet, x.x.x.127 and x.x.x.254. Now our hosts can be x.x.x.2 through x.x.x.126 and x.x.x.129 through x.x.x.253. As you can see, for the convenience of turning our class C network into two subnetworks, we've given up the use of four host IP addresses.

Things of course get more complex as we create four subnets. The host bits in nnhhhhhh add up to 63, so we end up with the following four subnet ranges: x.x.x.0 through x.x.x.63, x.x.x.64 through x.x.x.127, x.x.x.128 through x.x.x.191, and x.x.x.192 through x.x.x.255. Once again, we lose x.x.x.0 and x.x.x.255 to the overall network address and broadcast address. We also lose x.x.x.1, x.x.x.64, x.x.x.128, and x.x.x.192 to network addresses; x.x.x.63, x.x.x.127, x.x.x.191, and x.x.x.254 to broadcast addresses. Table 4.5 lays out the address ranges for each subnetting possibility and the addresses lost as well.

Table 4.5 **Host and Special Addresses Among IP v4 Class C Subnets Two Through Thirty-Two, Assuming That x.x.x.0 and x.x.x.255 Are Always Lost for Network and Broadcast Addresses**

Number of Networks	Network Numbers	Broadcast Addresses	Host Addresses
2	x.x.x.1, x.x.x.128	x.x.x.127, x.x.x.254	x.x.x.2 – x.x.x.126, x.x.x.129 – x.x.x.253
4	x.x.x.1, x.x.x.64, x.x.x.128, x.x.x.192	x.x.x.63, x.x.x.127, x.x.x.191, x.x.x.254	x.x.x.2 – x.x.x.62, x.x.x.65 – x.x.x.126, x.x.x.129 – x.x.x.190, x.x.x.193 – x.x.x.253
8	x.x.x.1, x.x.x.32, x.x.x.64, x.x.x.96, x.x.x.128, x.x.x.160, x.x.x.192, x.x.x.224	x.x.x.31, x.x.x.63, x.x.x.95, x.x.x.127, x.x.x.159, x.x.x.191, x.x.x.223, x.x.x.254	x.x.x.2 – x.x.x.30, x.x.x.33 – x.x.x.62, x.x.x.56 – x.x.x.94, x.x.x.97 – x.x.x.126, x.x.x.129 – x.x.x.158, x.x.x.161 – x.x.x.190, x.x.x.193 – x.x.x.222, x.x.x.225 – x.x.x.253
16	x.x.x.1, x.x.x.16, x.x.x.32, x.x.x.48, x.x.x.64, x.x.x.80, x.x.x.96, x.x.x.112, x.x.x.128, x.x.x.144, x.x.x.160, x.x.x.176, x.x.x.192, x.x.x.208, x.x.x.224, x.x.x.240	x.x.x.15, x.x.x.31, x.x.x.47, x.x.x.64, x.x.x.79, x.x.x.95, x.x.x.111, x.x.x.127, x.x.x.143, x.x.x.159, x.x.x.175, x.x.x.191, x.x.x.207, x.x.x.223, x.x.x.239, x.x.x.254	x.x.x.2 – x.x.x.14, x.x.x.17 – x.x.x.30, x.x.x.33 – x.x.x.46, x.x.x.49 – x.x.x.63, x.x.x.65 – x.x.x.78, x.x.x.81 – x.x.x.94, x.x.x.97 – x.x.x.110, x.x.x.113 – x.x.x.126, x.x.x.129 – x.x.x.142, x.x.x.145 – x.x.x.158, x.x.x.161 – x.x.x.174, x.x.x.177 – x.x.x.190, x.x.x.193 – x.x.x.206, x.x.x.209 – x.x.x.222, x.x.x.225 – x.x.x.238, x.x.x.241 – x.x.x.253

continues

Table 4.5 **Continued**

Number of Networks	Network Numbers	Broadcast Addresses	Host Addresses
32	x.x.x.1,	x.x.x.7,	x.x.x.2 – x.x.x.6,
	x.x.x.8,	x.x.x.15,	x.x.x.9 - x.x.x.14,
	x.x.x.16,	x.x.x.23,	x.x.x.17 – x.x.x.22,
	x.x.x.24,	x.x.x.31,	x.x.x.25 - x.x.x.30,
	x.x.x.32,	x.x.x.39,	x.x.x.33 – x.x.x.38,
	x.x.x.40,	x.x.x.47,	x.x.x.41 - x.x.x.46,
	x.x.x.48,	x.x.x.55,	x.x.x.49 – x.x.x.54,
	x.x.x.56,	x.x.x.64,	x.x.x.57 - x.x.x.63,
	x.x.x.64,	x.x.x.71,	x.x.x.65 – x.x.x.70,
	x.x.x.72,	x.x.x.79,	x.x.x.73 - x.x.x.78,
	x.x.x.80,	x.x.x.87,	x.x.x.81 – x.x.x.88,
	x.x.x.88,	x.x.x.95,	x.x.x.89 - x.x.x.94,
	x.x.x.96,	x.x.x.103,	x.x.x.97 – x.x.x.102,
	x.x.x.104,	x.x.x.111,	x.x.x.105 - x.x.x.110,
	x.x.x.112,	x.x.x.119,	x.x.x.113 - x.x.x.118,
	x.x.x.120,	x.x.x.127,	x.x.x.121 - x.x.x.126,
	x.x.x.128,	x.x.x.135,	x.x.x.129 – x.x.x.134,
	x.x.x.136,	x.x.x.143,	x.x.x.137 - x.x.x.142,
	x.x.x.144,	x.x.x.151,	x.x.x.145 – x.x.x.150,
	x.x.x.152,	x.x.x.159,	x.x.x.153 - x.x.x.158,
	x.x.x.160,	x.x.x.167,	x.x.x.161 – x.x.x.166,
	x.x.x.168,	x.x.x.175,	x.x.x.169 - x.x.x.174,
	x.x.x.176,	x.x.x.183,	x.x.x.177 – x.x.x.182,
	x.x.x.184,	x.x.x.191,	x.x.x.185 - x.x.x.190,
	x.x.x.192,	x.x.x.199,	x.x.x.193 – x.x.x.198,
	x.x.x.200,	x.x.x.207,	x.x.x.201 - x.x.x.206,
	x.x.x.208,	x.x.x.215,	x.x.x.209 – x.x.x.214,
	x.x.x.216,	x.x.x.223,	x.x.x.217 - x.x.x.222,
	x.x.x.224,	x.x.x.231,	x.x.x.225 – x.x.x.230,
	x.x.x.232,	x.x.x.239,	x.x.x.233 - x.x.x.238,
	x.x.x.240,	x.x.x.247,	x.x.x.241 – x.x.x.246,
	x.x.x.248	x.x.x.254	x.x.x.249 – x.x.x.253

Perhaps after taking time to look over this table you might see why we stopped at breaking up addressing space at thirty-two subnets. There are only five host addresses available for each subnet when we reach this point, so breaking it up further would just bring us down to even smaller networks with less and less useful numbers of hosts.

IPv4 Routing Issues

As we all know, when you have a large network, address space is paramount. Not only do you have to break your subnets into identical pieces with IP v4, but even worse, you cannot utilize the first and last subnets. Therefore, even though a two-part subnet was included in Table 4.5, you could not even use these subnets in IP v4. So your four-part subnet is really two. Your eight is really six. The sixteen is fourteen, and the thirty-two is thirty. In this case, you actually give up less bulk address space by creating more subnets; however, you lose so many host IP addresses to new network and broadcast subnet addresses that it's not a useful trick.

The other thing to keep in mind is the information that an IP v4 router carries. All the external router knows is the network address and the netmask for that network. When the data reaches your internal routers, they then can send information appropriately to the correct subnet.

Classless IPv4 Addressing

While many of the tenets of IP v4 addressing apply here, such as there being 32 bits in an address divided into four bytes, separated by dots, the new concept you need to become familiar with is *Classless Interdomain Routing* (CIDR). This subset of IP v4 adds such words to our vocabularies as *supernetting* and *Variable Length Subnet Masks* (VLSM). So, buckle your seatbelts—it's going to be a fun ride.

Differences Between Classful and Classless IPv4 Addressing

There is no class A, B, and so on in CIDR IP v4. No, this does not cause chaos. Instead, all xxx.xxx.xxx.xxx (decimal) combinations come in turn with a *bit mask* (also called a prefix length). While this item is utilized in IP v4 as a shortcut instead of typing out the whole netmask, we chose to cover the math behind it in the following section, "Classless IP v4 Math," because calculating these values is an absolutely necessary skill. Everything has limitations. Classless IP v4 does not allow you unfettered ability to assign address blocks as you see fit. We'll get more into this when we actually start doing the math in the next section.

In Classful (original) IP v4, there are 32 bits (8 bits per byte x 4 bytes) in an address, and we use a subnet structure similar to what's shown in Figure 4.2. All subnets are the same size and are contained within a single larger network. While handy, this is a pretty rigid framework that leads to much loss of host addresses and prevents any further subdivisions.

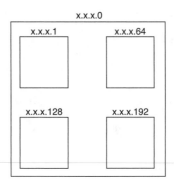

Figure 4.2   Subnetting from the Classful IP v4 perspective.

Classless IPv4 Math

As was said before, almost all of CIDR works properly because of bit mask or prefix length assignments. A bit mask is written in the format /xx, where the x's merely represent digits. In IP v4, only /8, /16, or /24 bit masks exist. These values correspond to the number of bits used for the network portion of the IP address. So, for a class A, you have nnnnnnnn.hhhhhhhh.hhhhhhhh.hhhhhhhh, or /8. For class B, you have nnnnnnnn.nnnnnnnn.hhhhhhhh.hhhhhhhh or /16, and for C you have nnnnnnnn.nnnnnnnn.nnnnnnnn.hhhhhhhh or /24.

Classless IP v4 tosses the whole address class thing out the window. However, as you were warned, there are still limits on what you can do. The number of addresses you give to a network in this system must be a power of two: 2, 4, 8, 16, 32, 64, 128, 256, 512, and so on. Notice that this didn't say the bit mask has to be a power of two. We're talking about addresses right now.

So, how do you figure out what bit mask to use for a particular host range? Once again, let's look at the IP address template xxxxxxxx.xxxxxxxx.xxxxxxxx.xxxxxxxx. The bit mask (network bits) and host bits must add up to 32, as there are 32 bits in the addressing scheme. Let's say that for our campus setup we need an address block of 4096. It would take 12 bits to express 4096 unique addresses because 2 to the 12th power is 4096. So, that's 12 host bits, which leaves the remaining 20 for network bits. So this address ends in a /20. It doesn't matter what the network bits are. In CIDR, machines do not assume anything from the network bits. We'll keep repeating this because it is one of the biggest changes you'll have to get used to.

Though we can't entirely get rid of the netmasks, it's pretty easy to make them. Let's go back to our /20 network, which looks like nnnnnnnn.nnnnnnnn.nnnnhhhh.hhhhhhhh. We're using all of the network bits in the first and second bytes so they both have a decimal value of 255. The third bytes only has the first four network bits in use, and their positions add up to 128 + 64 + 32 + 16, or 240. The last position is entirely host bits, so it's 0. That gives us a netmask of 255.255.240.0. Table 4.6 gives the bit mask and netmask particulars for a range of CIDR possibilities.

Table 4.6   **The Bit Mask, Netmask, and Number of Addresses Within a Range of Classless Domain Possibilities**

Bit Mask	Netmask	Host Addresses
/17	255.255.128.0	32,766
/18	255.255.192.0	16,382
/19	255.255.224.0	8,190
/20	255.255.240.0	4,094
/21	255.255.248.0	2,046
/22	255.255.252.0	1,022
/23	255.255.254.0	510
/24	255.255.255.0	254
/25	255.255.255.128	126
/26	255.255.255.192	62
/27	255.255.255.224	30
/28	255.255.255.240	14
/29	255.255.255.248	6

Notice that the host addresses are all a power of 2 minus 2. Because a network still needs a network address and a broadcast address, this accurately represents how many hosts you get per piece.

Applying Classless IPv4 Addressing Across Subnets

The concept of subnets might not seem to make a lot of sense when we start talking about classless networking, but it's still there. After all, what if we're assigned an address chunk and need to break it down into smaller pieces? Further still, maybe we don't want all of our subnets to be exactly the same size. Here's where we get into those Variable Length Subnet Masks (VLSMs).

In VLSM, you can apply multiple subnet masks to the same overall network to create subnets of different sizes. We do this in a hierarchal way. We create a collection of same-size larger subnets, and then where we need smaller networks, we subnet the subnet. We can keep breaking these down into smaller networks as far as we need to.

Here is where the *extended-network-prefix* comes in. Let's go back to that /20 network we discussed in the previous section. The /20 is the bit mask, as we already discussed. So the network bits and bytes are structured like nnnnnnnn.nnnnnnnn.nnnnhhhh.hhhhhhhh. Now that we have such a large address space—capable of containing 4,094 hosts—we need to break it down further. In the case of our example network, we have a huge autonomous system for the entire university that contains two smaller but still huge routing areas, one for the campus and one for the dorms.

So first we want to divide our 192.168.240.0/20 network into two large subnets, one for each. As you know, 2 is 2 to the power of 1, which means that we only need a single bit to handle this subnetting. We now need to use a new series of symbols to help keep everything clear in our address bits. The n stands not just for network, but for the main network—the bit mask portion of the network. We'll now add an e for the extended-network-prefix to the mix. So we now have nnnnnnnn.nnnnnnnn.nnnnehhh.hhhhhhhh.

We just need the network addresses for the subnets now. This is actually easier than you'd think. The first network is 192.168.240.0/21, and the second is 192.168.248.0/21, as shown in Figure 4.3.

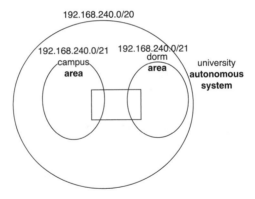

Figure 4.3 The beginning of our hierarchal Classless IP v4 networking scheme.

As you already know from the previous chapters, each building has its own router because it has its own network. Therefore, we need to divide each of the subnets above further into subnets for each building. Let's start with the campus area. There are seven different buildings defined here. We might add more some day. To break on a bit boundary, we want a power of two. The two closest and bigger than seven powers of two are eight and 16, and while it would be nice to break 192.168.240.0/21 down into 16 subnets to leave plenty of room to maneuver, this would limit us to just 126 machines per network (/25) rather than 254 (/24). How do we know this? The network bits for 192.168.240.0/21 are nnnnnnnn.nnnnnnnn.nnnnehhh.hhhhhhhh, and if an f is used to represent this subnet, then there are two choices:

- Eight subnets will require three more bits and give me nnnnnnnn.nnnnnnnn.nnnnefff.hhhhhhhh or /24.

- Sixteen subnets will require four more bits—including those used for the eight subnet option—and give me nnnnnnnn.nnnnnnnn.nnnnefff.fhhhhhhh or /25.

Because eight has been chosen, the first of the eight subnets is 192.168.241.0/24 (nnnnnnnn.nnnnnnnn.nnnne001.hhhhhhhh)—where we already know that the third bit's nnnne is 240. The full list of eight subnets is detailed in Table 4.7.

Table 4.7   **The Eight Campus Subnets Taken from Network 192.168.240.0/21, with Only the Changing Bits Displayed**

Subnet	Bit-wise	Network
Ag	.nnnne000.hhhhhhhh	192.168.240.0/24
Eng	.nnnne001.hhhhhhhh	192.168.241.0/24
Phys	.nnnne010.hhhhhhhh	192.168.242.0/24
Hum	.nnnne011.hhhhhhhh	192.168.243.0/24
Arts	.nnnne100.hhhhhhhh	192.168.244.0/24
Chem	.nnnne101.hhhhhhhh	192.168.245.0/24
Math	.nnnne110.hhhhhhhh	192.168.246.0/24
spare	.nnnne111.hhhhhhhh	192.168.247.0/24

In each subnet, you get 254 addresses—if this seems like a class C to you, it is; a class C is just a /24 network. From here, you can actually subnet further for different departments or whatever suits your needs.

On the dorm side there are six buildings. This means once again that if you want one subnet per building, the closest you can get is eight. The dorm network is 192.168.248.0/21. Its eight subnets are calculated exactly the same way, and the results are given in Table 4.8.

Table 4.8   **The Eight Dorm Subnets Taken from Network 192.168.248.0/21, with Only the Changing Bits Displayed**

Subnet	Bit-wise	Network
Runk	.nnnne000.hhhhhhhh	192.168.248.0/24
East	.nnnne001.hhhhhhhh	192.168.249.0/24
Trud	.nnnne010.hhhhhhhh	192.168.250.0/24
Wash	.nnnne011.hhhhhhhh	192.168.251.0/24
Wall	.nnnne100.hhhhhhhh	192.168.252.0/24
Poin	.nnnne101.hhhhhhhh	192.168.253.0/24
spare	.nnnne110.hhhhhhhh	192.168.254.0/24
spare	.nnnne111.hhhhhhhh	192.168.255.0/24

In this case, you might decide to have a subnet for each floor in the dorm or not make any subnetworks at all. Figure 4.4 shows you what our new network-addressing scheme looks like.

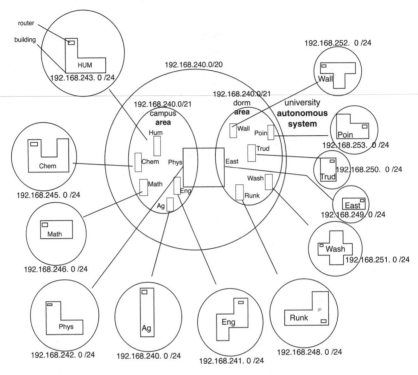

Figure 4.4   The current hierarchal Classless IP v4 networking scheme.

Classless IPv4 Routing Issues

It might sound like Classless IP v4 puts a huge burden on the Internet's routers. Even worse, it could explode the routing tables into an unmanageable size that slows down all Internet traffic. Fortunately this is not the case. Not only does Classless IP v4 allow you to create subnets of subnets of subnets, it also allows you to hide the layers from the outside world—if you plan your network correctly. See Chapter 7, "Planning Router Layout and Function," for further information.

A well-planned VLSM setup includes *route aggregation*, a concept that allows you to hide subnetting from the outside world. Let me break down the VLSM subnets created in the previous section, "Applying Classless IP v4 Addressing Across Subnets," to demonstrate this concept. Each of the subnet layers was mathematically derived from its parent layer. We started with the overall network 192.168.240.0/20. The 20-bit mask translates to nnnnnnnn.nnnnnnnn.nnnnhhhh.hhhhhhhh, where n is a network bit and h is a host bit. This means that you have access to the address range 192.168.240.0 through 192.168.255.255.

The two subnets within this network are 192.168.240.0/21 and 192.168.248.0/21. Both of these network addresses are within the main network's address range. Therefore, no matter which subnet the traffic ultimately needs to go to, it first has to go to network 192.168.240.0/20 according to how the IP v6 routing works. No router outside the main university router (prime) needs to know that there are any subnets at all.

Our major subnets have their own address ranges. The campus subnet, 192.168.240.0/21, has the bit mask nnnnnnnn.nnnnnnnn.nnnnehhh.hhhhhhhh. This gives it the address range 192.168.240.0 through 192.168.247.255. The dorm subnet, on the other hand, is 192.168.248.0/21 and gets 192.168.248.0 through 192.168.255.255. Take a look back at Tables 4.7 and 4.8. Every network address listed there falls within one of these two major subnets' available address ranges. Therefore, every network address in the campus and dorm buildings can be sent just to the main router, then to just the campus or dorm router, then to the appropriate building, and then directly to the correct machine.

In each case, only the router above the subnet layer needs to know that there are subnets involved at all. This is a good example of route aggregation, a term mentioned earlier. It is also the key to CIDR success. The more routing information that we can keep hidden at local levels, the smaller the overall routing tables need to be.

Routers under Classless IP v4 must carry information that IP v4 routers simply would not understand. While Classful IP v4 requires the netmask, Classless IP v4 needs the bit mask. The technique the routers use from that point is called *longest match*. The router looks at the address the information is trying to get to—let's say 192.168.250.52—and looks for the entry in its routing table that is closest to this number. The best it's going to find in a main routing table in this case is 192.168— remember that our parent network (the supernet) is 192.168.240.0/20.

Longest match isn't well demonstrated at the beginning. Rather than sending the data to 192.168.0.0, the router trying to send the data to 192.168.250.52 will have to look up 192.168.240.0/20 in the routing tables unless all of 192.168.0.0 is owned by a single ISP that then hands out parts of the addressing to others. Let's say that this is the case. The packet meant for 192.168.250.52 gets sent to the ISP that owns 192.168.0.0.

When the packet arrives at the ISP's routers, they don't see a longest match for 192.168.250.x. They do have 192.168.240.0/20 in their routing tables, however, so off the packet goes to our router Prime. Prime doesn't have a longest match for 192.168.250.x either. However, it has in its routing tables that the network 192.168.248.0/21 exists, so now the packet is sent to router East.

Now, when router East looks for a longest match for 192.168.250.x, it finds one. That's the network range assigned to the Trud router. The packet is sent to Trud, which immediately knows where to send data to 192.168.250.52. Once again, not only does this example illustrate the longest match concept, but it also shows just how much routing table information the routers outside of our campus don't need. As long as they can get the data to router Prime, it can do the rest.

What About Hosts That Don't Understand CIDR?

Not all machines can handle CIDR out of the box. This includes Linux. We'll get into the `route` command in depth in Chapter 6, "Inside The Commands," but you might already be familiar with the data `route` requires. This command wants to know the network address, gateway address, IP address, and netmask. It has no place for a bit mask. Therefore, it assumes a class for every IP address. This just won't do if you're using Classless IP v4. In fact, take a look at the other commands as well—and the kernel. You'll run into the same problem throughout.

The first Linux kernel series to have built-in Classless IP v4 support is 2.2.x. However, the Classless IP v4 module in this case is still labeled experimental. If you must have this host able to understand Classless IP v4, recompile the kernel with the Classless IP v4 modules attached and then go to `http://www.tazenda.demon.co.uk/phil/net-tools/` to download the latest version of the net-tools package. This Tarball contains all of the basic utilities you'll need for networking with Linux, and versions 1.52 and later add support for Classless IP v4. Be sure to read all README files before installing these programs.

IPv6 Addressing

We are in the midst of a large-scale change on the Internet. For many years now, many of us have worked to come to grips with the subtleties of IP addressing, subnetting, and more. Meanwhile, IP address space has approached exhaustion much sooner than anyone anticipated. When software and operating systems get outdated, what do we do? We upgrade them. The same goes for protocols that begin to show the signs of age and not being able to serve what is needed for the times. Classless IPv4 has helped, but it's not enough. IP has now been upgraded to version 6—also called IP next generation (IPng)—and the great migration has begun.

Introduction to IPv6 Addressing

IP v6 is not built upon the building blocks of IP v4. Instead, it's an entirely new mechanism for IP network addressing. Addresses are now 128 bits long rather than 32. This gives us a lot more room for individual hosts. There is also no broadcast address anymore in IP v6. Instead, you have a choice between unicast, multicast, or anycast. This last option allows for having more than one interface assigned the same IP address and sends the data meant for that address to the closest of these interfaces. The ability to assign more than one address to an interface also is built into IP v6.

IPng addresses are not displayed in IP v4 format. Instead, they're broken into eight parts. Each part contains two bytes—or sixteen bits—separated by a colon. Therefore, bit-wise they look pretty ominous:

xxxxxxxxxxxxxxxx:xxxxxxxxxxxxxxxx:xxxxxxxxxxxxxxxx:xxxxxxxxxxxxxxxx:xxxx
xxxxxxxxxxxx:xxxxxxxxxxxxxxxx:xxxxxxxxxxxxxxxx:xxxxxxxxxxxxxxxx, where "x" stands for one bit. Byte-wise, it isn't as overwhelming: bb:bb:bb:bb:bb:bb:bb:bb, where "b" stands for one byte.

To complicate things even further, IP v6 addressing isn't typically discussed in terms of bits and bytes. IP v6 addresses are written in hexadecimal—base 16, compared to a bit's base 2 and decimal's base 10. A single byte is equivalent to one hexadecimal pair, so what we end up with is something that looks more like the following in terms of placeholders: HHHH:HHHH:HHHH:HHHH:HHHH:HHHH:HHHH:HHHH, where H is one half of a hex pair.

Because the world of IP v6 is so different from IP v4, let's take a moment to go over some of the basics that we didn't need to look at for IP v4. These issues revolve around special numbers, what types of addresses all interfaces have to have, and how to recognize different address types. This chapter will not get into the many shortcuts for how to write IP v6 addresses, however. See RFC 2373 for more information on this front.

There are a few special host addresses in IP v6 just as there are in IP v4. One of these is the loopback address, 0:0:0:0:0:0:0:1, which is equivalent to IP v4's 127.0.0.1—you also can write the IP v6 loopback address using a shorthand technique as ::1. Another is the unspecified address, 0:0:0:0:0:0:0:0, which is utilized when no address has been given yet.

There are, however, special IP v6 addresses for broader use. There are prefixes that mark addresses of note, which are called Format Prefixes. Many of these are reserved but don't yet have a specific function—see section 2.4 in RFC 2373 for that set. Table 4.9 lists those that have already been assigned a meaning.

Table 4.9 **IPv6 Reserved Prefixes That Have an Assigned Purpose**

Decimal Prefix	Hexadecimal Prefix	Reserved Purpose
00000000	00	Not used.
00000010	02	For use by the Network Service Access Point (NSAP)—if you're interested in learning more about NSAP, see RFC 1706.
00000100	04	For use by Internet Package eXchange (IPX), a Novell networking protocol.
00100000	40	For use by the new Unicast aggregation features available in IP v6—see RFC 2374.

continues

Table 4.9 **Continued**

Decimal Prefix	Hexadecimal Prefix	Reserved Purpose
11111110 10	FE8+	For local use by linking items such as routers.
11111110 11	FEC+	For local use within a site.
11111111	FF	For multicast addressing.

Introduction to Hexadecimal Math

Notice that they have been given both binary and hexadecimal (hex) values in Table 4.9. Let's see how to get between these two bases because you'll require a solid foundation in this to work with IP v6. The things to remember when dealing with hex are

- Hexadecimal math is base 16, as compared to binary's base 2 and decimal's base 10.

- The digits you have available in hex are 0-9 and then A-F, as compared to binary's choices of only 0 or 1, and decimal's 0 through 9.

- In our case, it's easiest to think of a hexidecimal value as four bits, or half a byte.

- Hexadecimal values aren't typically discussed in singles, so we'll be talking about pairs of hex values, which means a full byte.

So let's see how we got at the numbers in Table 4.9. The first one is easy. 00000000 is decimal 0, and is hex 0000. For the second, we start with 00000010 binary. To convert this to decimal, we use the formula discussed in the section, "IP v4 Math Review":

$0x127 + 0x64 + 0x32 + 0x16 + 0x8 + 0x4 + 1x2 + 0x1 = 2$

But let's convert straight from binary to hexadecimal. We have two hex digits in this single byte, so we're really looking at 0000 and 0010. The first, 0000 binary, just becomes 0 hex. For the second we have to do just a wee bit of math. In this case, we'll use:

$0x8 + 0x4 + 1x2 + 0x0 = 2$

So, we get 02 in the end for this pair. For the rest we have:

$$00000100 = 0000\ 0100$$
$$= 0\ |\ 0x8 + 1x4 + 0x2 + 0x1$$
$$= 04$$

$$00100000 = 0010\ 0000$$
$$= 0x8 + 1x4 + 0x2 + 0x1\ |\ 0$$
$$= 40$$

$$11111110\ 10 = 1111\ 1110\ 10$$
$$= 1x8 + 1x4 + 1x2 + 1x1\ |\ 1x8 + 1x4 + 1x2 + 0x1$$
$$|\ 1x8 + 0x4 + ?x2 + ?x1$$
$$= (15\ decimal)(14\ decimal)8?$$
$$= FE8+$$

11111110 11 = 1111 1110 11 = 1x8 + 1x4 + 1x2 + 1x1 | 1x8 +
        1x4 + 1x2 + 0x1 | 1x8 + 1x4 + ?x2 + ?x1
        = (15 decimal)(14 decimal) (12 decimal)?
        = FEC+

11111111 = 1111 1111
        = 1x8 + 1x4 + 1x2 + 1x1 | 1x8 + 1x4 + 1x2 + 1x1
        = (15 decimal)(15 decimal)
        = FF

What do the plus signs—the ones up against the numbers, not the ones used for addition—represent? You must have four bytes to make a hex pair. The missing bits will determine what the final hex digit is. So the 8+ actually is 8 + ?x2 +_?x1 to give the actual hex digit.

Reading IPv6 Addresses

Most of us these days can read a Classful IP v4 address in our sleep. Sometimes when the first byte is near a boundary it's necessary to look up the borders between classes A, B, and C but generally speaking, it's usually a no-brainer. Those involved with Classful IP v4 multicasting know that any class D IP address is a multicast channel. Moving to Classless IP v4 wasn't much of a change. Most folks were already familiar with the basics of the bit mask, so even that part wasn't too traumatic.

Reading an IP v6 address does have a few similarities to reading an IP v4 address:

- The prefix—the bits at the beginning—determine what type of address you're talking about. (You might have already guessed this from the discussion in the previous section about reserved prefixes.)
- There is still a bit mask notation available.

To read an IP v6 address, work from left to right. You'll be pleased to see that it is much easier to distinguish multicast and unicast addresses from one another in IP v6. If the address begins with FF, you're looking at a multicast address. Anything else is unicast or anycast. Both of these addressing designations—unicast and anycast—look the same at a glance.

Let's focus on the unicast addresses because they're more commonly used. The possibilities for a unicast address type are detailed in Table 4.9 but here they are quickly (plus the one additional type that isn't there): aggregatable, IPX, link local, NSAP, site local, and—the new one—IP v4 capable. In general, host machines really don't know anything about these distinctions. Routers have to, however, to direct data from place to place.

The IP v6 rules as laid out in RFC 2374 for aggregatable global unicast addresses are

- **The first three bits express the initial prefix.** This prefix comes from Table 4.9, and for unicast is often 001. One more bit is required to complete the first hex digit.

- **The next 13 bits show the top level identification information required to initially tell routers where to send data.** This value is assigned by the Internet Assigned Numbers Authority (IANA) or a designated registration organization to large, well-interconnected sites that carry a lot of data that's going elsewhere.

- **The next eight bits don't yet have a purpose.** Their contents will be set when the time comes, but for now they are just 00000000.

- **The next 24 bits show the second level identification information.** Each top level designate gets the full 24 bits to utilize when handing out identification numbers to the sites it serves—note that this space is almost the same as is available for the total number of IP v4 networks. Some top level designates might choose to break this space into subnet-like portions.

- **The next 16 bits show the identification information assigned by the individual sites to their networks.** Notice that there's plenty of hierarchy involved in IP v6. A site can choose to apply subnet-like sections to this address space if they wish.

- **The last 64 bits show identification (ID) information for the interface itself.** This portion of the IP v6 address must be done in EUI-64 format, which is set by the Institute of Electrical and Electronics Engineers, Inc.'s (IEEE) Registration Authority Committee (RAC).

Remember once again that four bits is a single hex digit, eight bits is a hex pair, and 16 bits is a hex quad—which is the basic unit that makes up each portion of the IP v6 address.

Now, how does one build the interface ID according to the EUI-64 standard? The first thing to understand is that an interface ID can be either global or local. A global ID involves a unique set of numbers that represent the interface(s). We can have more than one interface with the same number in IP v6, if you remember, due to the anycast address type.

Another important concept is that an interface ID is typically built using the interface's Media Access Control (MAC) address. In the case of an Ethernet card, the MAC is a 48-bit value. So that means there are another 16 bits available to identify the interface. How you manipulate this data depends on what kind of address you're trying to create. For a global use interface ID, you take the 48-bit MAC address, split it in half, and then place the hex digits FF FE in the middle. You also take the EUI-64 standard 64-bit interface identifier and flip the very first bit. So if the first bit is a 0, make it a 1, or vice versa. It's as simple as that.

Now, what about the local use addresses? There are two designations for these in IP v6: *link-local*, and *site-local*. Both of these are specifically utilized within subnets, where external routers are aware of how to send data to the subnetwork itself but know nothing of the structure within that subnetwork.

Every interface on a host machine utilizing IP v6 must have a link-local address. This identifier is used to transmit information between the host and another entity, usually a router, or for getting the interface's global address information from a router automatically. You can recognize a link-local address by its first 10 bits, as given in Table 4.9: 11111110 10. No other machines aside from the router and the host need be aware of the link-local address.

The site-local address is a bit farther reaching. Each interface on a host gets one, and this value is useable by any machine in the network, including subnets. However, the router doesn't advertise a site-local address to the outside world. Once again, it's only for internal use. You'll know a site-local address by its first 10 bits, as usual: 11111110 11.

You might even see IP v6 addresses that end in an obviously IP v4 address. IP v6 does have a built-in mechanism for piggybacking IP v4 data, which enables the powers that be on the Internet to slowly begin migrating from IP v4 to IP v6 without causing undue hardships.

IPv6 Routing Issues

One good thing about routing issues with IP v6 is that this new addressing scheme can work within the same routing protocols we're used to: RIP-2, OSPF, and so on. There are some new features to IP v6 routing that definitely make an administrator's life more interesting. Most of them allow a finer control over what's happening with your data than you could get in IP v4.

An IP v6 packet contains a special header for routing instructions, unlike IP v4 packets. Each packet might, for example, contain information on every router it passed through on its way from one point to another. That information can actually be reversed to send data back exactly the way it came, if this is a feature you require. This feature can actually be utilized to track a mobile networking user's location when they log on—something that some will like and others will be very uncomfortable with.

One of the best new features by far is the ability of an IP v6 router to auto-configure an interface's address information. Once a host knows what an interface's link-local identifier is, that host sends an Internet Control Message Protocol for IP v6 (ICMPv6) neighbor request containing that information. If no other host responds claiming that it already has that address, the machine sends out an ICMPv6 router request message to find its router. When the network's router responds, it includes the network's IP v6 global prefix.

From here, the host builds the interface's global IP v6 address all on its own using the interface ID. If for some reason another interface claims to already have the original link-local identifier, then you'll have to configure that interface by hand.

Summary

You've learned a lot in this chapter. Hopefully by now your head is not swimming with numbers in three different bases. The important thing, here, is that you're now aware of all three addressing schemes that are currently in use and are ready to make use of whatever is appropriate for your situation—not to mention you're much better prepared for the continuing migration to CIDR and IP v6.

Linux Routing Issues and Technologies

5

Inside The Unicast
Kernel 2.2.x Daemons

T HERE ARE A NUMBER OF DAEMONS available to fulfill your Linux routing needs, and each of these has a wealth of features. Because it is not possible for me to work every single one of these into this book's examples in context, this chapter provides a central resource for a couple of the daemons you have to choose from and frees us up in later chapters to skip the basics and just get down to business. So, let's take a look at some of the routing daemons available to you for managing unicast routing under the Linux kernel 2.2.x series.

Guide to *routed*

The routed that comes with Linux kernel series 2.2.x by default—though it is not usually installed by default—only handles unicast IPv4. If you intend to use RIP within an IPv4 context, this is the only version you'll need. Be aware that in this tool's own manual under the BUGS section, it says the following: "routed is of dubious value. Consider using gated(8) or zebra(8)." As usual, it's a matter of choosing the right tool for the job. Sometimes routed is all you need.

How *routed* Works

The routed routing daemon typically starts at boot time—you'll want to be sure that it is set up to do so on the Linux box you use for your router. After finding out which network interfaces are active, the router looks at how many interfaces it has to deal with. If there is more than one, routed determines that it will have to deal with multiple internal networks rather than the single internal network that only one interface requires.

At this point, routed looks to each of the interfaces to see what types of packets they support. In this case, the only two packet types of consequence are unicast and broadcast. If the interface can only handle unicast data, the router sends a *request* packet out through it to the machines defined in its /etc/hosts file. Broadcast packets are the preferred solution, however. If the interface can handle a broadcast packet, the request packet goes as a broadcast message—which means that it goes to the network's broadcast IP address, and all machines capable of receiving broadcast traffic pick it up.

After the requests are sent, routed enters a listening loop. At this point the daemon is receptive to two types of packets: *request* and *response*. A request packet tells routed to build a list of its routing table contents with the following information for each route:

- The network or host IP address to which this table entry refers.

- The netmask for this network.

- The RIP cost (see Chapter 1, "Unicast Protocols," for more information) to send data along this particular route.

After the list is completed, it is returned to the machine that sent the request in the form of a response packet.

When routed receives a response packet from another machine, however, it has to do a bit of thinking before it knows what to do with the information. Figure 5.1 illustrates the decision-making process involved.

In the meantime, every 30 seconds routed has been sending out copies of its routing tables, according to the unicast/broadcast issues discussed earlier in this section. All of the other routed routers within your network, if you have more than one, have been doing the same. Whenever one of these packets arrives, its contents overwrite their counterparts' in the current table because they are considered definitive. This means that if any of the network or host entries in routed's table do not match what just arrived, it is replaced with the new entry. Brand new routes are added also at this point if they don't already exist. When data is changed in this manner, its last change time is reset to zero.

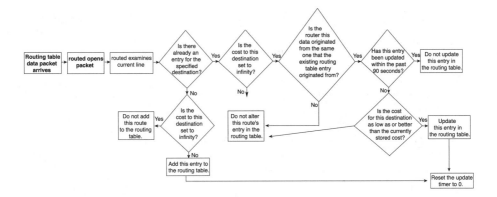

Figure 5.1   A flow chart illustrating how `routed` analyzes a response packet.

If any table entry's last change time advances to 180 seconds, routed sets the cost for the route to sixteen—which you might remember invalidates the route in RIP—and flags it for deletion. This entry is not actually removed until it has been flagged in this manner for another 60 seconds, which corresponds to two sends of the router's routing tables to its neighbors. After these 60 seconds, if no new response packets give information that this route is up and active, it is deleted from this router's tables. The router then must choose another valid route from itself to the specified destination from those available.

Configuring *routed*

The `routed` RIP routing daemon builds its own routing tables utilizing the method described in the earlier section, "How `routed` Works," so you do not need to start it with a list of defaults. There is a file that you can create, however, if you have some gateways that need to be defined as *active* or *passive*. An active gateway is able to respond to routing queries; a passive one is not. That is the "simple" difference between the two.

Given that a passive router is not going to respond to request packets, `routed` will never learn of it if it is not explicitly told. To enter this information, first create the file `/etc/gateways` as root. You then must add a line for each passive gateway in the format:

```
address name gateway cost passive
```

All but the last item in this line of code must be replaced with the appropriate values:

- **address**. The IP address of the host or network this entry refers to.
- **name**. The hostname as set in `/etc/hosts`, the network name as set in `/etc/networks`, or the full name for the machine in the format host.domain.extension.

- **gateway**. The name or IP address for the gateway that traffic must pass through to get to *address*.
- **cost**. The RIP cost of going through this gateway, determined according to the rules discussed in Chapter 1.

Passive gateway information is loaded at boot time—when routed starts. It is not reloaded unless you restart the routing daemon.

Running *routed*

The routed daemon, as mentioned earlier, should be set to start at boot time. You do this either through a file, such as rc.local, or by adding an initialization script pointer for the run levels that require the routing daemon. In either case, there are flags available so you can specify particulars about how this program should run. Table 5.1 lists the options and their functions.

Table 5.1 **Flags and Options Available for the IPv4 Version of *routed***

Option	Result
-d	Saves extensive debugging information.
-g	Sets a default route, such as –g 192.168.52.1. Typically used to point to external destinations that routed may not be able to find on its own, such as the Internet or a router using another protocol.
-s	Supplies routing information even if there is only one network interface, which normally tells routed to assume that it is not an internetwork router.
-q	Does not supply routing information even if there are multiple network interfaces.
-t	Runs routed linked through the terminal, so packet information is shown on STDOUT and the process can be killed using Ctrl-C. Used for testing purposes.
filename	If you end the line with a filename, that file is used to log routed's behavior.

Guide to *gated*

Another program you have heard much about in earlier chapters is gated. There are actually three different versions of this program. You can utilize gated for either unicast or multicast use, for either IPv4 or IPv6, or any combination of these you require—just make sure you have the correct version (see Table 5.2) for each. This routing daemon comes with many versions of Linux, though it might be on a second disk or among supplementary materials. If this is the daemon you decide to use and don't have it, want the latest version, or need a capability that didn't come with the version packaged with your distribution, go to `www.gated.org` or `www.gated.merit.edu` to obtain them.

Table 5.2 **Versions of *gated* and Their Capabilities**

Version	Enables
gated-ipv6	Static IPv6 routing, RIPng, and BGP4MP.
gated-multicast	IGMP, MP-BGP, MDSP (check to see if this implementation is complete), DVMRP, PIM-SM, and PIM-DM.
gated-public	EGP, BGP, RIP-1, RIP-2, and OSPF. The public version is a slightly older but very stable version.
gated-unicast	EGP, BGP, RIP-1, RIP-2, OSPF, and Intermediate System to Intermediate System (IS-IS).

The public version is a slightly older but very stable version. The unicast, multicast, and IPv6 versions are all newer and available through the main site as well. Access to the public version's source code is possible but not to the newer versions unless you obtain a license—if you require source code access, the `zebra` (`http://www.zebra.org`) daemon might be a better choice for you.

It is the public version we'll focus on in this chapter.

How Public *gated* Works

Like most routing daemons, the `gated` routing daemon typically starts at boot time—you'll want to be sure that it is set up to do so on the Linux box you use for your router. See the section "Running Public `gated`" for ideas on using the `gdc` program to interface with the daemon rather than directly starting it by hand.

When `gated` starts, it first determines how much space it needs in memory for its arrays and other data structures. After it knows how much room it needs, `gated` is assigned a virtual machine with a 32-bit address space in either RAM or on a hard drive (this is how Linux handles all processes). The daemon then reserves a section of its space to hold the information and then clears out anything already stored there—a process called *initializing memory*. After this, it reserves another section of its space for each of the threads it will use to keep track of its state and serve other functions. The `gated` daemon then creates the memory framework for the data structures, such as routing tables, to which it needs fast access.

After the entire framework is in place, `gated` reads the kernel's routing tables into its own RAM—something it won't do again unless specifically instructed or restarted. It then finds the interfaces on this specific machine and records both their addresses and whether they are currently up or down.

Now the individual threads—multithreading programs are made up of the various things a program must swap between doing—have to get initialized. The `gated` dae-mon first sets values for all of the global variables for each thread. It then reads its con-figuration file, `/etc/gated.conf`, into memory. Because `gated` is modular, it does not load the capability to run every single protocol it supports. Instead it looks in `/etc/gated.conf` for the protocols that have been enabled and sets up a framework to run each, including loading the appropriate modules of code.

When you configure `gated`'s behavior, one thing you do is set up rules for how it imports routes it learns from outside sources. At this point, these rules are loaded into memory. After this occurs, `gated` loads the rules for how you want it to handle export-ing routes to other routers and protocols.

At this time all initializations are complete. The `gated` daemon enters what the pro-grammers call *the forever loop*, which means it enters its actual running state—and it will stay there until you tell it to do otherwise. It first sets all of the timers required for different protocol behaviors. The daemon then looks to the *sockets*, which are files used to transfer information between programs, that `gated` is interested in and loads any pertinent data from them. If any resulting tasks have to be run, they are queued to start when it's their turn.

Finally, `gated` runs the tasks that happen in the *foreground* and *background*. Foreground tasks are visible to the administrator and are items that only need to run once. They're often requests from protocol modules to take care of something when-ever CPU time is available. In contrast, background tasks are hidden away and may run constantly or at regular intervals.

Configuring Public *gated*

The `gated` configuration file is `gated.conf`. Statements within this file can stretch beyond one or more lines and so are terminated with a semicolon (;). There are also two different kinds of comments you'll run into here. One is the standard hash (#), which comments out the entire line. The other is the C-like pair: `/*` to start the com-ment and `*/` to end it. Now, with the basics out of the way, let's look at how this file is built.

One of the most important things to keep in mind is statement type order. There are a number of main statement types that must be used in the proper order and two additional ones that can be liberally scattered throughout as needed. The statement types and the items within these types are briefly defined in Table 5.3 for reference's sake.

Table 5.3   Types of Statements Available for *gated.conf*, Sorted by Order Requirements

Type	Order	Statements
options	First	`options`
definition	Second	`autonomoussystem, martians, routerid`
control	Third	`aggregate, export, generate, import`
directives	Third	`%directory, %include`
interfaces	Third	`interfaces`
protocol	Third	`bgp, egp, icmp, isis, kernel, ospf, redirect, rip, snmp`
static	Third	`static`
trace	Third	`traceoptions`

The *options* Statement

The typical `gated.conf` file starts with an `options` statement, which sets global values that apply to everything that follows. You do not have to have an `options` statement at all if you don't see the need. These items do not have to be in any specific order within the overall statement.

Table 5.4   Values Available in the *gated.conf options* Statement

Option	Purpose	Format	Value(s)
`mark`	Writes a timestamp to the `gated` logfile every specified interval.	`mark time`	Number of seconds to wait between timestamps.
`noresolv`	Specifies not to try to convert IP addresses into host.domain.extension.	`noresolv`	N/A
`nosend`	Specifies not to send out packets. Just listen to the network traffic. Used only for staying out of RIP traffic.	`nosend`	N/A
`syslog`	Sets the amount of data that `gated` should log through syslog. There are two different syntax options. The first logs only the level listed, and the second logs all levels from the lowest to the specified level.	`syslog level` `syslog upto level`	Logging level, listed from least to most problematic: `debug`, `info`, `notice`, `warning`, `err`, `crit`, `alert`, and `emerg`. The lower the level you decide to log, the more data you wil generate.

A `gated` `options` statement is written in the following format:

```
options
    setting1
    ...
    settingN
;
```

The *interfaces* Statement

After you set (or don't set) your global options, it's time to tell `gated` about the network interfaces available on this machine. Doing this involves a set of nested statements, the first of which is the `interfaces` statement. This item provides a framework for all of the rest of the interface configuration in the following manner:

```
interfaces {
    statement1
        settings
    ;
    ...
    statementN
        settings    -
    ;
}
```

There are three kinds of statements you have available to you within the `interfaces` statement: `options`, `interface`, and `define`. While there are no strict requirements on the order in which you utilize these three statements, it's a good idea to stick with what we've listed here. The first is, once again, `options`. This is not the same as the global `options` but instead is a set of options local to all of the interfaces—which it seems would make them global interface options. You have two choices here, as shown in Table 5.5.

Table 5.5   Values Available in the *gated.conf options* Portion of the *interfaces* Statement

Option	Purpose	Format	Value(s)
scaninterval	Sets how often `gated` checks the kernel's files for new or removed interfaces. Default is every 15 seconds.	scaninterval *time*	The number of seconds to wait between checks.

Table 5.5 Continued

Option	Purpose	Format	Value(s)
strictinterfaces	Sets how gated behaves if it finds an interface that was added after boot time but isn't specifically defined in its configuration file. Default is to give an error but continue running. If you include this option, gated will crash in this circumstance.	strictinterfaces	N/A

Next among the `interfaces` statements is one or more `interface` statements. Yes, this could get confusing. Make sure to double-check that you don't get these two items turned around. You can configure multiple interfaces together in the same statement if you want or break them up if you need some to have different settings than others. The `interface` statement itself is in the format `interface` *list*, where *list* is a series of IP addresses belonging to each interface you want to configure with this specific collection of settings. The items you can configure within the `interface` statement are listed in Table 5.6.

Table 5.6 Values Available in the *gated.conf interface* Portion of the *interfaces* Statement

Option	Purpose	Format	Value(s)
down preference	Sets the preference value—how favored or unfavored this interface is—in the case where gated has marked the interface as potentially malfunctioning.	down preference *value*	The higher the integer *value*, the less likely gated will choose this interface. Default is 120.
passive	Prevents gated from changing this interface to the down preference value.	passive	N/A

continues

Table 5.6   Continued

Option	Purpose	Format	Value(s)
preference	Sets the `preference` value—how favored or unfavored this interface is—in the case where `gated` has marked the interface as functioning properly.	`preference value`	The lower the value, the more likely `gated` will utilize this interface. Default is 0.
simplex	Prevents the interface from hearing its own broadcast packets and therefore from using them to determine whether it is functioning properly or not.	`simplex`	N/A

Finally, there is the `define` statement within the `interfaces` statement. You need to include this item if you set `strictinterfaces` in the `interfaces option` statement earlier. For each interface that `gated` needs to utilize but that may not be up and running when the routing daemon starts, you'll need to create a `define` statement that tells `strictinterfaces` that this interface may be added to routing tables. The `define` statement itself is used in the format define *address*, where *address* is the IP address for this interface. See Table 5.7 for a list of the options you have available within `define`.

Table 5.7   **Values Available in the gated.conf** *define* **Portion of the** *interfaces* **Statement**

Option	Purpose	Format	Value(s)
`broadcast`	Tells `gated` that the interface can handle broadcast messages— both Ethernet cards and Token Ring cards can do this—and what address to use.	`broadcast address`	The broadcast IP address this interface has access to.
multicast	Tells `gated` that the interface can handle multicast traffic.	multicast	N/A

Table 5.7   **Continued**

Option	Purpose	Format	Value(s)
netmask	Tells gated what netmask applies to this interface for IPv4. Invalid if pointopoint is set.	netmask *address*	The network mask for the interface.
pointopoint	Tells gated that this interface is a modem or other device using SLIP or PPP.	pointopoint *address*	The local address for this interface. In this case, the define address would have to refer to the remote address for the interface.

So, since you are probably a bit confused about what a typical interfaces statement might look like, here's a more fleshed out example:

```
interfaces {
    options
        strictinterfaces
    ;
    interface 192.168.232.*
        simplex
    ;
    interface 192.168.251.*
        simplex
        passive
    ;
    define 192.168.232.*
        broadcast 192.168.232.255
        netmask 255.255.255.0
    ;
    define 192.168.251.*
        broadcast 192.168.251.255
        netmask 255.255.255.127
    ;
}
```

Notice that not all of the IP information is strictly in the form of an IP address. You have a few different formats you can use:

- all. The word all is the same as using just the wildcard *.
- xxx.xxx.xxx.xxx. Full IP address.
- xxx.xxx.xxx.*, xxx.xxx.*, xxx.*. Partial IP addresses with a wildcard at the end.

- `eth*.` Wildcarded device name.
- `eth0.` Nonwildcarded device names.

While the `gated` documentation also discusses referring to "symbolic names" (`host.domain.extension` format), doing so can be problematic because that name may not always correspond to the same interface. Therefore, the practice is not recommended.

The Definition Statements

There are three definition statements available, all of which must be used before any of the statements defined later in this chapter—if you decide to make use of them. These statements are `autonomoussystem`, `routerid`, and `martians`. The first two of these statements are required only under certain conditions, and the last is never absolutely required. Table 5.8 outlines the purpose of each of these statements and how to use them.

Table 5.8 **Definition Statements Available in** `gated.conf`

Statement	Purpose	Format	Value(s)
`autonomoussystem`	Sets the AS number that this AS border router serves. Required with BGP and EGP.	`autonomoussystem` `number;`	The AS number assigned to your autonomous system by the Network Information Center (NIC).
`martians`	Used to filter out known bad routes.	`martians {` `bad1` `...` `badN` `}`	As specified in the discussion on route filtering.
`routerid`	Sets an IP address that points to this router.	`routerid address;`	The default is the first IP address `gated` finds, but better still is a loopback address that is not 127.0.0.1.

If you decide to utilize the `martians` statement, you'll need to understand how *route filtering* works in `gated` to get the most use out of it. However, because we're talking specifically about `martians`, only the three filtering components that apply in this case will be covered. The simplest and least useful in this context is:

```
martians {
    all;
}
```

This keyword would quite literally filter out every single piece of network and host information it received for its routing tables. A more useful item is:

```
martians {
    network rules;
}
```

For the *network* portion, you specify the IP information for the network in question. The *rules* in this case are either the keyword `exact`, or the keyword `refines`. These two keywords govern how the *network* information is interpreted. An `exact` tells `gated` to interpret network information in the `martians` statement strictly by overall network, ignoring netmasks that are not on class boundaries and therefore ignoring subnets. Hosts also are ignored. However, if you use `refines` for *rules*, the mask and host information is utilized—though in this case the mask is implied as a class mask.

A more complex version of this format is as follows:

```
martians {
    network mask mask rules;
}
```

Here, the `refines` option for *rules* makes more sense. The *mask* item refers to the netmask. An even more refined version is as follows:

```
martians {
    network masklen bit_mask rules;
}
```

You might remember discussions in Chapter 4, "IPv4 and IPv6 Addressing," in the beginning of the section, "IPv6 Math," where the bit mask was introduced. A Class A bit mask is /8, Class B is /16, and C is /24. From there, the bit masks get fancier for subnets and IPv6. It's this value that goes in the bit mask slot.

A `martians` statement doesn't have to be just one line. You can mix and match all of the network definitions you see here within the statement. There is also one more item you have access to: You can set particular addresses or ranges within a blocked out range as valid using the `allow` option at the end of any of these items. For example, the following ignores routing information from the entire class B 192.168.0.0 except specifically from the Class C subnet 192.168.10.0:

```
martians {
    192.168.0.0 exact;
    192.168.10.0 mask 255.255.255.0 refines allow;
}
```

RIP Configuration

Each routing protocol must be individually configured in `gated`. Let's start with the oldest and simplest one: RIP. Regardless of whether you want this router to be able to speak with RIP-1 or RIP-2 routers or not, start the RIP configuration section with the following:

```
rip status
```

The *status* entry can be one of the following:

- `no;`. Do not handle RIP traffic.
- `off;`. Do not handle RIP traffic.
- `on {`. Handle RIP traffic.
- `yes {`. Handle RIP traffic.

It is not mandatory that you set any more information than this. You could have the following whether on or yes:

```
rip on;
```

However, using the curly brace to build a statement gives you more control over how gated deals with RIP. The options for what you use within the rip statement are listed in Table 5.9.

Table 5.9   Options Available in the *gated.conf rip* Statement

Option	Purpose	Format	Value(s)
broadcast	Sets gated to broadcast RIP packets even if there is only one active interface in this machine.	broadcast;	N/A
defaultmetric	Sets the default RIP *cost* for routes learned from a different protocol.	defaultmetric *cost;*	The RIP *cost* to utilize. Default is 16, which means the route is unavailable.
interface	Sets a specific interface's behavior for RIP. This item is covered in more detail in the chapter itself.	interface *list value1* ... *valueN;*	In this case, the *values* are another set of options, and *list* refers to the specific interface(s) this rule covers. The *values* are covered separately in Table 5.10. For the *list*, use all if you want to match everything, the format xxx.xxx.xxx.xxx to match a full IP address, the formats xxx.xxx.xxx.*, xxx.xxx.*, or xxx.* to match partial IP addresses, eth* to use a wildcarded device name, or the full name of the device such as eth0.

Table 5.9   **Continued**

Option	Purpose	Format	Value(s)
no broadcast	Sets gated not to broadcast RIP packets even if there are multiple active interfaces in this machine.	nobroadcast;	N/A
nocheckzero	Sets gated to not reject RIP-1 packets who have nonempty reserved fields.	nocheckzero;	N/A
preference	Sets the preference level for a route that gated learned of through RIP (as compared to other routes).	preference *value*;	The preference level goes in place of *value*. The default is 100. In the case of gated, the lower the preference, the more likely this route will be used.
query authentication	Sets whether gated should be fussy or not about RIP-2 queries that come from nonrouters.	query authentication *value*;	The *value* for this option is one of the following: none (default), simple, or md5 (which is at best not much better than just using a password). If you choose either of the last two, you also must include a password at the end before the semi-colon.
Sourcegateways	Sets which routers gated should send unicast data to instead of broadcasting.	sourcegateways *machines*;	The *machines* value consists of one or more space-separated IP addresses.
Traceoptions	Sets what gated logs.	traceoptions *settings*;	The *settings* value can consist of a mix of general protocol gated tracing options and RIP-specific gated tracing options. These two option sets are covered in Tables 5.11 and 5.12.

continues

Table 5.9 **Continued**

Option	Purpose	Format	Value(s)
Trustedgateways	Sets what routers gated accepts RIP updates from.	trustedgateways *machines;*	The machines value consists of one or more space-separated IP addresses.

As you can see, the RIP setup for gated can get quite complex. Two of the options defy quick explanation in the form of a table. These are the interface option (a different one than the interfaces interface option) and both kinds of tracing options discussed in this section.

Under the rip statement, the interface option takes the following form:

```
rip on {
    options
    interface list
        settings
    ;
    options
};
```

Building the *list* follows the same rules given in the interface coverage of the earlier section, "The interfaces Statement." The options available for the rip version of interface are listed in Table 5.10. Remember that each of these items is relative to the network interface specified in the section. You can have multiple interface statements if you need various network connections to have different settings.

Table 5.10 **Options Available in the *gated.conf rip interface* Statement**

Option	Purpose	Format	Value(s)
authentication	Sets the one or two forms of authentication used for router connections. Utilized only for RIP-2.	*which* authentication *rule*	The *which* value is blank if you want to use primary or secondary. The *rule* value is one of none, md5, or simple. For md5 and simple, you must have a password after the rule.
broadcast	Sets gated to send RIP-2 data compatible with RIP-1 routers as broadcast packets to RIP-1 routers.	broadcast	N/A

Table 5.10 **Continued**

Option	Purpose	Format	Value(s)
metricin	Sets the RIP cost for sending RIP-1 or RIP-2 traffic to this interface(s).	metricin *cost*	An integer between 1 and 15 if you want the route to stay in the tables or 16 if you want to disable any routes found out about through this interface. Default is 1.
metricout	Sets the RIP cost for sending RIP-1 and RIP-2 traffic from the interface(s).	metricout *cost*	An integer between 1 and 15 if you want the route to stay in the tables or 16 if you want to disable any routes found out about through this interface. Default is 1.
multicast	Sets that gated communicates with other RIP-2 routers through multicast packets.	multicast;	N/A
noripin	Sets that gated should ignore RIP packets arriving on the interface(s).	noripin;	N/A
noripout	Sets that gated should not send RIP information from the interface(s).	noripout;	N/A
ripin	Indicates to accept RIP traffic through the specified interface(s). Default.	ripin;	N/A
ripout	Specifies to send RIP traffic through the specified interface(s). Default.	ripout;	N/A
version 1	Sets gated to send RIP-1 packets through the specified interface(s).	version 1;	N/A
version 2	Sets gated to send RIP-2 packets through the specified interface(s).	version 2;	N/A

Another difficult statement to pin down is `traceoptions`. One reason for this awkwardness is that there are two sets of values available: one that applies `gated`-wide (see Table 5.11) and another that only applies to RIP traffic (see Table 5.12). There are also global tracing options available, but they have no meaning in a specific protocol statement such as `rip`.

Table 5.11   Tracing Options Available for all Protocols in _gated_—Though Some of These Make No Sense for Particular Protocols

Option	Purpose
all	To enable every option in this table for this protocol statement. If an option makes no sense for the protocol, it is ignored.
general	To enable the `normal` and `route` options.
normal	To log regular protocol activity as well as abnormal happenings.
policy	To log policy information for imported and exported routes.
route	To log routing table changes.
state	For protocols that use various router states (RIP is not one of them), to log information about these state changes.
task	To log information about interface use and processor use by this protocol.
timer	To log timer use by this protocol.

Table 5.12   _gated_ Tracing Options Specific to RIP

Option	Purpose
other	To log packets not specified by the other options.
packets	To log all RIP packets.
request	To log RIP information-requesting packets.
response	To log RIP information-containing packets.

Open Shortest Path First (OSPF) Configuration

One of the more popular internal unicast routing protocols is OSPF. As you might remember from Chapter 1, this protocol includes features such as designated routers and routing areas. Due to this level of complexity, OSPF involves even longer sets of code to configure. So let's get started.

You begin the OSPF configuration statement with the following:
`ospf status`

The *status* entry for `ospf` has the same options as the `rip` statement had:

- `no;`. Do not handle OSPF traffic.
- `off;`. Do not handle OSPF traffic.

- on {. Handle OSPF traffic.
- yes {. Handle OSPF traffic.

Typically, the first substatement within `ospf` is `defaults`, so the beginning of the statement often looks like the following:

```
ospf on {
    defaults {
```

The items available within the `defaults` statement are listed in Table 5.13.

Table 5.13 **Options Available Within the** *defaults* **Portion of the** *gated ospf* **Statement**

Option	Purpose	Format	Value(s)
cost	Sets the cost value for a route taken from the gated routing tables that was not learned through OSPF.	cost *value;*	An integer specifying how much to add to the route's cost. Default is 1.
ospfarea	Tells gated that all of the interfaces are within the same OSPF area.	ospfarea *location;*	The *location* value can be either backbone or the ID you assigned to this specific area. OSPF specifies that an area ID of 0 is the backbone, and other area IDs must be a 32 bit number. An IP address or network number in the format xxx.xxx.xxx.xxx can be utilized as an area ID.
preference	Sets how much gated prefers routes it learned from OSPF over other protocols.	preference *value;*	The *value* is a number from 0 to 255, with lower values reflecting a higher preference. The default preference for OSPF routes is 10.
router-prio	Allows this router to participate in OSPF designated router elections.	router-prio;	N/A

continues

Table 5.13 **Continued**

Option	Purpose	Format	Value(s)
tag	Allows you to assign a tag to the data this router originates through OSPF.	`tag valueL;` or `tag as valueS;`	The two values here are the long value (*valueL*), and short value (*valueS*). The long value can be 32 bits, while the short value must be only 12 bits considering your AS number is also included.
type	Allows you to specify whether your AS is a type 1 or 2, as discussed in the section "How It Works" in the OSPF coverage in Chapter 1.	`type num;`	1 or 2.

After you set the `defaults`, you can then move on to the main portion of the `ospf` statement after closing the defaults statement like so:

```
ospf on {
    defaults {
        option1;
        ...
        optionN;
    };
```

The main `ospf` options are listed in Table 5.14.

Table 5.14 **Options Available Within the** *ospf* **Statement of** *gated.*

Option	Purpose	Format	Value(s)
backbone area	Sets up the OSPF backbone rather than a specific area.	`backbone area value {` `option1;` `...` `optionN;` `};`	The *value* is the number assigned to the backbone area. See the chapter text for a further explanation of this complex statement. Its options are defined in Table 5.15.

Table 5.14 **Continued**

Option	Purpose	Format	Value(s)
exportinterval	Sets how long gated waits between sending out OSPF updates about external systems.	exportinterval *time;*	The number of seconds between broadcasts. The default is 1.
exportlimit	Sets how many routes gated sends out at once in an OSPF update.	exportlimit *number;*	The number of routes. Default is 100.
monitorauthkey	Sets the password used for using the ospf_monitor tool to check on your OSPF routing behavior.	monitorauthkey *value;*	The password to use. By default, there is no password.
traceoptions	Sets how gated logs OSPF interactions.	traceoptions *options;*	Options available to all protocols are listed in Table 5.11, and options available specifically in the ospf statement are listed in Table 5.16.

Another complex substatement within `ospf` is the `backbone` statement. You must set up your OSPF backbone if you have more than one area because it's the backbone that carries inter-area communications. Following along with the earlier format examples, let's add to it:

```
ospf on {
    defaults {
        option1;
        ...
        optionN;
    };
    statement1;
    ...
    statementN;
    backbone area value {
        option1;
        ...
        optionN;
    };
};
```

The *value* as mentioned in Table 5.14 is the area number you assigned to the area serving as your AS backbone. Within the `backbone area` statement there is a small collection of options you can set to define how this backbone interacts with the rest of the AS. These options are outlined in Table 5.15.

Table 5.15 **Options Available Within** *backbone area* **Substatement of the** *ospf* **Statement, for** *gated*

Option	Purpose	Format	Value(s)
authtype	Sets the authentication type used in the OSPF backbone area.	authtype type;	There are four potential values for *type*. Use none if you don't want to use an authentication scheme or simple if you want to use passwords.
networks	Sets the boundaries of this OSPF area.	networks { rule1; ... ruleN; {;	There are a few different ways to specify the *rules* in a networks statement. All of these should be familiar. You can have just a network number such as 192.168.15.0;, a network number followed by the word mask and then the netmask, such as 192.168.15.0 mask 255.255.255.0;, a network number followed by the word masklen and then the bit mask, such as 192.168.15.0 masklen 24;, or even just a single host IP address with the word host in front of it as in host 192.168.15.5;. At the end of each of these statements for OSPF, you can add the word restrict if you don't want the specific item advertised outside of this OSPF area.

Table 5.15 **Continued**

Option	Purpose	Format	Value(s)
stub	Specifies that this area has only router leading in and out.	stub; or stub cost cost;	The *cost* is the OSPF cost for sending data through this router into the area.
stubhosts	Specifies the hosts within a stub that you want to have advertised outside this area.	stubhosts { address cost cost; ... address cost cost; };	Each *address* is the IP address of the host interface you're defining, and each *cost* is the OSPF cost for sending data through that address.

Table 5.16 **OSPF-Specific *traceoptions* Statements Available in *gated***

Option	Purpose
ack	To log OSPF ack packets.
dd	To log OSPF database description packets.
hello	To log OSPF HELLO packets.
lsabuild	To log OSPF link state advertisement creation activities.
lsu	To log OSPF link state update packets.
request	To log OSPF link state request packets.
spf	To log OSPF shortest path first calculations.

EGP Configuration

If you need to exchange routing information with networks outside your own, you'll need to use one of the border routing protocols. One choice is EGP, as you learned in Chapter 3, "Introduction to Border Routing Protocols." Fortunately gated can handle this job as well as internal routing. Just be sure to set this aspect up only on your external border router(s).

Given that we've covered the general opening for these protocol configuration statements twice now, we'll just start the EGP setup statement with what you'd use if you intended to activate EGP:

egp on {

The statements available to you in the egp configuration section are outlined in Table 5.17. As usual, some of these are too complex to explore fully in a single table. Specifically, group and its neighbor substatement are just covered in a simplified manner in the table.

Table 5.17 **Options Available Within the** *egp* **Statement in** *gated*

Option	Purpose	Format	Value(s)
defaultmetric	Sets the EGP cost assigned to routes this border router advertises to neighbors.	defaultmetric *cost;*	An integer from 1 to 255. If you assign the *cost* as 255, some border routers might assume your network is unreachable, so beware.
group	Tells gated who its EGP neighbors are and how to interact with them.	group *options* { neighbor *settings;* };	The format shown is a very simplified version of the group statement, which is covered in more detail in the chapter itself.
packetsize	Sets the initial value of how large of a data packet EGP expects to receive from neighbors.	packetsize *value;*	The *value* is the number of bytes gated expects from EGP neighbors. If a packet is larger than this value, it gets truncated and therefore dropped. However, when this happens, *value* is automatically increased to be large enough to receive a packet of this size next time. The default is 8192 bytes.
preference	Sets how important routes learned from RIP are to this border router.	preference *value;*	The lower the *value*, the more important RIP routes are. Default is 200.
traceoptions	As usual, sets how the EGP portion of gated logs data.	traceoptions *settings;*	Options available to all protocols are listed in Table 5.11, and options available specifically in the egp statement are listed in Table 5.18.

As noted in Table 5.17, the egp options available in gated are covered in Table 5.18.

Table 5.18 **EGP-Specific *traceoptions* Statements Available in *gated***

Option	Purpose
acquire	To log the ACQUIRE and CEASE packets used to start and end EGP sessions.
hello	To log the HELLO and I-HEARD-U packets used to keep tabs on EGP neighbors.
packets	To log all EGP packets.
update	To log the POLL and UPDATE packets used in EGP to request and receive routing table updates.

The group statement has many possibilities. To define the EGP neighbors in an autonomous system, you start with something as simple as the following (you might have more than one because there is more than one way to send data in and out of your AS or you need these border routers to allow internal networks using different protocols to talk to one another):

```
group options {
```

There are two *options* available in the group statement itself:

- maxup *number*. Sets the *number* of EGP neighbors gated needs to connect to—especially useful if you don't need this router to necessarily connect to all of your other EGP routers.

- peeras *number*. Tells gated the AS number it's a part of.

Inside the curly braces is where the real work begins. Here you must set up a series of neighbor statements, each of which specifically defines one of the other EGP routers in your AS. You must have all of them defined here—which is handy if you're using gated for all of your EGP routers because you can just copy this section for the other machines and make a couple of adjustments. So now the initial statement looks like:

```
group options {
    neighbor machine1
        option1
        ...
        optionN
    ;
    ...
    neighbor machineN
        option1
        ...
        optionN
    ;
};
```

The *machine* entry in a `neighbor` statement is pretty straightforward; it's the IP address for the EGP router you're telling `gated` about. Everything else in a neighbor statement is optional, depending on the level of detail you need to configure for each machine. Table 5.19 lists and defines the available options.

Table 5.19 **Options Available for the *gated group* Statement's neighbor Substatement**

Option	Purpose	Format	Value(s)
exportdefault	Sets gated to include the *default route* in EGP updates. The default route is 0.0.0.0.	exportdefault;	N/A
importdefault	Tells gated to accept a default route if another EGP router includes it in an update.	importdefault;	N/A
lcladdr	Sets the interface on this machine that will communicate with this neighbor.	lcladdr *address*;	The IP address for the local interface.
metricout	Sets the EGP cost to assign to routes advertised to this neighbor.	metricout *cost*;	The *cost* integer.
minhello	Sets how long gated will wait for a HELLO packet from its EGP neighbor before giving up.	minhello *value*;	The *value* is the number of seconds that gated waits after sending a HELLO packet before trying again to acquire that neighbor. After three of these transmissions with no answer in the given *value*, the neighbor is marked as unreachable. The default is 30 seconds.

Table 5.19 **Continued**

Option	Purpose	Format	Value(s)
minpoll	Sets how long gated will wait between polls to its neighbor.	minpoll *value;*	The value is the number of seconds that gated waits before sending each poll to ensure that its neighbor is still alive. After three of these transmissions with no answer in the given value, the neighbor is marked as unreachable and its routes are removed from this machine's routing table. The default is 120 seconds.
nogendefault	Tells gated not to generate the default route.	nogendefault;	N/A
preference	Sets how gated's EGP implementation views routes learned from this neighbor compared to others.	preference *value;*	The lower the *value*, the more important routes learned from this neighbor are.
preference2	A tie-breaking subsetting for preference.	preference2 *value;*	Once again, the lower the *value*, the more likely routes from this neighbor will be chosen over others. Default is 0.
traceoptions	Sets how gated logs data for this specific EGP neighbor.	traceoptions *settings;*	Options available to all protocols are listed in Table 5.11, and options available specifically in the egp statement are listed in Table 5.18.
ttl	You typically will not need this item. It's used to override the default IP time-to-live setting.	ttl *value;*	If an EGP neighbor ignores packets from this router, try setting *value* to 2 instead of the default 1.

One thing to note is that you're seeing layers upon layers of the same settings here. There are multiple places, for example, that you can set `traceoptions`. The most local version of this setting is the one that takes hold. If you've set `traceoptions` for a specific neighbor, then that's the setting used even if the overall `egp` statement says differently.

BGP Configuration

Another potential border routing protocol is appropriately named the Border Gateway Protocol (BGP), which you should be familiar with from Chapter 3. If you would rather run a BGP border router than an EGP, `gated` can still do the job. You activate this capability by creating a `bgp` statement starting with:

```
bgp on {
```

The main substatements available in the `bgp` statement are listed in Table 5.20. You will notice that much of the meat in the setup is not this set of statements, but is instead in the child statements within substatements.

Table 5.20   **Options Available Within the *bgp* Statement in *gated***

Option	Purpose	Format	Value(s)
defaultmetric	Sets the BGP cost assigned to routes this border router advertises to neighbors.	defaultmetric *cost;*	An optional value that can add a *cost* to routes advertised from this border router.
group type	Enables you to create a group of like BGP peers. Use more than one group type statement to make more than one grouping.	group type *details* { allow { *options* }; peer *options;* }	This is a very simplified version of what a group type statement looks like. See the chapter text for a more detailed discussion.
preference	Sets how important gated sees routes learned from RIP.	preference *value;*	The lower the *value*, the more important these routes are to gated when utilizing BGP. Default is 170.
traceoptions	Sets how gated logs data for this specific BGP router.	traceoptions *settings;*	Options available to all protocols are listed in Table 5.11, and options available specifically in the bgp statement are listed in Table 5.21.

Table 5.21 **BGP-Specific *traceoptions* Statements Available in *gated***

Option	Purpose
keepalive	To log BGP KEEPALIVE packets.
open	To log BGP OPEN packets.
packets	To log all BGP packets.
update	To log BGP UPDATE packets.

The most complicated statement within `bgp` is `group type`. Let's piece this one together step by step. This statement starts as you might expect:

```
group type
```

After this there are five different ways you can continue, depending on the nature of the machines you're trying to connect:

- `external peeras`. Defines a group of BGP routers outside the autonomous system.
- `igp peeras`. Defines a group of routers within your autonomous system that are not border routers but that BGP needs to exchange information with.
- `internal peeras`. Defines a group of routers within your autonomous system that do not utilize an IP-based routing protocol.
- `routing peeras`. Defines a group of BGP routers within your autonomous system used with your internal routers to resolve address forwarding.
- `test peeras`. Defines a test BGP router that you can use to make sure information is propagating properly.

So, depending on which type of `group` you're setting up at the moment, you begin with one of the following lines to start your statement:

```
group type external peeras
group type igp peeras
group type internal peeras
group type routing peeras
group type test peeras
```

The word, "begin," is used here because you're not done with the initial line yet. No matter which of these you choose, the next item is the AS number to which this particular group belongs. So now you have:

```
group type gtype peeras as
```

If you're setting up an `external`, `internal`, or `test` group the first line is finished. For a routing or test group you have two new items to add. You start with:

```
group type gtype peeras as proto
```

The name of the interior protocol this specific group uses to communicate goes after `proto`, with the options being `rip`, `ospf`, or `isi`—see the sidebar, "gated and the IS-IS Protocol," for more information on this last option. Finally, if you're setting up the `group type` routing statement, you can choose to give specific interface information, which first involves expanding the statement to:

```
group type routing peeras as proto prot interface
```

After the `interface` term, include the IP information for specific internal interfaces that you want to have treated as though they are external.

At this point you need to start the `group type` substatement, which you do by adding a curly brace, so you might now have:

```
group type external peeras as
{
```

There are actually only two clauses that go within the `group type` substatement: `allow` and `peer`. You must include both of these items to properly set up the `bgp group type`. The `allow` clause gets inserted into the substatement as follows:

```
group type blahblahblah
{
    allow
    {
```

Every option in the `allow` clause involves identifying hosts and networks belonging to this particular `group type`. We've covered the various ways of specifying machines for `gated` a number of times now so we're just going to fill out the `allow` clause with one of each of the possible formats, giving us:

```
group type blahblahblah
{
    allow
    {
        192.168.15.0
        192.168.15.0 mask 255.255.255.0
        192.168.15.0 masklen 24
        all
        host 192.168.15.5
    };
```

The next clause in the `group type` substatement is `peer`, which gets added like so:

```
group type blahblahblah
{
    allow
    {
        192.168.15.0
        192.168.15.0 mask 255.255.255.0
        192.168.15.0 masklen 24
        all
        host 192.168.15.5
    };
    peer hostIP
        option1
        ...
        optionN;
```

The extensive list of options available within the `peer` clause are listed in Table 5.22. You'll recognize a number of these from other sections of `gated.conf`.

Table 5.22   **Options Available for *gated*'s *peer* Clause Within the *egp* Group Type Substatement**

Option	Purpose	Format	Value(s)
analretentive	Tells gated to issue warnings for events that it normally ignores, such as duplicate update packets.	analretentive	N/A
gateway	Tells gated that the BGP neighbor isn't directly attached and to send data through another router to communicate with the neighbor.	gateway *IP*	IP address of the interface that needs to act as the intermediary.
holdtime	Sets how long gated waits for proof of life before disconnecting from a BGP neighbor.	holdtime *value;*	The number of seconds to wait, from 0 to 3.
indelay	Sets how long a route must be advertised as the same before gated will add it to its BGP routing tables.	indelay *value;*	The number of seconds to wait. Default is 0.
keep all	Tells gated to place routes in its BGP routing tables even if those routes have your AS number.	keep all;	N/A
keepalivesalways	Tells gated to send keepalive messages even when its BGP neighbor should assume an UPDATE is enough.	keepalivesalways;	N/A

continues

Table 5.22 **Continued**

Option	Purpose	Format	Value(s)
lcladdr	Tells gated what interface to use when connecting to this BGP neighbor.	lcladdr *IP;*	The rules for *IP* vary depending on what kind of group type you are using. An external type requires an address on the same network as the peer or its specified gateway. For any other type, the network information does not matter.
localas	Tells gated which AS this BGP router handles.	localas *AS;*	The AS number this border router governs. Default is what was set in the global autonomoussystem option.
logupdown	Adds a log file entry each time gated's BGP function enters the ESTABLISHED state or leaves it.	logupdown;	N/A
metricout	Sets the BGP cost assigned to routes sent to this neighbor.	metricout *cost;*	The BGP cost for sending data through this neighbor.
noaggregatorid	Prevents gated from including the router ID information in routing packets to this neighbor, so the routes cannot be aggregated into a larger statement.	noaggregatorid;	N/A
noauthcheck	Tells gated to ignore the authentication portion of incoming BGP packets. This section is set to fully on by gated but not by all gated implementations.	noauthcheck;	N/A

Table 5.22 **Continued**

Option	Purpose	Format	Value(s)
outdelay	Sets how long a route must be in the routing table as the same before gated advertises it to its neighbors.	outdelay *value*;	The number of seconds to wait. Default is 0.
passive	Tells gated that this BGP router should not respond to other BGP routers' OPEN packets but can send its own.	passive;	N/A
preference	Sets how gated's BGP implementation views routes learned from this neighbor compared to others.	preference *value*;	The lower the *value*, the more important routes learned from this neighbor are.
preference2	A tie-breaking subsetting for preference.	preference2 *value*;	Once again, the lower the *value*, the more likely routes from this neighbor will be chosen over others. Default is 0.
ttl	You typically will not need this item. It's used to override the default IP time-to-live setting.	ttl *value*;	If a BGP neighbor ignores packets from this router, try setting *value* to 2 instead of the default 1.
traceoptions	Sets how gated logs data for this specific BGP peer.	traceoptions *settings*;	Options available to all protocols are listed in Table 5.11, and options available specifically in the peer and group type statements are listed in Table 5.21.
version	Tells gated which BGP version to use.	version *value*;	There are three supported BGP versions: 2, 3, and 4. Default is 4.

The IS-IS Protocol

There is one protocol `gated` supports that is not being covering in any detail, but you should be aware of in case you require it. It's the Intermediate System-Intermediate-System (IS-IS) protocol. This routing protocol is for internal use in cases where there is a large variety of subnets running on many kinds of networking hardware and software.

IS-IS is a *connectionless* protocol, meaning that it does not maintain open connections with the machines it exchanges information with—making it more like UDP than TCP, to give you a reference point. If you think you might require the use of this protocol, you can learn more about it starting with RFC 1142 or preferably the ISO DP 10589 parent document.

Configuring SNMP Interaction

Let's switch gears away from routing protocols and look at the Simple Network Management Protocol (SNMP). Administrators use this tool to aid in managing large computer networks. The `gated` daemon does not actually run the SNMP protocol, but it does allow your Linux (or other) routers to interface with SNMP if you are using it as part of your network management solution. See RFC 1157 for more about SNMP itself.

The configuration statement for SNMP interactions is actually quite short. It starts, predictably, with:

```
snmp on {
```

Within the parentheses, there are only three options available:

- `debug;`. If you are having troubles with the SNMP daemon on your Linux box, add this line to activate the debugging features.

- `port value;`. If you are running SNMP but have set it to use a port that is not the default port 167, use this statement to tell `gated`.

- `traceoptions options`. As usual, you use this statement to configure logging. You have access to all of the items available in Table 5.11, as well as those listed in Table 5.23.

Table 5.23 **Options Available for the *traceoptions* Portion of *gated's* SNMP Setup**

Option	Purpose
receive	To log SNMP requests that come from the Linux SNMP daemon, as well as the responses sent to them.
register	To log SNMP requests to create new variables.
resolve	To log SNMP requests for the contents of a variable.
trap	To log SNMP trap messages.

Configuring Static Routing

While most Linux users know how to use the standard routing commands for their static routing on their individual machines, it's a good idea to make sure and give the static information to `gated` as well. Doing this allows your network to be more efficient by sparing individual hosts from having to do as many lookups.

You start a static routing statement (there can be more than one in a `gated.conf` file) with:

```
static {
```

Notice that there is no `on` or `off`. Static routing by its very nature is always available. There isn't a long list of options available within the `static` statement. Instead, there are a lot of variations of format you can use and a few options along with that. The substatement types available to you start with one of the following mostly familiar sequences:

- **default gateway *gateIP*.** Informs `gated` that one specific interface, whose IP address fills *gateIP*, is the default for sending data.

- **host *hostIP* gateway *gateIP*.** Informs `gated` that traffic for the host whose IP address fills *hostIP* should pass through the interface specified by *gateIP*.

- ***netIP* mask *netmask* gateway *gateIP*.** Informs `gated` that traffic for the network specified in *netIP*, which is narrowed down by the netmask contained in the `netmask` portion, should pass through the interface specified by *gateIP*.

- ***netIP* masklen *len* gateway *gateIP*.** Informs `gated` that traffic for the network specified in *netIP*, which is narrowed down by the mask length contained in the *len* portion, should pass through the interface specified by *gateIP*.

- ***netIP* mask *netmask* interface *interface*.** Informs `gated` that traffic for the network specified in *netIP*, which is narrowed down by the netmask contained in the *netmask* portion, goes to the interface specified by *interface*.

- ***netIP* masklen *len* interface *interface*.** Informs `gated` that traffic for the network specified in *netIP*, which is narrowed down by the mask length contained in the *len* portion, goes to the interface specified by *interface*.

- ***netIP* interface *interface*.** Informs `gated` that traffic for the network specified in *netIP* goes to the interface specified by *interface*.

- **interface *interface*.** Sets the default interface that `gated` should use for routing traffic.

The `gateway` statements are specifically for when you want to send data through a particular interface to get to particular destinations. On the other hand, if you have hosts or routers that are sharing a single interface but pretending they have different IP addresses, you need to use the `interface` statement.

After you have this initial portion set up, you fill in the rest of the substatement in the format:

```
specifier gateway gateIP options;
```

The options available here are listed in Table 5.24.

Table 5.24 **Options Available for** *gated's static gateway* **Substatements**

Option	Purpose	Format	Value(s)
blackhole	Drops all packets headed for the specified destination(s).	blackhole	N/A
interface	The only valid gateways for the specified destination(s) are those listed after this keyword.	interface values	Use all if you want to match everything, the format xxx.xxx.xxx.xxx to match a full IP address, the formats xxx.xxx.xxx.*, xxx.xxx.*, or xxx.* to match partial IP addresses, eth* to use a wildcarded device name, or the full name of the device such as eth0.
noinstall	If the static route for this destination has the lowest preference setting, don't store this route in the kernel's route forwarding table.	noinstall	N/A
preference	Sets how preferred the route specified is compared to others.	preference value	An integer—the lower the number, the more preferred the route. Default is 60.
reject	Drops all packets headed for the specified destination(s); or if they're undeliverable, returns them with an error message.	reject	N/A

Table 5.24 **Continued**

Option	Purpose	Format	Value(s)
retain	Do not erase this route from the kernel's route forwarding tables during shutdown.	retain	N/A

Configuring Route Importation

Your routers don't just advertise your network's information to the Internet or external networks. They also receive advertisements from the outside containing vital data for directing packets from place to place. This data is not just collected blindly into a routing table by gated. You have to set up the rules for how the importation of routes operates on each gated router.

The gated.conf file allows you to set up different rules for each protocol type. They're covered here in the order they were covered in Chapters 1 and 3. That means the first item of interest is how you set up how RIP routes are imported.

You start the RIP import statement in the following format:

```
import proto rip
```

From here, you might prevent routes from being imported from other routers using the following structures:

- restrict;. Do not install any RIP routes matching in the routing table.
- interface *ilist* restrict;. Do not install any RIP routes that match ilist in the routing table. To build ilist: use all if you want to match everything; the format xxx.xxx.xxx.xxx to match a full IP address; the formats xxx.xxx.xxx.*, xxx.xxx.*, or xxx.* to match partial IP addresses; eth* to use a wildcarded device name; or the full name of the device such as eth0.
- gateway *glist* restrict;. Do not install any RIP routes that match glist in the routing table. To build glist, use the same rules as discussed previously but apply them to the gateways that matching data packets would travel through rather than the interface from which they were first sent.

Alternatively, you might instruct gated to import routes in a similar fashion. Once again, it starts with:

```
import proto rip
```

After this you have one of two options:

- interface *ilist*. Install RIP routes that match *ilist* in the routing table.
- gateway *glist*. Install any RIP routes that match *glist* in the routing table.

Subsequently, you might have one of these two lines so far:

```
import proto rip interface ilist
import proto rip gateway glist
```

Next you have the choice of adding or not adding preference *value*, which is used to assign how preferred a route from RIP matching the given rules is compared to its alternatives. The default is 100. So now you might have one of the following four statements:

```
import proto rip interface ilist
import proto rip gateway glist
import proto rip interface ilist preference value
import proto rip gateway glist preference value
```

No matter which of these you choose, you now add an opening curly brace ({) at the end of the line and drop down to the next line. This new line of code starts with one of the standard ways of specifying a host or network, which will be illustrated by repeating the example formats given earlier:

```
192.168.15.0
192.168.15.0 mask 255.255.255.0
192.168.15.0 masklen 24
all
host 192.168.15.5
```

After starting the line with one of the above structures, you might end it with only a semicolon, or you might proceed with one of the following additions:

- restrict;. Do not import the routes that meet this rule.

- preference *value*;. Import the routes that meet this rule and assign them the specified preference *value*.

Finally, at the very bottom of the statement, add:

```
};
```

Build as many of these RIP rules as necessary. You can put multiple statements between the curly braces, as long as each of these is meant to match the same list of interfaces or gateways. If you want to set other rules for other interfaces or gateways, you need to build a whole new statement.

Handling Redirect Routes

The simplest protocol on the Internet is the Internet Control Message Protocol (ICMP). This protocol sends packets with one single command inside. For example, the packet might contain the command `echo`, which means it's a ping packet, and the receiving machine will send back a response, giving the originator a metric for how long it took the data to get to the recipient and back. Another command an ICMP packet can contain is `redirect`.

At certain times there are temporary reasons that a nondefault router is suddenly a better choice for sending data to a specific machine than the default—typically for reasons of overlapping network space or when there are multiple subnets running on the same hardware. In this case, an ICMP redirect message is sent to the default router, telling it that all traffic for the target should go through this other router instead of the original default. After the original router, destination router, and destination machine are all notified, the data travels efficiently.

Redirects are typically set with low times-to-live. A redirect routing table entry in `gated` often lasts only three minutes.

Now you need to tell `gated` how to handle incoming routing data from OSPF. The first thing to understand is that `gated` has no control over what routes it imports from OSPF within the area and autonomous system—also referred to as ASE. However, you can control the information imported from outside your AS. You start this statement with:

```
import proto ospfase
```

After this, you might or might not want to add **tag** *value* afterwards. An OSPF tag consists of the originating router's ID, plus a checksum value that helps to ensure that the packet's contents have not been mangled during transmission. So, if you want to watch for routing updates from a specific router within another AS, add this item on the end of your `ospfase` statement.

If you want to use this rule to prevent any external AS OSPF routes from being imported, then just end this statement in `restrict;`, such as:

```
import proto ospfase restrict;
```

However, if you want to use this rule to enable a specific collection of external AS OSPF routes to be imported, you need to continue the statement longer. First, if you don't want the preference for OSPF routes learned from external autonomous systems to be 150, continue the statement by adding `preference value`. At this point, you start a clause with a curly brace:

```
import proto ospfase
     options {
```

The first term(s) within the curly brace specify the networks and hosts that this rule applies to, using the same five formats shown in the example earlier. So, now you may have something such as:

```
import proto ospfase
     options {
          192.168.15.*
```

After you specify which networks, hosts, and so on this rule applies to, you can add either the word `restrict` to prevent these specific routes from being imported or `preference value`—where once again the default preference is 150. The final format looks similar to:

```
import proto ospfase
    options {
        192.168.15.* preference 200;
    };
```

Now we move on to telling `gated` how to handle routes advertised through EGP and BGP. As usual, there are a number of ways to accomplish this. You start either statement with the now familiar:

```
import proto
```

If you're configuring EGP route importation, you continue this with:

```
import proto egp autonomoussystem
```

Next add the AS number for the autonomous system to which you want this rule to apply. After this, if you do not want to save routes learned from this AS through EGP in your routing tables, complete the phrase as follows:

```
import proto egp autonomoussystem value restrict;
```

If you want to allow routing for items that match this rule, then you have a choice. You can either add the phrase `preference value` after the `autonomoussystem` *value* entry or stick with the default of a 200 preference for EGP. Then, expand the statement to the familiar format:

```
import proto egp autonomoussystem value
preference value {
```

This statement ends in the usual manner. Inside the curly braces you define the networks, hosts, and so on to which you want the rule to apply and then end the statement with one of the following: the word `restrict`, the phrase `preference value`, or neither. In the end, you'll have something similar to:

```
import proto egp autonomoussystem value
preference value {
    all;
};
```

You can use the same exact formats for BGP as you do for EGP; you just use `bgp` in place of `egp`. However, BGP contains some additional features. The other type of BGP configuration statement allows you to tell `gated` how to handle importation of a wider variety of routing protocol data into its routing tables. This statement type begins with the following:

```
import proto bgp aspath value
    origin type
```

The *value* variable contains a regular expression that contains a list of autonomous systems to which this rule applies. In this case, we're not looking for which AS the data comes directly from—though this information can be included here too. Instead, *value* contains AS numbers that the data may have passed through.

Choosing what to place in the *type* variable's place is a bit more straightforward. The following settings are available:

- `blank`. You can choose to put nothing at all here.
- `any`. Sets that this rule applies to routes no matter from which protocol group they come.
- `egp`. This rule refers to External Gateway Protocols, or EGPs.
- `igp`. This rule refers to Internal Gateway Protocols, or IGPs.
- `incomplete`. This rule refers to routes where the given data is not complete.

You can actually have one or more of `egp`, `igp`, and `incomplete` if necessary.

On the next line, you'll have the following to finish the rule if you want to prevent the defined routes from being imported:

```
restrict;
```

There's another format of this statement available that allows you not only to set protocol types, but also data about which routes the rule should apply. It starts with what we just covered:

```
import proto bgp aspath value
        origin type
```

Now decide whether you want to use the default BGP preference of 170 or start the next line with:

```
preference value {
```

You need the curly brace even if you don't set a preference. Proceed now to the next line and use the usual formats to set the list of routes you want to import. For each of these routes, start the line with the data that defines the address(es) to which you want the rule to apply, so you might start the next line with:

```
host 192.168.15.5
```

Then, set whether you want to save this route to the routing tables by ending the line with one of the following:

```
host 192.168.15.5;
host 192.168.15.5 preference value;
```

Or, tell `gated` that this item points to data that should not be saved to the routing tables with:

```
host 192.168.15.5 restrict;
```

After you've entered all of the address lines for this rule, close it with:

```
};
```

Configuring Route Exports

If the rest of the Internet is to know how to reach you, `gated` or another border router has to export information to go into others' routing tables. This doesn't mean that you have to let everyone under the sun know about every single one of your machines. At the very least, though, the outside world must know how to reach your network gateway. Just as with the `import` statement, the `export` statement allows for specific rules to be applied to each routing protocol.

As usual, let's start with RIP. There are two ways you can specify an RIP `export` statement that refers to how `gated` shares data with external RIP routers, but both start with:

```
export proto rip
```

If you instead want to use this rule to set how `gated` exports routes learned from RIP, then change the first line to:

```
proto rip
```

The second line is also identical regardless of which type of RIP `export` statement you're building. If you want to specify a collection of addresses that this rule applies to, you have a choice of two different items you can place on this line:

```
interface ilist
gateway glist
```

You actually don't have to put anything here at all. If you don't require the second line items just covered, then ignore them and treat the second line as though it's the third. To set this rule so that it tells `gated` not to export data that matches, end the statement with:

```
restrict;
```

Otherwise, if you want this rule to set what data can be exported through RIP, decide if you want to assign an RIP cost for the data hop from this border router to its neighbor. If you do, make the next line:

```
metric value {
```

If you don't want to apply a cost, leave the `metric value` out and just use the curly brace. On the next line and as many after as necessary, use the structure:

```
elist;
```

All list values are built in the same format. It's just what you're representing that's different. The *ilist* refers to the specific interfaces on this router that this rule refers to. The *glist* applies to the external gateways that this `export` rule refers to. Finally, the *elist* is a set of values that specify which routes—networks, hosts, netmasks, and more—this rule fits.

After you've finished specifying the lists, close the statement with:

```
};
```

Now let's take a look at handling `gated` interaction with external OSPF routers. You start this type of rule with:

```
export proto ospfase
```

You may not need to add anything else to this line. It depends on your needs. If you want this rule to apply to networks that have cost metrics that are compatible with OSPF, then expand this line to:

```
export proto ospfase type 1
```

On the other hand, if you want this rule to apply to networks that have incompatible costs when compared to OSPF, expand it to:

```
export proto ospfase type 2
```

You don't have to use either of these types if you are unsure. Finally, when it comes to the first line, if you want to limit this rule to an OSPF router within a specific AS, add the following to the end:

```
tag asnumber
```

Now you finish the line with one of the following structures, both of which should look familiar. Use this one if you want the rule to refuse to export matching routes:

```
restrict;
```

Alternatively, use this one if you want to use this rule to allow for exporting, where the metric item and its value are optional:

```
metric value {
    evalue1;
    ...
    evalueN;
};
```

Then there's the case of exporting routes learned by OSPF. You start these statements with one of the two following lines:

```
proto ospf
proto ospfase
```

If you don't want anything matching this rule exported, end the statement with only:

```
restrict;
```

Otherwise, if you want to add a cost metric to the OSPF or OSPFASE routes you export, and then end this line with metric value { (the curly brace must be there even if metric value isn't). Then, move to the next line and add the first in a potential series of lines defining the specific routes to which this rule applies. Each one of these lines starts with one of the usual network and host definition items and then has either restrict; or metric value; at the end—or nothing to use the default cost. After the statement is complete, close it with };. An example of what you might end up with is:

```
proto ospfase {
    192.168.15.*;
    host 192.168.15.2 metric 300;
    host 192.168.15.9 restrict;
};
```

Now we can move on to export rules for both EGP and BGP. In this case, both egp and bgp are interchangeable as far as plugging these items into the format. We'll use _gp for the examples. First we'll look at how to set up rules for exporting data to EGP or BGP from other autonomous systems. If you don't want to export anything to external EGP or BGP routers, use the rule:

```
export proto _gp as asnum
    restrict;
```

If you want more individual control so you can explicitly list which routes should be exported to EGP or BGP, then use the following format:

```
export proto _gp as asnum
    metric value {
        elist1;
        ...
        elistN;
    };
```

The `metric value` clause is optional as usual because you can just leave it to the defaults. You also need rules for how to handle exporting routes learned from BGP or EGP. To prevent these from going out, use the structure:

```
proto _gp autonomoussystem asnum
    restrict;
```

To individually control which routes are exported and which are not, use the structure:

```
proto _gp autonomoussystem asnum
    metric value {
        route1;
        ...
        routeN;
    };
```

Once again, the `metric value` clause is optional. At the end of each route line, you can have either `metric value` or `restrict`. As you can tell by now, even though some of the details are different from protocol to protocol, the structure for the statements is pretty much the same.

There are some additional situations you can set up with `export` as well. You don't have to do everything according to protocol. In fact, not every route on your network was learned using a protocol at all. To apply routing according to specific interfaces, start with the following:

```
proto
```

After `proto`, you have one of three choices:

- `direct`. Refers to the interfaces on this router.
- `kernel`. Refers to data installed using the `route` command.
- `static`. Refers to data installed using `gated`'s `static` statement.

So now let's say that you have:

```
proto static
```

After this, drop down to the next line. You may or may not place here the structure:

```
interface ilist
```

Add this item only if you want this rule to be specific to one or more particular interfaces. On the next line (or this one if you didn't use the `interface` clause) you put `restrict;` to end the statement if you want to use this rule to prevent exportation. Otherwise, you may want to make the next line:

```
metric value {
```

Even if you don't use the `metric` clause, you need the open curly brace. Now drop down to the next line. You start this one with the information that specifies what exact route to which you're referring. As usual, you can have multiple lines here in the format:

```
route1;
...
routeN;
};
```

If you don't want to use the default metric, you have the usual two options for the end of each line (before the semi-colon):

- `metric value`. Set the cost for using this interface instead of using the default costs of 0 for `direct`, 40 for `kernel`, or 60 for `static`.

- `restrict`. Do not allow routes matching this rule to be exported.

Configuring Route Aggregation

As we discussed in Chapter 4, you can advertise a network address to the outside world as though it is a single-piece entity, when in fact it is broken down into smaller networks with subnets or IPv6. As long as `gated`, your router, understands where to send the data once it reaches the overall network, everything will work fine.

You start a route aggregation section with one of the following lines of code:

```
aggregate default
aggregate networkIP
aggregate networkIP mask netmask
aggregate networkIP masklen bitmask
```

You should already be familiar with the terms *networkIP*, *netmask*, and *bitmask* by this point. The second line also has a number of combinations you might use:

```
{
preference value {
brief {
preference value brief {
```

You only use the `preference` option if you don't want to use the default setting of 130 for aggregate routes. Also you only need the brief term if you want the path specified for the AS to be truncated down to a common denominator.

From here, you have a series of lines that denote which routes should and should not be advertised. No matter which type of rule you're setting up, it starts with the term `proto`. After this you might utilize one of six different options:

- `aggregate`. This rule applies to any route that `gated` has made an aggregate rather than advertising the individual components.

- `all`. This rule applies to all types of routes.

- `direct`. This rule applies to the interfaces attached to this router.

- `kernel`. This rule applies to routes placed into the routing table with the `route` command.

- `static`. This rule applies to routes assigned with a `static gated` statement.
- `value`. This rule applies to the specified routing protocol out of those supported by `gated`.

Another item available for placing after `proto` (with or without what you see in the preceding list) is a choice of one of the following:

- `as asnum`. This rule applies to the specified autonomous system.
- `as asregexp`. This rule applies to the autonomous systems that match the regular expression.
- `tag value`. This rule applies to the routes that have the specified tag.

Now is when you decide where you're going with this rule. If it is only meant to prevent a single aggregation, just end it with:

```
restrict;
```

However, if you want to build a series of rules according to what networks and hosts you're looking at, then you next have to decide if you want to use the default aggregate preference value of 130 or if you want to change it for this rule as an overall new default. If you do, start the next line with:

```
preference value {
```

If not, just use the curly brace on this line. On the next line, you use the very familiar format:

```
        route1;
        ...
        routeN;
    };
```

As usual, with each route you can add at the end either `restrict` or `preference` *value*. Build as many `proto` statements as you need within the overall `aggregate` statement, and then close it all out with an ending:

```
    };
```

Running Public *gated*

Fortunately, the most complex part of dealing with `gated` is the configuration. After you reach the point of actually being ready to run the daemon, it's time to make sure that the router is working as you anticipated. Only then you can finally rest. What I recommend here is typing things manually at the command line and taking notes for what works and what doesn't. As soon as you know the exact format you need to use when running `gated`, add the command to `/etc/rc.local` or to the daemon `init` script according to how you prefer to start your network services.

As a general rule, you don't tend to work directly with `gated` at this point. One of this daemon's companion programs is `gdc`, which is the `gated` controller. Even if you've already installed `gated`, you might not have `gdc`. It seems that some distributions don't include `gdc` as part of the `gated` package, nor even in a separate one. However, `gdc` does come with the main `gated` public source, which you can get by going to `www.gated.org`.

Starting gdc

The `gdc` program itself doesn't run continuously. Each time you want to use it, you have to use the necessary flags and commands. The flags are listed in Table 5.25. As soon as you have `gdc` and its flags typed in, add the commands specified in the following section. This allows you to manipulate `gated` without having to actually touch the daemon itself. Doing this can save a lot of angst and heartache down the road.

Table 5.25 **Command-Line Switches Available When Starting** *gdc*

Flag	Purpose	Format	Value(s)
-c	Sets the maximum allowed size of a gated coredump— only when gated is started using gdc.	-c *size*	Size in bytes.
-f	Sets the maximum allowed size of a gated state dump file—only when gated is started using gdc.	-f *size*	Size in bytes.
-m	Sets the maximum allowed data segment size for gated—only when gated is started using gdc.	-m *size*	Size in bytes.
-n	Sets gated to not alter the kernel forwarding table.	-n	N/A
-q	Sets gated to run in quiet mode, sending nothing to STDOUT. Error messages are logged according to settings in syslog.conf.	-q	N/A

continues

Table 5.25 **Continued**

Flag	Purpose	Format	Value(s)
-s	Sets the maximum allowed stack size for gated—only when gated is started using gdc.	-s *size*	Size in bytes.
-t	Sets how patient gdc is when waiting for gated to complete certain tasks.	-t *time*	Number of seconds gdc should wait for gated to complete instructions. Default is 10.

Items -c, -f, -m, and -s are all used primarily to fix problems with gated running out of space when it tries to run.

Testing *gated.conf*

One of the first things you'll probably want to do after you finish configuring gated is to utilize gdc to check /etc/gated.conf for syntax errors and other such concerns. You accomplish this with the commands listed in Table 5.26. One thing to keep in mind is that this routing daemon actually keeps multiple versions of gated.conf in storage. The first time you utilize gated, you'll have it loading your original gated.conf. After that make sure you work with the correct file—don't just delete gated.conf when you're changing configuration settings and do not work directly on gated.conf itself. There's more on this in the section, "Manipulating gated," in this chapter.

Table 5.26 *gated* **Testing Commands Available Through** *gdc*

Command	Purpose
checkconf	Tells gdc to examine /etc/gated.conf for syntax errors.
checknew	Tells gdc to examine /etc/gated.conf+ for syntax errors. Configuration file cycling—the creation of /etc/gated.conf+—is covered in the section, "Manipulating gated."
COREDUMP	Tells gdc to copy the entire contents of gated's memory to a file and then shuts off gated.
dump	Tells gdc to ask gated to save a data snapshot of its current settings and other information to the file /usr/tmp/gated.dump.
interface	Tells gdc to instruct gated to immediately check the status of all directly connected network interfaces—usually Ethernet cards as of this writing.
rmcore	Tells gdc to delete the latest gated core dump file.
rmdump	Tells gdc to delete the latest gated state dump file.

Table 5.26 **Continued**

Command	Purpose
rmparse	Tells gdc to delete the latest file containing the list of gated.conf syntax errors.
running	Tells gdc to determine whether gated is currently running or not.
toggletrace	Tells gdc to either turn on or shut off gated behavior tracing capabilities.

The bird and zebra **Routing Daemons**

Routing daemons are so complex that it is not possible to cover all of those you might want to utilize in this book unless we cut out a lot of more useful information. One of the daemons that had to have in-depth coverage cut is the BIRD Internet Routing Daemon, or bird (http://bird.network.cz/). This daemon is capable of supporting both IPv4 and IPv6 static routing as well as the protocols RIP, OSPF, and BGP. It also provides tools for route filtering.

Another daemon that didn't make the cut but is popular in its own right is GNU's zebra (http://www.zebra.org/). This one also supports IPv4 and IPv6, RIP-1, RIP-2, OSPF, and BGP. The great thing is that these two daemons are also open source and tested under Linux. This gives you a wide range of options.

Manipulating *gated*

The gdc handler has many other functions that exist to help you to both start and stop the gated daemon as well as alter its behavior and even update it's current data. These commands are outlined in Table 5.27. One thing it is important to understand here is that gated maintains three copies of its configuration file, /etc/gated.conf, after you've updated its settings at least once. These copies entail:

- /etc/gated.conf+. The new configuration file you want gated to load.
- /etc/gated.conf. The current configuration file in use by gated.
- /etc/gated.conf-. The last gated configuration file you used.

Table 5.27 *gated* **Manipulation Commands Available Through** *gdc*

Command	Purpose
backout	If /etc/gated.conf- is empty or doesn't exist or if there is already a /etc/gated.conf+ file, this command does nothing. Otherwise, this command "backs up" through the configuration files, moving /etc/gated.conf to /etc/gated.conf+, moving /etc/gated.conf- to /etc/gated.conf, and then loading the older configuration file.

continues

Table 5.27 **Continued**

Command	Purpose
BACKOUT	If /etc/gated.conf- is empty or doesn't exist, this command does nothing. Otherwise, this command "backs up" through the configuration files, moving /etc/gated.conf to /etc/gated.conf+, moving /etc/gated.conf- to /etc/gated.conf, and then loading the older configuration file.
createconf	If /etc/gated.conf+ exists, this command does nothing. Otherwise, gdc creates the empty file /etc/gated.conf+ and sets it to be owned by the user root and the group, gdmaint, with the permissions 664.
KILL	Tells gdc to do a kill -9 on gated.
modeconf	Tells gdc to set all of the gated configuration files to be owned by the user root and the group, gdmaint, with the permissions 664.
newconf	If /etc/gated.conf+ does not exist, this command does nothing. Otherwise, this command overwrites any existing /etc/gated.conf- with the current /etc/gated.conf, and then moves /etc/gated.conf+ to /etc/gated.conf.
reconfig	Tells gdc to have gated load the current /etc/gated.conf and alter its settings appropriately.
restart	Tells gdc to stop the gated process if it is already running, and then start a new gated process. If gated is not already running, this command still calls start.
start	If gated is already running, this command exits with an error. Otherwise, it tells gdc to run the gated program and then wait for the appropriate number of seconds (10 by default, see Table 5.25) before exiting with an error if the daemon does not start properly.
stop	If gated isn't running, this command exits with an error. Otherwise, tells gdc to send a shutoff command to gated and then wait for the appropriate number of seconds (10 by default, see Table 5.25). If gated does not properly exit within this wait period, gdc then sends the same shutoff command and waits once again. If after this gated still does not manage to exit, then gdc sends the equivalent of a kill -9 to force the issue.
term	Tells gdc to tell gated to shut down each of its protocols one by one and then exit. If gated fails to shut down and you issue term a second time, gdc sends the equivalent of a kill -9 to force the issue.
version	If gated is running, this command fails. Otherwise, this tells gdc to display information about the gated version currently in use.

Summary

Well, there you have it. Everything you could possibly want to know about utilizing the public `gated` routing daemon was covered in this chapter. This tool, as well as others such as `zebra` (`http://www.zebra.org/`), allows you a great amount of control over how your router behaves, including the ability to sit back and just configure some basics and not bother with the higher end issues if you don't need them.

Now that we've gotten familiar with one of the popular unicast routing daemons, in Chapter 6, "Inside The Multicast Kernel 2.2.x Daemons," we tackle some of the multicast routing daemons used in the 2.2.x kernel series.

6

Inside the Multicast Kernel 2.2.x Daemons

I F YOU WANT TO PROVIDE MULTICAST services or even just want to receive them, you need to have the routing infrastructure in place to direct multicast packets. There are a number of daemons available to serve this purpose under Linux. What we've chosen to cover here is a pair of daemons, each of which serves a specific purpose in the Linux multicast routing world. These are `pimd` for Protocol Independent Multicast-Sparse Mode (PIM-SM) and `mrouted` for Distance Vector Multicast Routing Protocol (DVMRP).

The PIM-SM Linux Daemon: *pimd*

For your PIM-SM routing pleasure, we chose to cover `pimd` (`ftp://catarina.usc.edu/pub/pim/pimd/`). As you'll learn in this chapter's sidebars, you do have other options available under Linux, but this one made the most sense to cover here. `pimd` is a single-purpose, single-protocol daemon. After seeing how complex the public `gated` is to configure in Chapter 5, "Inside the Unicast Kernel 2.2.x Daemons," you will probably find this fact a blessing.

PIM-SM seems destined to be a favorite among the multicasting community. It is a low-overhead protocol and handles directing of traffic efficiently, especially in Sparse Mode situations where people listening to any given multicast channel are on machines widely spread network-wise (instead of in close proximity).

Multi-Protocol, Multicast Routing with the Multicast gated

The multicast version of gated (www.gated.org) handles PIM-SM, Protocol Independent Multicast-Dense Mode (PIM-DM), DVMRP, and Multicast Source Discover Protocol (MSDP) all in a single program. It's not featured in this chapter because it's not freely available, but for many this program is worth the cost. This is especially true if you need to run more than one multicast protocol, which you might just need to do. The reasons for this are discussed in the section, "The DVMRP Linux Daemon: mrouted."

Configuring *pimd*

Since pimd is a single-function daemon, the configuration is really not that complex—at least when compared to a monster tool such as gated. The configuration data is kept in the file /etc/pimd.conf. While the order of the statements does not have to strictly follow what is about to be presented, I'll walk you through the contents you might want to add to this file.

The /etc/pimd.conf file begins with the following statement:

```
default_source_preference value
```

Routers hold elections to determine which gets to be a site's upstream router. Because pimd is such a focused tool, you generally don't want it to win over something more general. Using a *value* of 101 here is a minimum for making sure that gated and other routing tools are going to win the election and leave pimd to do its PIM-SM handling. The next line is

```
default_source_metric value
```

This item sets the cost for sending data through this router. You want only PIM-SM data to go to this daemon; so once again, a high *value* is recommended to prevent accidental usage. The preferred default value is 1024.

Though you can swap the first two statements around, you must have the next statement after you set default_source_metric. This item starts with

```
phyint interface
```

phyint refers to physical interface. You fill in *interface* with a reference to the ethernet card or other network interface you're telling pimd about, either with the device's IP address or name (for example, eth0). If you just want to activate this interface with default values, you don't need to put anything else on the line. However, you do have some additional items you can add. The items are, in the order you would need to use them, as follows:

- **disable**. Do not send PIM-SM traffic through this interface nor listen for PIM-SM traffic from this interface.

- **preference** *pref*. This interface's value in an election. It will have the **default_source_preference** if not assigned.

- **metric** *cost*. The cost of sending data through this interface. It will have the **default_source_metric** if not assigned.

Add one `phyint` line per interface on this router. If you don't do this, `pimd` will simply assume that you want it to utilize all interfaces on the machine with the default values. If you set `phyint` for one or more interfaces but not for all, the missing ones will be assigned the defaults. After you have done this, start the next line with

`cand_rp`

cand_rp refers to Candidate Rendezvous Point (CRP). This statement specifies which interface on this machine should be included in RP elections. Additional options to choose from are, listed in the order used, as follows:

- *ipadd*. The default is the largest activated IP address. If you don't want to utilize that interface, add the IP address of the interface to use as the next term.

- **time** *value*. The number of seconds to wait between advertising this CRP. The default value is 60 seconds.

- **priority** *num*. How important this CRP is compared to others. The lower the value here, the more important the CRP.

The next line begins with

`cand_bootstrap_router`

Here you give the information for how this machine advertises itself as a Candidate BootStrap Router (CBSR). If you need to, add the *ipaddr* and/or `priority` items as defined earlier after `cand_bootstrap_router`. What follows is a series of statements that start with

`group_prefix`

Each `group_prefix` statement outlines the set of multicast addresses that CRP, if it wins an election, will advertise to other routers. The two items you might include here are, listed in order, as follows:

- *groupaddr*. A specific IP or network range this router will handle. Remember that a single multicast network is written as a single IP address.

- **masklen** *len*. The number of IP address segments taken up by the netmask. Remember that a multicast address is a Class D and has a netmask of 255.255.255.255, which means its length is 4.

After this comes

`switch_data_threshold rate `*rvalue*` interval `*ivalue*

This statement defines the threshold at which transmission rates trigger the changeover from the shared tree to the RP tree; starting the line with `switch_register_threshold` does the opposite in the same format. (See Chapter 2, "Multicast Protocols," for more details on the two PIM-SM trees.) Regardless of which of these you choose, the `rvalue` stands for the transmission rate in bits per second, and `ivalue` sets how often to sample the rate in seconds—with a recommended minimum of five seconds. It's recommended by the `pimd` programmers to have `ivalue` the same in both statements.

For example, I might end up with the following (these are real IP addresses; don't use them for actual testing purposes):

```
default_source_preference 105

phyint 199.60.103.90 disable
phyint 199.60.103.91 preference 1029
phyint 199.60.103.92 preference 1024
cand_rp 199.60.103.91
cand_bootstrap_router 199.60.103.92
group_prefix 199.60.103.0 masklen 4
switch_data_threshold rate 60000 interval 10
switch_register_threshold rate 60000 interval 10
```

Running *pimd*

After you've set up the configuration file, you're ready to actually run the PIM-SM daemon, pimd. As usual, we tend to recommend that you run this by hand for testing purposes and then later add the daemon, with any startup flags it needs, to your system's startup scripts.

The format for running this daemon is

```
pimd -c file -d level1,...,levelN
```

Both of the flags with their values are optional:

- **-c *file***. Utilize the specified configuration file rather than the default, /etc/pimd.conf.

- **-d *level1,...,levelN***. Specifies the debug level(s) to utilize when running this daemon. Type **pimd -h** to see a full list of these levels.

The DVMRP Daemon: *mrouted*

For your DVMRP routing fun, we chose to cover mrouted (ftp://parcftp.xerox.com/pub/net-research/ipmulti/). Once again, this is not the only tool available for the job, but we've chosen to cover it because it is single purpose and freely available, just as with pimd. See the chapter sidebars for other DVMRP options.

The multicasting community has found that DVMRP does not quite suit their needs for internal use. Mainly, the protocol does not perform well when put under heavy load—whereas PIM-SM is quite scalable. Today, this protocol comes into play when connecting your network to the MBONE (http://www.live.com/mbone/), which exclusively uses DVMRP.

While I am not including SNMP coverage, mrouted does support this tool. If you intend to utilize SNMP and mrouted hand-in-hand, see the file mrouted.conf.dist that comes with the package itself.

> **Multi-Protocol, Multicast Routing with** *zebra*
>
> Another daemon that's useful in both the unicast and multicast worlds is GNU's zebra. For unicast, this daemon handles BGP4, OSPF, RIP-1, RIP-2, and more. However, in this case, the multicasting functionality has not been added to the main zebra release quite yet. You can keep up with its progress at http://www.zebra.org/.

Configuring *mrouted*

Once again, we're dealing with a single-function daemon. This gives us the benefit of a pretty straightforward configuration process. The configuration file for mrouted is /etc/mrouted.conf. Some of these settings must be presented in a specific order. The chapter will make it clear when this is the case. The rest doesn't matter; so if you don't see any directions about ordering, the options are presented in the sequence as they are typically used.

The mrouted configuration file often begins with one or more options of the name statement. You utilize this command in the format

```
name boundaryname boundaryadd/masklen
```

These three variables are

- **boundaryname.** The name that you choose to assign to the particular collection of addresses for which you want to set rules.
- **boundaryadd.** The network or subnet address you're naming.
- **masklen.** The number of binary 1s at the beginning of the netmask for the network or subnet that you're naming.

Typically, the next line involves the cache_lifetime option. It's used in the format

```
cache_lifetime seconds
```

seconds sets how long information learned through DVMRP is stored in the kernel. The default is 300, and the guidelines state that you should keep it between 5 minutes (300 seconds) and 1 day (86,400 seconds). After this statement tends to come one of the following two lines:

```
pruning on
pruning off
```

These two statements control whether or not your DVMRP router supports tree pruning, as you might have guessed.

You can actually end the file right here if you prefer. The mrouted program by default activates all interfaces capable of transmitting multicast data and assigns them default values. Alternatively, you can proceed to set up one or more interfaces. The next command typically used is phyint, which should look familiar if you just read the pimd configuration material. The initial format for phyint in mrouted's case is

```
phyint IPaddr
```

IPaddr tells `phyint` which physical interface you're referring to and can be an IP address or an interface name, such as `eth0`. After this, you have a collection of options that you can add to suit your needs:

- **disable**. Indicates to route no DVMRP traffic through this interface.

- **metric** *metric*. The cost for sending data from the multicast source to this interface. For an interface to be valid, the metric should be below 31. It's often recommended to use 1.

- **threshold** *threshold*. The minimum Internet Protocol (IP) time-to-live setting the packet must have before `mrouted` will bother sending this packet along to the interface. This value is given in seconds.

- **rate_limit** *rate_limit*. The rate in Kbits/second that this interface will accept multicast traffic, if you want to limit this.

- **boundary** *boundaryname*. Apply this set of rules to the network block defined earlier with the `name` statement. You can have more than one of these options.

- **boundary** *boundaryadd/masklen*. Apply this set of rules to the network block specified by these variables, which are utilized in the same way you would use them in the `name` statement. You can have more than one of these options.

- **altnet** *subnet/masklen*. If the interface in question leads to a number of subnets, you can refine the data path utilizing this option. *subnet* refers to the network address for the specific subnet you want to set up, and `masklen` is the same as it is defined in the `name` statement. You can have more than one of these options.

- **altnet** *subnet*. If the interface in question leads to a number of subnets, you can refine the data path utilizing this option. *subnet* refers to the network address for the subnet you want to set up and assumes that there is no netmask needed. You can have more than one of these options.

Now we finally get into an order issue. The final possibility here is the `tunnel` statement, which you can utilize to set up a unicast method of transporting your multicast data from one `mrouted` machine to another across unicast-only network space. You must define your tunnels after your physical interfaces. The base format for this item is

```
tunnel local remote
```

As you might guess, `local` refers to the connected interface on which to start the tunnel—either an IP address or device name—and *remote* refers to the IP address of the interface to connect to on the other end to receive the data. All of the additional options are identical to those available in `phyint`: `metric`, `threshold`, `rate_limit`, `boundary` *boundaryname*, and `boundary` *boundaryadd/masklen*. See the previous bulleted list for definitions of these options and how to set them.

For example, I might set up my configuration file to be as close as possible to the PIM-SM configuration file as follows:

```
name multi 199.60.103.0/32
cache_lifetime 21600
```

```
pruning on
phyint 199.60.103.90 disable
phyint 199.60.103.91 rate_limit 60 threshold 10 \
preference 1029 boundary multi
phyint 199.60.103.92 rate_limit 60 threshold 10 \
preference 1024 boundary multi
tunnel 199.60.103.92 210.17.105.9 rate_limit 60 \
threshold 10 preference 1024 boundary multi
```

Running *mrouted*

After you've set up the configuration file, you're ready to run the DVMRP daemon, mrouted. The usual recommendations apply, such as setting up the daemon to start and stop automatically at boot and shutdown, but not until you've run it manually at first to determine what combination of flags and settings works best for your needs. The format for running this daemon is

mrouted *flags*

Yes, that's it. The available flags are

- **-p**. Disable tree pruning.
- **-c *file***. Utilize the specified configuration file. Be sure to include the path in *file*.
- **-d**. Enter debug level 2. The debugging levels are outlined in Table 6.1.
- **-d *level***. Enter the specified debug level.

Table 6.1 Debugging Levels Available in *mrouted*

Level	Description
1	Send all `syslogd` messages to STDERR.
2	Level 1 plus send all messages marked "significant" to STDERR.
3	Level 2 plus send messages recording every packet's arrival and departure to STDERR.

Summary

You have a number of options available to you in the multicasting daemon world. If you want to set up wide-scale or internal multicasting, then typically you'll want to use PIM-SM to carry your traffic—or even PIM-DM if you have a very dense local setup. One simple method of setting up PIM-SM is to utilize `pimd`, a nice little single-function daemon. On the other hand, if you need to connect to the `mbone`, you have to use DVMRP, for which you have `mrouted`. You also can choose options such as getting access to the multicast `gated`, the multicast components of `zebra` when they are available, or try one of the additional options that will no doubt appear as multicasting gains ground. Considering the amount of bandwidth that unicasting data such as Internet radio consumes, those days aren't too far off.

7

Kernel Support Tools

THIS CHAPTER EXAMINES TWO SUPPORT DAEMONS for Linux: pppd and rip2ad.

pppd is the Point-to-Point Protocol (PPP) daemon that provides PPP support to the Linux kernel and Linux network processes. The pppd provides a transparent interface to the user; that is, network utilities and applications can be used without the utilities and applications having to have knowledge of the Point-to-Point Protocol or pppd.

pppd is a widely deployed Point-to-Point daemon for UNIX and Linux operating systems. Most versions of Linux use this version of pppd, with version 2.4.1 being the most recent release of the distribution. Before covering pppd, an overview of PPP and some design considerations will be presented.

rip2ad is a utility that allows Routing Information Protocol (RIP) advertisements to be sent out of an interface without running a full-blown routing daemon. rip2ad is an ideal tool on Linux routers that acts as an edge device that in turn acts as a gateway to RIP systems but does not require the complexity of RIP on the local systems.

We will begin with an overview of PPP, followed by sections on PPP for Linux and rip2ad.

PPP Overview

PPP was designed for serial connection protocols and has become the Internet standard for both dial-up and leased (nailed) line connections. PPP's open standard encouraged wide support by vendors and the Internet explosion, and use of serial links to connect to the Internet have created wide acceptance of the protocol—with very few interoperability problems. PPP is defined in RFC 1661, "The Point-to-Point Protocol (PPP)."

PPP's format is straightforward and takes advantage of the High-level Data Link Control (HDLC) protocol with the addition of a PPP header made up of one field containing the size of the packet and the protocol field, which defines the type or protocol of the packet being transported. PPP supports hundreds of protocols. Table 7.1 summarizes the common types seen in enterprise environments.

Table 7.1 **Common Protocols Supported by PPP**

Value	Protocol
0x0021	IP
0x002D	Van Jacobson Compressed IP
0x002F	Van Jacobson Uncompressed IP
0x003D	PPP Multilink Protocol (MP)
0x8021	PPP Internet Protocol Control Protocol (IPCP)
0xC021	Link Control Protocol (LCP)
0xC023	Password Authentication Protocol (PAP)
0xC223	Challenge Handshake Authentication Protocol (CHAP)

Logical View of PPP

PPP is not just the encapsulation of packets over the link; the PPP stack must support specific functionality throughout the lifetime of a PPP session. RFC 1661 defines this functionality in the term of phases, which are shown in Figure 7.1.

Link Dead Phase

The *link dead phase* is the phase entered before and after a PPP session. When triggered to leave this phase by the Link Control Protocol (LCP), covered shortly, PPP will enter the link establishment phase.

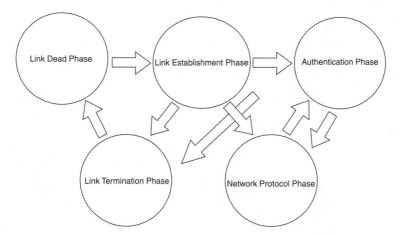

Figure 7.1 PPP phases.

Link Establishment Phase

LCP provides the *link establishment phase*. The connection is established with the bare minimum configuration options to bring the link up. Neither peer in the process is aware of particular options supported by the other—with the exception of authentication protocol selection. Should authentication be required for the link, the type of authentication will be determined (negotiated) during the link establishment phase.

LCP is defined in RFC 1661 with some added capabilities in RFC 1570, "PPP LCP Extensions." The LCP packet is made up of the LCP header and data and is encapsulated within the PPP packet as shown in Figure 7.2.

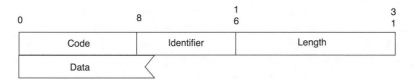

Figure 7.2 LCP packet.

The LCP header includes an LCP code that identifies the messaging type, which could be a rejection to a particular option request. The LCP codes are listed in Table 7.2.

Table 7.2 **LCP Protocol Codes**

Value	Message
1	Configure-Request
2	Configure-Ack
3	Configure-Nak
4	Configure-Reject
5	Terminate-Request
6	Terminate-Ack
7	Code-Reject
8	Protocol-Reject
9	Echo-Request
10	Echo-Reply
11	Discard-Request

The data field is determined by the LCP code. This means that each message has a particular data or payload portion that matches the message.

After the link establishment phase has been accepted by both parties, the authentication phase is entered.

Authentication Phase

Prior to accepting any option parameters, the nodes can authenticate one another. Although not required, there is no good reason to not use authentication. This is unless another form of authentication is deemed adequate, such as caller ID. Once both peers are satisfied with any required authentication, the *network layer protocol phase* is entered. (Most sites only have the central remote access server authenticate the remote site; however, authentication can be supported in both directions regardless of which node initiated the session.)

PPP supports two authentication methods: Password Authentication Protocol (PAP) and the Challenge Handshake Authentication Protocol (CHAP).

PAP is a simple username and password mechanism whereby the node sends the username and password in plain text. The user name and password are accepted or rejected by the remote node.

CHAP uses a more complicated 3-way handshake without sending clear text usernames or responses: challenge, response, and acknowledgement.

The node wishing to authenticate the remote host will send a challenge based on a secret phase that is known by itself and that also should be known by the remote node. The remote node uses the challenge and the secret phase with a hash function to compute the response. The response is then sent, and the node checks the response to ensure it is the same calculated response it computes itself and, should it match, acknowledges the authentication and allows the connection to continue.

Unlike PAP, CHAP never sends the secret phase, not even in encrypted form.

Network Layer Protocol Phase

The Network Control Protocol (NCP) determines the appropriate options for the protocols being supported. Each protocol supported by a node will have an NCP for the particular protocol. In addition, these NCPs can run in parallel. For example, IP and IPX options can be negotiated at the same time. Layer 3 traffic can be passed at this point within the phase, assuming the particular protocol was negotiated.

For IP over PPP, RFC 1172, "The PPP Internet Protocol Control Protocol (IPCP)" defines the standard for IP NCP.

IPCP uses the LCP packet format. However, only codes 1 through 7, shown in Table 7.3, are valid.

Table 7.3   **IPCP Protocol Codes**

Value	Message
1	Configure-Request
2	Configure-Ack
3	Configure-Nak
4	Configure-Reject
5	Terminate-Request
6	Terminate-Ack
7	Code-Reject

To distinguish IPCP packets from LCP, the protocol field in the PPP header is set to 0x8021.

In addition to determining that IP is supported on the link, the network layer protocol phase uses specifics of IPCP to determine the IP address of the local IP address of the link and whether compression should be used.

Although the IP address must not be determined with IPCP, most implementations of PPP allow the administrator to determine which IP address is required. Most sites require that the central remote access server provide the IP address to ensure proper routing within the network.

Link Termination Phase

Under ideal conditions, the *link termination phase* is signaled end-to-end using PPP terminate packets; however, the link termination phase also can be caused by a loss of carrier or an immediate shutdown by the system administrator.

It is interesting to note that although the states seem very sequential, a state can be entered in the "middle" of a session, which would be during the network layer protocol state. For example, authentication could be requested again after having already authenticated once. This is represented by the arrows pointing the various states in Figure 7.1.

Users tend to think of PPP as a client server protocol because it is often used to connect remote resources (a PC for example) to a central office (a network access server). However, the protocol, at least as defined by the standards, is a peer protocol with all options available to both peers. But despite this support, typical installations will often implement client server-type architectures. For example, the remote PC just mentioned will authenticate with the central resource, but the central Network Attached Storage (NAS) will not authenticate with the PC despite the protocol supporting the option. Additionally, some implementations of PPP will not support the bi-directional functionality on the "client" side. An example of such an implementation is Microsoft Windows Dial-Up networking's lack of authentication of the peer when dialing in to a remote site.

Advanced Uses of PPP

In addition to the vanilla dial-in access, there are many advanced uses of PPP that provide additional network capability or provide solutions to network problems. These applications and PPP are not dependent on each other from a standards perspective, but many vendors have tied the features so closely to PPP that they are often only supported with PPP or require PPP to take advantage of the full functionality.

Leased/Nailed lines

PPP offers good interoperability for leased lines between various vendor products. HDLC has not been proven successful due to vendor interoperability issues. (HDLC, unlike PPP, does not provide protocol negotiations.)

PPP over ISDN

Integrated digital services network (ISDN) has become very popular in Europe, and ISDN4Linux (`http://www.isdn4linux.de/`) has become quite popular for running PPP over ISDN connections. ISDN has very quick call setups, so it lends itself well to additional features such as caller identification, caller identification call-back, and some of the specific applications covered in the next sections.

Dial on Demand

When a dial-up connection, such as an asynchronous (modem) or ISDN connection, is used to provide a gateway to another network or the Internet, the router making the connection must initiate the connection. The initiation is usually created by traffic bound for the PPP interface. Besides this basic gateway functionality, dial on demand is often built upon to provide additional functionality such as dial backup and bandwidth on demand.

Dial Backup

Dial backup provides an alternate route to a network based on a network failure. The network failure can be determined based on an interface status or a condition reported by a network protocol, such as a network failure. Although not required, dial backup is usually used to back up a leased line connection.

Consider Figure 7.3. The Linux router, "sleepy," is connected to the router, "tired," via a fractional T1 line providing 256Kbps of bandwidth (without compression) for the dedicated connection.

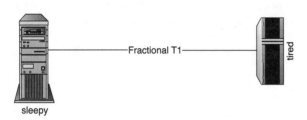

Figure 7.3   Dial backup network.

As shown in Figure 7.4, the leased line has failed. The backup connection has become active, providing continued connectivity between the sites.

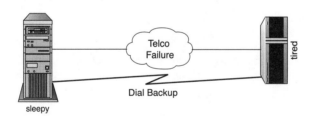

Figure 7.4   Dial backup network with failure.

Bandwidth on Demand

Bandwidth on demand uses a dial-up connection to provide additional bandwidth to a network by adding the bandwidth of a dial up to the already existing connection through a load-balancing algorithm. The bandwidth on demand is triggered by a utilization threshold on the main link.

The PPP multilink protocol can be used to bundle multiple PPP links together and is defined in RFC 1990, "The PPP Multilink Protocol (MP)."

PPP for Linux

pppd for Linux is available at `ftp://cs.anu.edu.au/pub/software/ppp/`.

The Linux kernel sources (2.2 and 2.4) have the necessary drivers for kernel support, and the PPP package contains the user daemon, supplemental programs, documentation, and example configuration files. (If MP support is needed, then kernel 2.4 is also needed.)

Most Linux distributions provide PPP support directly, or it is normally easily added with a package manager or sys admin tool; however, it is important to know how the standard `pppd` package works considering it is the basis for most distributions. An understanding of the package will help troubleshoot networking problems and the `pppd` wrappers that have become popular with most distributions.

Should the kernel need to be compiled, the serial and PPP support should be activated.

Compiling

Compiling `pppd` is very straightforward under Linux:

Place the `ppp` distribution downloaded from `ftp://cs.anu.edu.au/pub/software/ppp/` into a source directory such as `/usr/src/`.

Unzip the archive:

```
[root@lefty src]# gunzip ppp-2.4.1.tar.gz
```

And untar the tarball:

```
[root@lefty src]# tar xvf ppp-2.4.1.tar
```

This will create the source directory structure `ppp-2.4.1`. Move into the directory to compile the source code and install `pppd`:

```
[root@lefty src]# cd /usr/src/ppp-2.4.1
```

Execute the configure script:

```
[root@lefty ppp-2.4.1]# ./configure
```

Then run the make:

```
[root@lefty ppp-2.4.1]# make
```

Finally, install the distribution with `make install`:

```
[root@lefty ppp-2.4.1]# make install
```

File Location and Configuration

The installation will install files into two directories: `/usr/sbin/` and `/etc/ppp/`.

The files stored in `/usr/sbin/` are `pppd`, the PPP daemon; `pppdump`, a packet dump utility; and `pppstats`, a utility that reports the statistics for a given PPP interface.

The files stored in /etc/ppp/ from the installation are chap-secrets and pap-secrets, which contain user and authentication information; ip-up and ip-down, which are interface scripts; and options, which defines the behavior of pppd.

pppd supports 100+ options, guaranteeing interoperability with almost any implementation of PPP. Thankfully, most current generations of PPP support the standards requirements that options be negotiated. So many options are not required. However, some of the more common options are given in Table 7.4.

Table 7.4   *pppd* **Options**

Option	Description
auth	Requires the peer to authenticate. Should the Linux node have a default route already defined, the auth parameter is assumed or "default." If the Linux node does not have a default route and neither auth nor noauth are specified, pppd will not require authentication; but the peer must have an IP address within a network that the Linux node does not currently have a routing entry for.
call *name*	Tells pppd to read its options from /etc/ppp/peers /name. This is very useful for supporting connections to multiple sites.
connect *script*	Instructs pppd to use the script (or executable) given to communicate with the serial port and modem.
crtscts | nocrtscts	Turns hardware flow control on and off. Should it not be specified, the flow control will not be changed.
defaultroute	Causes the node to create a default routing entry to the remote peer. This is normally the behavior desired when the connection is to the Internet or as a route of last resort for a LAN connecting to a central remote access server.
file *file*	Instructs pppd to read the configuration parameters from *file*. The parameters are entered one per line in the text file.
lock	Instructs pppd to lock the serial port for its exclusive use.
Local IP:Remote IP	The local and remote PPP interfaces can be specified by placing the two addresses between a colon (:).
debug	Turns on additional debugging information to the syslog facility.

continues

Table 7.4 **Continued**

Option	Description
demand	Instructs pppd to operate in a dial–on–demand fashion. Should traffic be sent for the remote site, pppd will kick off the connection automatically without user interaction. This is the desired behavior for network gateways.
require-chap | require pap	Requires the peer to authenticate using the specified option.

Running *pppd*

pppd can be used to initiate a connection to a remote site or to wait on a connection from a remote site. When pppd is used to connect to a remote site, it is referred to as client operation, and when used to listen for a connection, it is referred to as the server. (Remember, this client/server model comes from the idea that a client initiates a session; from a protocol perspective, the two nodes are peers and not client and server.)

To initiate a PPP connection using pppd, several configuration options must be known and entered into the pppd configuration files. The following example is one that is typical for a connection to an ISP.

The configuration information needed is the PAP username and password or CHAP host name and password, the access telephone number, whether the IP address is assigned dynamically or statically, and the serial port to which the modem is connected.

Let's assume the following information for the configuration:

PAP username:	customer1
PAP password:	customerpassword
Access telephone number:	800-555-5555
IP address:	assigned dynamically
Serial port:	/dev/ttyS0

This information must now be entered into the appropriate files. Because this configuration uses PAP authentication, the /etc/ppp/pap-secrets would have the following entry:

```
#Secrets for authentication using PAP
# client      server  secret                  IP addresses
customer1     isp     customerpassword
```

The pppd does not provide direct-dial support, so an additional program is needed to dial. The chat program is normally used for this purpose. The chat program makes use of a chat script that, in the past, has played a very important role with remote access servers that required a login session to be initiated before PPP could be started. This is no longer the case with most remote access services—the majority can now start PPP immediately after the modem has picked up.

Nowadays, the chat program, for most ISP and enterprise connections, must only send any needed initialization strings to the modem and the dial command. The chat setting will be specified with the connect parameter. The connect parameter and a few other key parameters are included in the /etc/ppp/options file:

```
lock
debug
/dev/ttyS0
crtscts
defaultroute
connect '/usr/sbin/chat -v " " ATZ OK ATDT 8005555555'
```

The options were covered in Table 7.4, but briefly, the options file has defined that pppd needs to lock the serial port (lock option), log extra debug information (debug), use serial port /dev/ttyS0, turn on hardware flow control (crtscts), create a default route to the peer, and then connect using the chat command given.

The connection to the ISP can then be started by simply starting pppd:

```
[root@lefty /root]# pppd
```

Problems with pppd are generally either modem or authentication related. The first place to check for problems is the /var/log/messages file. For example, the following entries:

```
Jun  3 09:08:45 lefty pppd[11857]: pppd 2.4.1 started by root, uid 0
Jun  3 09:08:45 lefty pppd[11857]: Removed stale lock on ttyS0 (pid 11850)
Jun  3 09:08:46 lefty chat[11858]: expect ( )
Jun  3 09:09:31 lefty chat[11858]: alarm
Jun  3 09:09:31 lefty chat[11858]: Failed
Jun  3 09:09:31 lefty pppd[11857]: Connect script failed
Jun  3 09:09:32 lefty pppd[11857]: Exit.
```

would imply that the chat script failed, which can be caused by a typo or, in this case, the modem not responding.

The easiest way to test the modem is to run a chat script directly and turn up the volume to receive audio feedback from the script:

```
/usr/sbin/chat -v " " ATZ OK ATL2M2 ATDT 8005555555
```

With authentication problems, should the Linux router not be authenticated to the remote site, it will record "Failed to authenticate ourselves to peer." Should the remote site not authenticate with the Linux node, then Linux will report "Authentication failed."

Additional Network Services Considerations

For Linux routers acting as gateways, the network designer must determine what additional services should be run on the gateway. The additional services are based on need, expense, and management.

Email

Mail services are often run on the Linux gateway to provide mail delivery, especially to the Internet.

Linux does a very nice job of handling mail services, which might prove to be an ideal solution for a corporate mail system.

Gateways to the Internet should be considered carefully. Placing the mail server on the pppd server leaves the mail server open should the gateway be compromised.

Domain Name Services (DNS)

DNS is often a good candidate for running on the same gateway as pppd. Like a mail server, the DNS server (usually BIND), also is open to attack; however, DNS is not considered as risky as email for several reasons: It is less interesting to hackers, traditionally has fewer holes than mail servers (although this trend is subsiding as mail servers are continually being hardened), and typically only brings about a denial of service as opposed to a threat to resources.

A DNS server run in cache-only mode can be useful for both corporate and Internet gateways. A cache-only server simply caches all entries requested for later use. This saves query time for the next user that requests the particular host name and keeps the additional traffic off the gateway's WAN link.

For corporate gateways, it is worth considering loading the internal domains on the name server as well. This allows name server resolution to occur locally, as opposed to sending the request over the WAN link. There is a small additional load created by the name server pulling the zones on a timed basis, but the load is typically small and is often worth the trade-off if more than a few internal name resolution requests are required.

Placing a DNS server does have risks, though; and, like email, should be considered carefully to ensure that the advantages gained are worth the risk.

Web Caching

Web caching, like DNS, might be considered for both Internet and corporate connections. Under best circumstances, a 5%-10% hit rate can be expected on visited pages in larger sites. Many current web caching solutions allow predefined sites to be cached and common pages to be "mirrored," which can be very effective for storing local copies of corporate intranet sites.

rip2ad

rip2ad, written by Andrea Beck, is a RIP version 2 broadcast (actually multicast) utility available at http://www.ibh.de/~beck/stuff/ripper/. rip2ad provides RIP advertising functionality without having to run a full-blown routing daemon or having to support RIP on the local network. In the past, this functionality was often provided by bcastd; however, bcastd is no longer maintained and does not support RIP-2.

A *rip2ad* Example

Consider the network in Figure 7.5. The Linux router named "ritz" needs to tell the corporate router, "gate" about the local networks 192.168.0.0/24, 192.168.1.0/24, 192.168.2.0/24, and 192.168.3.0/24, which can be summarized as 192.168.0.0/22.

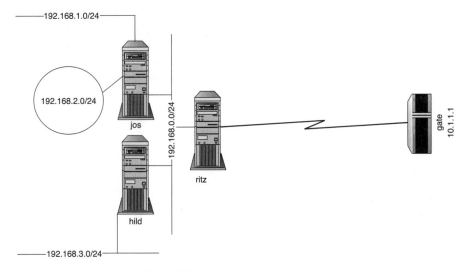

Figure 7.5   rip2ad network example.

The problem could be solved by running RIP within the remote network, having "ritz" run RIP with static routes pointed towards the other LAN networks, or having a static routing entry on "gate;" however, static routes might be prohibited by policy, which has the disadvantage of "gate" always further advertising the route, even when the link is not available due to an outage.

Running a routing protocol daemon on 'ritz' is overkill, but router 'ritz' can use rip2ad to tell corporate router 'gate' about the networks without RIP having to run on itself, 'jos,' or 'hild.'

Compiling and Installing *rip2ad*

`rip2ad` is simple to compile with a one-liner:

```
[root@lefty ripper]# gcc rip2ad.c -o rip2ad
```

The `rip2ad` executable can then be placed in an appropriate place, such as `/usr/local/sbin/`:

```
[root@lefty ripper]# cp rip2ad /usr/local/sbin/
```

`rip2ad` can be used with only command-line arguments, but the `-f` parameter allows a filename to be specified, which makes its use a bit easier.

For the network shown in Figure 7.5, the following `/etc/riptable` is entered:

```
192.168.0.0 255.255.255.0 0 1
192.168.1.0 255.255.255.0 0 1
192.168.2.0 255.255.255.0 0 1
192.168.3.0 255.255.255.0 0 1
```

This table is made up of the network address, the netmask, the IP address that advertised the route, and the metric. In this specific example, the `0` in the IP address field tells `rip2ad` to use the local IP address, which is fine with this example—it isn't important for 'gate' to know anything more specific.

To have `rip2ad` advertise these routes every 30 seconds, we use

```
[root@lefty ripper]# rip2ad -f /etc/riptable -c 30 &
```

If `tcpdump` is used to examine the packets, the advertisements will be seen to the RIP-2 multicast address:

```
[root@lefty ripper]# tcpdump
Kernel filter, protocol ALL, datagram packet socket
tcpdump: listening on all devices
09:33:38.311593 eth0 > 192.168.1.254.route > 224.0.0.9.route: rip-resp 4:
{192.168.0.0/255.255.255.0}(1) {192.168.1.0/255.255.255.0}(1)
{192.168.2.0/255.255.255.0}(1) {192.168.3.0/255.255.255.0}(1) [ttl 1]
1 packets received by filter
```

Because the connection between 'gate' and 'ritz' is a point-to-point link, the multicast just shown will not function. A unicast address is required, which `rip2ad` supports:

```
[root@lefty ripper]# rip2ad -f /etc/riptable -c 30 -d 10.1.1.1 &
```

And `tcpdump` shows the unicast:

```
[root@lefty ripper]# tcpdump
Kernel filter, protocol ALL, datagram packet socket
tcpdump: listening on all devices
09:41:35.679407 eth0 > 192.168.1.254.route > 10.1.1.1.route: rip-resp 4:
{192.168.0.0/255.255.255.0}(1) {192.168.1.0/255.255.255.0}(1)
{192.168.2.0/255.255.255.0}(1) {192.168.3.0/255.255.255.0}(1)
1 packets received by filter
```

As mentioned, the networks can be summarized as 192.168.0.0/22 (netmask = 255.255.252.0), so the following `/etc/riptable` can be used:

```
192.168.0.0 255.255.252.0 0 1
```

If `rip2ad` is started again with the new `/etc/riptable`:

```
[root@lefty ripper]# rip2ad -f /etc/riptable -c 30 -d 10.1.1.1 &
```

Then `tcpdump` will show the new route being advertised:

```
[root@lefty ripper]# tcpdump -n host 192.168.1.1
09:49:32.124445 eth0 > 192.168.1.254.route > 10.1.1.1.route: rip-resp 1:
{192.168.0.0/255.255.252.0}(1)
```

Summary

This chapter has provided a technical overview of PPP, the protocol of choice for point-to-point connections. We've also covered the Linux PPP daemon, `pppd`, and its configuration. Additionally, `rip2ad` has been covered, which lends itself to providing RIP gateway functionality without the complexities of a full-blown routing daemon.

8

Kernel 2.4.x Routing Daemons

IN THIS CHAPTER WE'LL LOOK AT some of the changes in the 2.4.x kernel series and how they affect routing services. We'll also take a look at some tools you might want to use to configure your Linux router.

Changes from 2.2.x to 2.4.x

The biggest change from the 2.2.x series of kernels to the 2.4.x series, at least as far as networking is concerned, is the migration from `ipchains` to the Netfilter architecture. Netfilter facilitates a new level of services, including stateful packet filtering and better NAT.

The introduction of Netfilter allows Linux to handle some of the more sophisticated routing through a Linux box. For anyone new to Linux, this is a huge boon with no real drawbacks. For experienced Linux admins, it means learning (again) a new set of tools to manage packet filtering and NAT. Of course, optimists will simply see it as job security and an interesting exercise in extending their current skills.

Stateful inspection of packets increases security and efficiency. It also, to some extent, increases complexity in configuration; but it's more than a fair trade-off for the capabilities you will have.

In the 2.2.x series of kernels, Source NAT (SNAT), Destination NAT (DNAT), and redirection aren't even options. However, Netfilter makes configuring these types of NAT relatively painless and dramatically improves the routing capabilities of Linux.

More on Netfilter

Netfilter/`iptables` is also used for IP Masquerading and setting up firewalls. Chapter 14, "Security and NAT Issues," walks you through the use of Netfilter/`iptables` to set up IP Masquerading, firewall rules, and NAT.

Enabling *ipfwadm* and *ipchains* Support

Though we cover kernel configuration more thoroughly in Chapter 13, "Building a Routing Kernel," we wanted to cover migrating your `ipfwadm` or `ipchains` setups here.

We think that `iptables` is a much better tool for setting up firewalls and NAT; but for ease of migration, the 2.4.x kernel provides compatibility modules for both `ipfwadm` and `ipchains`.

When compiling a new kernel, be sure to enable support for development drivers and code. When using `menuconfig` or `xconfig`, you'll find this option under the menu item, Code Maturity Level Options. The only choice given under this menu item is Prompt For Development and/or Incomplete Code/Drivers. Go ahead and select *y* for this option.

In the Networking Options menu, you will need to enable *IP: Netfilter Configuration*. In the 2.4.x kernel series, `ipchains` and `ipfwadm` support run on top of the Netfilter framework.

You can use `iptables`, `ipchains`, or `ipfwadm`, but you can't use them together. You'll have to disable all other options under `IP: Netfilter Configuration` or enable them as modules only to be able to enable either `ipchains` or `ipfwadm`. You can compile module support for all three if you want, but it's probably best to stick with one and recompile if you decide to migrate to `iptables`.

That's really all there is to it. After you've compiled the kernel, you can use either module to continue support for your old setup until you're ready to migrate to `iptables`.

Note: Development and Incomplete Code/Drivers

Don't worry! Selecting this option will not make your kernel unstable; it simply allows you to choose features or drivers that aren't considered "stable" yet. In many cases, you'll find that so-called "unstable" features are quite reliable, usually more so than some commercial-release software. The bar for "stable" with most Free Software or Open Source projects is considerably higher than for commercial software on many occasions. However, you will find that "unstable" code or drivers are often not feature-complete.

continues

continued

> If you're concerned about using these features, the best thing to do is search the kernel mailing list archives and your distribution's mailing lists and conduct a quick search on Google. If you belong to a Linux user group, posting a query to the mailing list isn't a bad idea either. If folks are having serious issues, they'll be talking about them. On the other hand, they might be talking about the success they're having. If you do encounter a bug down the road, be sure to give the developers a detailed report of the bug if it hasn't been reported already. You might have found a special case scenario that others haven't encountered yet.

Other Networking Linux 2.4.x Kernel Options

One thing you'll notice if you've compiled several 2.2.x kernels is that not much has changed. Ethernet bridging is no longer considered experimental, and a few options have either been moved around or dropped altogether; but for the most part there aren't any drastic changes in networking.

ATM Support

One notable addition is ATM (Asynchronous Transfer Mode) support, which is currently in experimental mode. Actually, ATM is (at the time of this writing) still hard to get running for some people and in Alpha or pre-Alpha development. If you're going to be using your Linux router as an edge router, you'll want to enable this option. To use ATM, you'll need several userspace programs that can be found at the ATM section on the Linux homepage at `http://icawww1.epfl.ch/linux-atm/`. There also is an ATM on the Linux mailing list that might be useful while getting up and running.

Explicit Congestion Notification Support

The `TCP Explicit Congestion Notification Support` option allows routers to notify clients about network congestion. Unfortunately, not all firewalls/routers on the Internet understand this feature. It's probably best to leave this feature disabled for the time being, as it may cause headaches when your users cannot connect to sites that refuse connections from clients with ECN enabled.

It's also possible to compile support for this option, but turn it off by issuing

`echo 0 > /proc/sys/net/ipv4/tcp_ecn`.

This might be the best scenario, as it will allow you to turn the feature on without recompiling the kernel if support for ECN improves. More than likely there will be some sites that "break" in response to this option for the foreseeable future.

WAN Interfaces

The 2.4.x kernel supports a wider variety of WAN interfaces. You'll need to explicitly enable WAN Interfaces Support and then look to find your device. With any luck, you'll be able to check to see if there is Linux support for your WAN card and then purchase the right device instead of hoping that your device is supported when trying out Linux.

Note: Oddly Placed Options

This has (as far as we know) little to do with routing or networking, but the option for Fibre Channel driver support can be found in the Network Device Support menu when configuring the kernel. Fibre Channel is a technology meant to replace SCSI but isn't directly related to networking (that we're aware of). Mainly we bring this up so that users won't wonder if this is something that should be enabled or not. Unless you're using Fibre Channel devices, just choose n.

There are some high-speed networking devices that operate over fiber or copper, specifically Fiber Distributed Data Interface (FDDI) and High Performance Parallel Interface (HIPPI). Those options are also located in the Network Device Support menu, and if you're going to be using those technologies, be sure to enable support for them in the kernel.

Wireless LAN

Though wireless LAN equipment is still a bit pricey, it's good to know that it is supported. The 2.4.x kernel adds wireless LAN support and support for several Aironet cards/adapters, the AT&T/Lucent WaveLAN, and Metricom's starmode radio IP. If you're using a Personal Computer Memory Card International Association (PCMCIA) card with wireless support, you also might need to enable support for a specific PCMCIA device as well as support for PCMCIA itself.

In most cases, you will be able to say *no* to Wireless LAN support. However, if you have special needs that require mobility on your LAN or just want to surf around the house on your laptop, this is the way to go.

USB Support

The 2.4.x kernel series adds support for many USB devices previously unsupported. This includes USB modems, ethernet devices, and other network devices. These devices will be excellent additions to your Linux arsenal in time, but right now we'd suggest sticking with PCI or PCMCIA Ethernet cards and "traditional" devices unless you have a compelling reason for venturing into USB devices. Most USB networking devices are in the experimental stage; and with product life cycles being what they are, by the time they're fully supported, the devices themselves are likely to have been replaced by newer-generation devices. Unless the manufacturer supports Linux directly, you're probably better off avoiding USB in the short term. (Note that we're writing this in the Summer of 2001. By the time you read this, the situation might have changed dramatically.)

Virtual Private Networks

Another of the more advanced functions you can implement with Linux is a Virtual Private Network (VPN). VPNs are becoming a popular solution as security becomes more and more of an issue in information technology.

In this section we'll look at a popular VPN solution for Linux and discuss one of the more popular commercial alternatives as well.

PoPToP

If you're looking to set up a VPN over PPTP with Linux, one of the tools you should take a look at is PoPToP. PoPToP is a PPTP implementation for Linux, and there are ports available for Solaris, OpenBSD, and FreeBSD—which might be of interest if you happen to be working in an environment with those operating systems in addition to Linux.

Because many commercial environments are a mixture of Linux servers and work-stations with Windows clients, PoPToP supports Windows clients as well as Linux. So far, PoPToP supports Windows 95, 98, NT, and 2000. The price is also right, as PoPToP is licensed under the GNU General Public License—so no worries about license fees.

Getting the Code

As of this writing, the most recent stable version of PoPToP is 1.0.1. There is also an unstable version with more cutting-edge features available, but we recommend you stick with the stable code unless there's a feature that you desperately need in the development version, or if you want to assist with finding bugs and contributing code. You can find PoPToP at `http://poptop.lineo.com/`.

At the site you'll find source code for Linux, Solaris, and other operating systems. There are also RPMs compiled for i386 and source RPMs if you're running a distribution that uses RPM. If you'll be connecting from Windows clients, there are a few patches you'll want to grab. To enable Microsoft Encryption (MPPE) or Microsoft Authentication (MSCHAPv2), you'll need to download and install the appropriate patches, which are also available from the web site.

Installing PoPToP

In this section we'll show you how to install PoPToP on Linux from source. After you have the PoPToP code, `cp` it to the `/tmp` or `/usr/local/src` directory, depending on your personal preference.

Make sure that you're logged in as `root`, uncompress the tarball that you retrieved, and then `cd` to the new directory. Then run

```
./configure
make
make install
```

Assuming there have been no compiler errors, you should now have the PoPToP binaries in /usr/local/bin. You also will need to be root to launch the PPTP daemon pptpd.

Configuring and Debugging PoPToP

After everything has been compiled and installed, you'll need to edit three files to tweak everything for your installation. The files are /etc/pptpd.conf, /etc/ppp/chap-secrets, and /etc/ppp/options.

The /etc/ppp/chap-secrets is a text file containing the username, password, servername, and valid IP addresses that they can connect from. You'll want to add one or more users to this file so that they can connect to the server.

There is a sample /etc/pptpd.conf file included with the source download, which you can customize to your own tastes. You'll use this file to set the local and remote IP addresses, speed at which clients can connect, ports at which the daemon will listen, and debugging level. Make sure that you restart syslogd after starting pptpd to enable logging.

Finally, you'll need to edit /etc/ppp/options that is included with the source distribution to reflect the options in /etc/ppp/chap-secrets.

If you have any problems setting up PoPToP, you might want to check the PoPToP web site for troubleshooting tips or workarounds for particular clients. Right now there are several HOWTOs and setup guides for various Windows clients.

Commercial VPN Solutions

If you're looking for a quick-and-easy solution to your routing and VPN needs, there are a few commercial solutions available that you might find easier to set up.

Most of these are based on the Open Source and Free Software tools but include slicker configuration tools. There are also some Linux-based hardware solutions that you might find to be interesting alternatives to Cisco routers.

NetMAX VPN Server

One outstanding commercial product is the NetMAX VPN Server. It's a customized Linux distribution with web-based setup tools that allow you to quickly and easily set up an IPSec VPN solution. It also includes Windows client software, so you can easily set up a client to connect to your VPN. The downside, however, is that the NetMAX solution does come with per-client and per-server license fees. Legally, you can't buy one copy of NetMAX VPN server and install it on multiple machines, or install the client software on unlimited machines. Also there is no Linux client software, so if some of your road warriors are on Linux machines you'll still have to hand-configure those clients.

On the other hand, the NetMAX software is very easy to use and is fairly reasonably priced compared to other proprietary solutions. It might be worthwhile to look into if you're going to be setting up several VPNs—or just one in a hurry.

Summary

In this chapter we've taken a quick look at some of the changes that affect routing/networking in the Linux 2.4.x series. There are far too many special cases to provide a comprehensive look at every scenario, but we hope that this will give you a general idea of what to expect from the "new" kernel.

When compiling a new kernel, be sure to read through Chapter 13, "Building a Routing Kernel," which gives a thorough overview of compiling the Linux kernel.

We've also taken a look at some of the "advanced" routing tools for Linux and setting up a basic VPN. Though by no means an exhaustive look at VPNs, this should serve to get you started if you decide to implement a VPN on your Linux router.

9

Inside the Commands

LINUX PROVIDES AN ARRAY OF NETWORKING commands to support network troubleshooting, IP configuration, and routing tasks. This chapter covers ifconfig, route, ping, traceroute, arp, netstat, and tcpdump. With the exception of tcpdump, these commands will likely be installed with a standard install of most Linux distributions. These commands (again with the exception of tcpdump) have their roots in earlier versions of BSD and AT&T's System V commands.

ifconfig

ifconfig is the command used to bring interfaces into service and specify Layers 1 through 3 attributes, such as media type, speed, and network addresses. (Layer 1 covers the physical aspects of the network, such as twisted pair or coaxial cabling, and Layer 2 covers the data layer, including the media dependent network, such as Ethernet frames and media access control in Ethernet networks.) ifconfig is normally located in the /sbin/ directory, but the program can be run by nonroot users. However, only configuration changes can be carried out by root. With most versions of Linux, the ifconfig command is provided by the net-tools distribution, which is available at http://www.tazenda.demon.co.uk/phil/net-tools/.

In addition to interface configuration, ifconfig is also used to report interface status; therefore, ifconfig's functionality can be grouped into two sections: interface reporting and interface configuration.

Interface Reporting

Most often ifconfig is used for interface reporting to assist in network troubleshooting. The basic command without any parameters proves very useful:

```
[root@lefty /sbin]# /sbin/ifconfig
eth0      Link encap:Ethernet   HWaddr 00:E0:29:4B:AC:0C
          inet addr:192.168.1.254  Bcast:192.168.1.255  Mask:255.255.255.0
          UP BROADCAST RUNNING MULTICAST  MTU:1500  Metric:1
          RX packets:9833 errors:0 dropped:0 overruns:0 frame:0
          TX packets:10195 errors:0 dropped:0 overruns:0 carrier:0
          collisions:306 txqueuelen:100
          Interrupt:10 Base address:0xb800

lo        Link encap:Local Loopback
          inet addr:127.0.0.1  Mask:255.0.0.0
          UP LOOPBACK RUNNING  MTU:3924  Metric:1
          RX packets:18 errors:0 dropped:0 overruns:0 frame:0
          TX packets:18 errors:0 dropped:0 overruns:0 carrier:0
          collisions:0 txqueuelen:0
```

ifconfig has reported all interfaces recognized by the kernel and configured for use. (Linux ifconfig, unlike other versions of UNIX, does not require an additional parameter to see all interfaces.) On the eth0 we can easily determine that the interface is Ethernet based on the interface name (eth0), the Link encap:Ethernet, and the 6-byte (48 bits) address. The IP address is reported on the next line with the broadcast address and netmask used.

The third line reports that the interface is currently running (UP), which means it can send and respond to network traffic. It is running in broadcast (standard for Ethernet) and additionally is configured to listen to multicast traffic. The multicast configuration is required to allow multicast traffic to be examined by the kernel and user applications such as RIP-2 because RIP-2 uses the RIP multicast address of 224.0.0.9.

The maximum transmission unit (MTU) is 1500 bytes, a standard length for Ethernet frames, and ifconfig has reported this is the size the kernel is configured to. As the name, maximum transmission unit, implies, this is the largest packet size that will be transmitted out of that interface. Should the administrator manually lower the size of the MTU, it will only affect the outgoing packets, which means the system will still recognize the incoming packets that are within the largest MTU supported by the topology. Common MTU sizes are shown in Table 9.1.

Table 9.1 **Network Topology and Maximum Transmission Unit**

Topology	MTU
Ethernet	1500
Fiber Distributed Data Interface (FDDI)	4352
Point-to-Point (PPP)	1500
Serial Line IP (slip)	1006
Token Ring	4464

Lines 4 through 6 report traffic statistics that are extremely useful in troubleshooting networking problems. Here, there seems to be a high number of collisions based on the amount of traffic, which could imply a mismatch between a half-duplex and full-duplex port with the Linux router and the Ethernet switch. The final line reports the resources used by the network interface card for low-level device driver support. This particular NIC uses interrupt 10 to speak to the CPU and has a memory segment starting at 0xb800.

Due to Ethernet's popularity, the `ifconfig` output just described is very typical of what is found in most enterprise networks, but a closer examination of other hardware supported by Linux shows Linux's wide support of network topologies.

Hardware Types

Table 9.2 lists hardware types supported by the Linux operating system.

Table 9.2 **Network Media (Hardware) Types Supported by Linux and *ifconfig***

Media	hwtype abbreviation
Adaptive Serial Line IP	`Adaptive`
Amateur NET/ROM	`netrom`
Amateur ROSE	`rose`
Amateur X.25	`ax25`
ARCnet	`arcnet`
Ash	`ash`
Cisco HDLC	`hdlc`
Compressed Serial Line IP	`cslip`
Compressed Serial Line IP 6 bit	`cslip6`
Econet	`Ec`
Ethernet	`ether`
Fiber Distributed Data Interface	`fddi`
Frame Relay Access Device	`frad`
Frame Relay DLCI	`dlci`
High-Performance Parallel Interface	`hippi`
IP in IP Tunneling	`tunnel`

continues

Table 9.2 **Continued**

Media	hwtype abbreviation
Ipv6 in IPv4 Tunneling	`sit`
IrLAP	`irda`
LAPB	`lapb`
Local Loopback	`loop`
Point-to-Point Protocol	`ppp`
Serial Line IP	`slip`
Serial Line IP 6 bit	`slip6`
Token Ring	`tr`

A closer look at the more common interfaces follows.

Serial Line IP—slip

`slip` (see RFC 1055, "A Nonstandard For Transmission Of IP Datagrams Over Serial Lines: Slip") is a serial connection-oriented protocol that has been replaced with PPP in most networks. Variants of `slip` that are supported under Linux include `cslip`, which is a compressed serial line IP based on the compression techniques described in RFC 1144, "TCP/IP Headers for Low-Speed Serial Links," also known by the author's name: Van Jacobson Compression. Another variant is `slip6` and a compressed version of `slip6`, aptly named `cslip6`.

Point-to-Point Protocol (PPP)

PPP is the de facto standard for serial link connections and has moved into other networking topologies, including IP over SONET. PPP (covered thoroughly in Chapter 7, "Kernel Support Tools").

IP over IP Tunneling (IPIP)

IP over IP tunneling is often used for connecting autonomous networks through a transit network. IP over IP also can be used for creating virtual private networks (VPNs).

Logical Loopback Device—Loop

Loopback interfaces exist to allow applications that require network connections to communicate with services residing on the local host without requiring or passing through a physical interface.

Token Ring (TR)—(IEEE 802.5)

Token Ring, which operates at 4- or 16Mbps, had an early advantage over Ethernet of not replying on a broadcast domain. This advantage has been overcome by Ethernet's speed increases and Ethernet switching technology. However, Token Ring is still supported in many organizations—especially industries such as banking and financial institutions that IBM has strongly penetrated. (IBM sold a lot of Token Ring given that their early mainframes did not support Ethernet.)

Returning to ifconfig's output listed previously, notice the IP address is IP version 4. In addition to IPv4, Linux also supports other protocols and their addressing. Some of the more popular protocols and ifconfig's corresponding output are shown in Table 9.3.

Table 9.3 **Linux and *ifconfig* Protocols Supported**

Protocol	ifconfig abbreviation	Reference
IPv6	`inet6`	RFC 2373, "IP Version 6 Addressing Architecture"
Amateur [radio] X.25	`ax25`	AX.25 Amateur Packet-Radio Link Layer Protocol Version 2.2, November 1997 `http://www.tapr.org /tapr/html/Fax25.html`
Internetwork Packet Exchange	`ipx`	Novell `http://www.novell.com/`
AppleTalk Datagram Delivery Protocol	`ddp`	"Inside Macintosh" by Apple Computers `http://developer.apple. com/techpubs/mac/Network ingOT/NetworkingWOT- 66.html`

Configuration Using *ifconfig*

ifconfig is also used to configure Linux network interfaces. Most Linux distributions have text or X Windows-based wrappers to initially fill configuration tables used by Linux during bootup, which are then used with the ifconfig command to configure the network interface for use. The commands covered here will have immediate effects on network configuration; however, it is still necessary to make the appropriate changes to configuration and network startup scripts, which is not covered here. Because configuration changes using the ifconfig command are immediate, the command can interrupt or even stop network traffic to and from the Linux node.

Bringing Interfaces Up and Down

Likely the most basic and useful configuration command using ifconfig is shutting down and bringing up an interface. This could be performed to ensure no network connections are made during a software upgrade. It is also often the first set taken when the NIC is suspected of having trouble. To shut eth0 down, use

```
[root@lefty /root]#ifconfig eth0 down
```

To return the Ethernet NIC to service, use

```
root@lefty /root]#ifconfig eth0 up
```

Changing IP Addresses

To change a node's IP address, `ifconfig` is also used. (Remember that a gateway address also might need to be changed using the `route` command.) The following `ifconfig` command will change the IP address to 192.168.1.253:

```
root@lefty /root]#ifconfig eth0 192.168.1.253
```

And to change the IP address and netmask:

```
root@lefty /root]#ifconfig eth0 192.168.1.253 netmask 255.255.255.248
```

Multiple IP Addresses

When multiple IP addresses need to be assigned to an interface, such as when Linux is used to support multiple web servers, `ifconfig` also is used to add the additional IP addresses to the interface. A logical interface must be configured to be recognized by the kernel in order to assign the IP address to it. This logical interface is often called a *virtual* or *alias interface*. Linux naming convention for logical interfaces is the interface name followed by a colon and the logical interface number. For example, the first local interface name on `eth0` would be `eth0:1`.

The `ifconfig` to assign an interface does not look much different except that it uses the logical interface name:

```
root@lefty /root]#ifconfig eth0:1 192.168.1.250 netmask 255.255.255.0
```

This will assign 192.168.1.250 to the network interface `eth0:1` and bring up the interface. A look at all the interfaces shows the new assignment:

```
[root@lefty /root]# ifconfig
eth0      Link encap:Ethernet  HWaddr 00:E0:29:4B:AC:0C
          inet addr:192.168.1.254  Bcast:192.168.1.255  Mask:255.255.255.0
          UP BROADCAST RUNNING MULTICAST  MTU:1500  Metric:1
          RX packets:169 errors:0 dropped:0 overruns:0 frame:0
          TX packets:125 errors:0 dropped:0 overruns:0 carrier:0
          collisions:0 txqueuelen:100
          Interrupt:10 Base address:0xb800

eth0:1    Link encap:Ethernet  HWaddr 00:E0:29:4B:AC:0C
          inet addr:192.168.1.250  Bcast:192.168.1.255  Mask:255.255.255.0
          UP BROADCAST RUNNING MULTICAST  MTU:1500  Metric:1
          Interrupt:10 Base address:0xb800

lo        Link encap:Local Loopback
          inet addr:127.0.0.1  Mask:255.0.0.0
          UP LOOPBACK RUNNING  MTU:3924  Metric:1
          RX packets:18 errors:0 dropped:0 overruns:0 frame:0
          TX packets:18 errors:0 dropped:0 overruns:0 carrier:0
          collisions:0 txqueuelen:0
```

There are several things to be aware of with logical interfaces under Linux. From the `ifconfig` output it is obvious that the statistics are all reported under the global interface, `eth0` in this case.

Logical interfaces are also shut down with the primary interface, which means an `ifconfig eth0` down also will shut down `eth0:1`.

Unlike the physical interface to which they are assigned, logical interfaces do not remain in the `ifconfig` list when they are shut down, so an `ifconfig eth0:1` down (or even `eth0` as mentioned in the previous paragraph) will remove the logical device. As a result, the next `ifconfig` will no longer show `eth0:1` as an interface.

Specifying Media Type

Ethernet can support multiple media types that require specific physical interfaces and attributes. Examples include 10base2, which is 10Mbps Ethernet that uses coaxial cable and British Naval Connectors (BNC); and 10baseT, which is 10Mbps Ethernet run on twisted pair with a RJ-45 connector. The various Ethernet media and interfaces supported by Linux are shown in Table 9.4. Some driver development has not included all media types for a particular card, or the developer might have chosen another method (such as passing parameters to the Kernel) to activate the media on the card or possibly hard-coded the media support into the driver.

Table 9.4   **Ethernet Media and Connector Support**

Name	Speed	Media	Connector
10base2	10 Mbps	Thin Coaxial	BNC
10base5	10 Mbps	Thick Coaxial	Attachment Unit Interface (AUI) connected to the Media Access Unit (MAU)
10baseT	10 Mbps	Twisted Pair	RJ-45
100baseT	100 Mbps	Twisted Pair	RJ-45

Generally it is not necessary to specify the media considering most modern cards and drivers that support multiple interfaces will sense the media connected an make the correct assignment at bootup; however, there are some exceptions.

Let's assume a card supports both an RJ-45 connection and an AUI, and you believe the card is not using the RJ-45 connection (because there is not a link light). To tell the driver to use the RJ-45 10baseT connection, the following `ifconfig` would be used:

```
[root@lefty /root]# ifconfig eth0 medi 10baseT
```

To tell the driver to use 100Mbps access, the 100baseT option could be used with the media parameter. Not all cards support this type of configuration, so refer to the documentation for the particular network interface card and driver.

All the parameters for `ifconfig` have not been covered here because their use is so seldom needed, but a quick overview will at least make you aware of them should the need arise.

The multicast functionality can be deactivated using `-allmulti`; generally this should be left on for Linux routers.

The `promisc` parameter can turn the interface to promiscuous mode and `-promisc` will turn it off. Generally this is only useful for developers. Most sniffers, including `tcpdump`, covered in this chapter, correctly activate and deactivate the promiscuous mode for the interface. Remember to turn `promisc` off should it be activated because performance is affected.

The `metric` parameter allows specific interfaces, in theory, to have higher priority should they be placed on the same network. This support depends on strong driver support in the case of virtual interfaces and strong routing protocol support in the case of a routing daemon.

The `mtu` parameter allows the administrator to change the size of the MTU. There are papers published from time to time on increasing performance through the tuning of the MTU on various operating systems, but the likely only real use of the parameter on a Linux router is to force compatibility in a network that is having MTU discovery problems created by multiple media types. An example of this would be to set the MTU of a Token Ring to Ethernet size as a work around to a router that does not support correct fragmentation or does not send back a `please fragment` message in the case of a packet with the `do not fragment` (DF) bit set.

The `broadcast` parameter allows a specific broadcast other than the address determined by the IP address of the interface combined with the netmask. This is most often used for historical reasons; an early version of BSD actually used the network address (all zeroes) for broadcast. In addition, some implementations of IP over ATM have also made use of all zeroes for broadcasts.

route

The `route` command is the interface used to access the Linux kernel's routing tables. The `route` command operates in three modes: display, add, and delete. When used to add or delete routes from the routing table, its use is generally limited to adding and removing static `route` entries.

Using *route* to Display Routing Information

When `route` is used with no parameters, the `route` command prints the routing table to `stdout`:

```
[root@lefty /root]# route
Kernel IP routing table
Destination     Gateway         Genmask         Flags Metric Ref    Use Iface
Lefty           *               255.255.255.255 UH    0      0        0 eth0
192.168.1.0     *               255.255.255.0   U     0      0        0 eth0
127.0.0.0       *               255.0.0.0       U     0      0        0 lo
default         192.168.1.1     0.0.0.0         UG    0      0        0 eth0
```

The Destination column when combined with the Genmask, which is the netmask of the destination network, identifies the network entry to be routed. The Gateway column identifies the gateway to be used for the particular network, should the G (gateway) flag be set in the Flags column. The Flags column tells the administrator how the kernel is going to interpret the routing entry. The various flags and their meanings are summarized in Table 9.5.

Table 9.5 *route* **Flags**

Flag	Description
!	Learned routes for this network are rejected.
A	Route added by addrconf, an IPv6 address configuration protocol. (http://www.ietf.cnri.reston.va.us/proceedings/95apr/charters/addrconf-charter.html)
C	Cache entry.
D	Route created by routing daemon (D) or ICMP redirect.
G	Use the gateway (G) identified in the Gateway column for traffic bound to the network identified in the routing entry.
M	route has been modified (M) by a routing daemon or ICMP redirect.
R	Reinstate routing to allow routing updates for this particular routing entry.
U	The network route is created (up) and will be used by the kernel to make routing decisions.

The route command without any parameters is equivalent to the netstat -r command covered later in this chapter.

-C

The -C option displays the cache statistics for routing entries as well as directly connected hosts. The output of the route command with -C also shows the source and destination addresses that triggered the route lookup. The -C parameter is used to see that routing entries are active and being used. Here is an example of route -C in action:

```
[root@lefty /root]# route -C
Kernel IP routing cache
Source        Destination    Gateway        Flags Metric Ref   Use Iface
lefty         host4.some.com 192.168.1.1        0     0    10 eth0
lefty         192.168.1.102  192.168.1.102      0     2     4 eth0
lefty         host4.some.com 192.168.1.1        0     0    10 eth0
```

Each entry shows the source, followed by the destination, and the gateway of the traffic that used the route. Notice in the second entry that the destination and gateway are actually the same address. This signifies a directly connected host. The Use column shows how many packets were sent for that particular entry, and the Iface column reports the local interface the traffic used.

–n

The –n option turns off name resolution so that all the entries printed with the route command are printed using IP addresses rather than host names.

–v

The –v option was originally used with the route command to provide additional information—most notably the netmask of the route entry; however, current versions of the route command provide the additional information without the –v. It is just covered here for your reference in case an older version of Linux or route command is used.

–V

The –V displays route's version, as well as the net tool version and the protocols supported:

```
[root@lefty /root]# route -V
net-tools 1.54
route 1.96 (1999-01-01)
+NEW_ADDRT +RTF_IRTT +RTF_REJECT +I18N
AF: (inet) +UNIX +INET +INET6 +IPX +AX25 +NETROM +ATALK +ECONET +ROSE
HW:  +ETHER +ARC +SLIP +PPP +TUNNEL +TR +AX25 +NETROM +FR +ROSE +ASH +SIT
+FDDI+HIPPI +HDLC/LAPB
```

Using *route* to Add Routing Entries

The real power of the route command is to add static routes that affect routing on the local node and, if a routing daemon is running on that local node, affect traffic within the autonomous system as well.

Adding Routes to Networks

The route command used to add routes takes the following format:

```
route add -net destination netmask netmask gw gateway address
```

For example, to route all traffic destined for 10.1.1.0/24 to the router at 192.168.1.253, use

```
[root@lefty /root]# route add -net 10.1.1.0 netmask 255.255.255.0 gw 192.168.1.253
```

To add a routing entry for a specific host, the –host parameter is used, and the routing entry does not need the netmask parameter. To add a route for 192.168.1.200 to 192.168.1.1, the route command would look like this:

```
[root@lefty /root]# route add -host 192.168.1.200 gw 192.168.1.1
```

This route command would then create an entry that would appear as the following when the route command is entered without any parameters:

```
[root@lefty /root]# route
Kernel IP routing table
Destination     Gateway         Genmask         Flags Metric Ref    Use Iface
192.168.1.200   192.168.1.1     255.255.255.255 UGH   0      0        0 eth0
```

For PPP networks it is sometimes necessary or preferable to route to a network interface rather than a gateway address. This is used to allow IP addresses to be saved by not using an IP transit network for the serial connection or to create a route when a nonbroadcast network is used. An example follows, but the subject is covered more thoroughly in Chapter 7, "Kernel Support Tools."

```
[root@lefty /root]# route add -net 10.10.10.0 netmask 255.255.255.0 ppp0
```

ping

ping is a network troubleshooting tool that reports whether or not a remote node is reachable. ping sends an ICMP echo request to the remote node that should then reply with an ICMP echo reply. Because ping and ICMP can be used very effectively to map out a network, many network packet filters and firewalls are configured to drop ICMP to provide tighter security.

Besides checking if a node is responding (or other simple conectivity issues), ping also can be used to troubleshoot other network-related matter. This section covers some of the more advanced parameters of ping that are not well documented. These parameters are based on the ping command that comes with the iputils collection by Alexey Kuznetsov available at ftp://ftp.sunet.se/pub/Linux/ip-routing/. iputils is supplied with most versions of Linux.

-d

To see additional debugging information provided by the ping command, use the -d parameter. It tells ping to report additional messages that would not be seen, such as an ICMP network unreachable message. The additional information can oftentimes give further insight into the network condition that is causing the ping to fail.

-f Flood

The -f parameter should be used with caution because it causes Linux to send as many ICMP echo requests as possible, which can quickly cause network problems on burdened networks. The parameter can be used to create a load that simulates a heavy network or to create an additional load on the target machine.

-i Interval

ping's normal operation is to wait one second before sending the next ICMP echo request. By using the -i interval (in seconds), ping can be told to wait a longer amount of time before sending the next ICMP echo request. This can be very useful in network scripts in which it is important to test the network connectivity yet the script needs to be as friendly as possible to the network.

-s Packetsize

The -s parameter can be used to send smaller or larger ICMP packets than the standard 64byte packet. This option combined with tcpdump (covered later) can be used to determined if IP datagrams are being fragmented, which is common in networks that contain various network topologies.

-I Interface IP Address

The -I parameter forces the ICMP echo request out of the specified interface, which is very useful on multihomed hosts where there are multiple routes to the destination.

Address Resolution Protocol (ARP)

The Address Resolution Protocol (ARP) maps Layer 3 IP addresses to Layer 2 MAC addresses. Understanding when and how ARP is used is important to fully utilize the arp command. Whenever a node wishes to send traffic to a particular IP address, it will use its own IP address and netmask to determine if the destination is on a directly connected network. If the destination address is not directly connected, the routing table is consulted. Assuming a route for the destination network exists (a default route can include the destination network), the host then determines the gateway for the routing entry. After the gateway is determined, an arp who-has request with the gateway's (router) address can be broadcast on the appropriate network interface, and the gateway will respond with its MAC address. The host will then direct traffic for the destination to the MAC address of the gateway.

Linux's tool to access the ARP table is the command arp. arp, like the ifconfig command, is provided in the net-tools distribution available at
http://www.tazenda.demon.co.uk/phil/net-tools/.

arp, like ifconfig, is very useful without any parameters:

```
[root@lefty /root]# arp
Address            HWtype  HWaddress          Flags Mask Iface
192.168.1.1        ether   00:20:78:CF:3D:66  C          eth0
speedy             ether   00:40:D0:08:6A:72  C          eth0
```

The output includes the Layer 3 (IP) address, the type of network interface (HWtype), the MAC address (HWaddress), and the interface where the MAC address was learned. The Mask was used with early versions of Linux but is now no longer used. The Flags entry C reports that the entry is completed—that is, that the IP address was learned. The arp's output is not completely consistent: an incomplete entry is actually shown with an (incomplete) entry as opposed to any entry being made in the Flags column in the arp table:

```
[root@lefty /root]# arp
Address            HWtype  HWaddress          Flags Mask Iface
192.168.1.5                (incomplete)                  eth0
192.168.1.1        ether   00:20:78:CF:3D:66  C          eth0
speedy             ether   00:40:D0:08:6A:72  C          eth0
```

arp supports many parameters to assist in network troubleshooting.

-*a* Host

The -a host parameter filters the arp command output to the specific host involved. The host can be either the host name of the particular node or the node's IP address. The following shows the MAC address assigned to 192.168.1.100:

```
[root@lefty /root]# arp -a 192.168.1.100
Address                HWtype  HWaddress          Flags Mask Iface
192.168.1.100          ether   00:20:58:CC:66:3D  C          eth0
```

The -a host combined with the -d option discussed in the following section run on several Linux nodes on the same network and can help to quickly identify two hosts configured with the same IP address—the IP addresses will be the same, but the MAC address will be different.

-*H* hwtype

The -H parameter specifies that only arp entries for the particular interface type should be printed. For example, to print all Ethernet entries, use

```
[root@lefty /root]# arp -H ether
Address                HWtype  HWaddress          Flags Mask Iface
192.168.1.1            ether   00:20:78:CF:3D:66  C          eth0
speedy                 ether   00:40:D0:08:6A:72  C          eth0
```

Or to see any Token Ring entries:

```
[root@lefty net]# arp -H tr
arp: in 2 entries no match found.
```

The media (hardware) types supported by the arp command are shown in Table 9.6.

Table 9.6 **Network Media Types Supported by Linux *arp* Command**

Media	Hardware Types Abbreviations
Adaptive Serial Line IP	Adaptive
Amateur NET/ROM	Netrom
Amateur ROSE	rose
Amateur X.25	ax25
ARCnet	arcnet
Ash	ash
Cisco HDLC	hdlc
Compressed Serial Line IP	cslip
Compressed Serial Line IP 6 bit	cslip6
Econet	ec
Ethernet	ether
Fiber Distributed Data Interface	fddi

continues

Table 9.6   **Continued**

Media	Hardware Types Abbreviations
Frame Relay Access Device	`frad`
Frame Relay DLCI	`dlci`
High-Performance Parallel Interface	`hippi`
IP in IP Tunneling	`tunnel`
Ipv6 in IPv4 Tunneling	`sit`
IrLAP	`irda`
LAPB	`lapb`
Local Loopback	`loop`
Point-to-Point Protocol	`ppp`
Serial Line IP	`slip`
Serial Line IP 6 bit	`slip6`
Token Ring	`tr`

-*i* Interface

arp also can display all the entries for a particular interface with the `-i` parameter. To view all the ARP entries learned on `righty`'s second interface card, the following `arp` command would be used:

```
[root@righty /root]# arp -i eth1
Address          HWtype  HWaddress          Flags Mask Iface
10.1.1.4          ether   00:40:68:CF:33:22  C          eth1
blue              ether   00:40:D7:08:6A:52  C          eth1
```

-*n*

-n turns off name resolution for the arp command so that IP addresses are not resolved to host names. Notice the arp command without the -n:

```
[root@lefty /root]# arp
Address          HWtype  HWaddress          Flags Mask Iface
192.168.1.1       ether   00:20:78:CF:3D:66  C          eth0
speedy            ether   00:40:D0:08:6A:72  C          eth0
```

The IP address for speedy is being resolved, and arp prints speedy as opposed to the IP address. Here is the same ARP table without name resolution:

```
[root@lefty /root]# arp -n
Address          HWtype  HWaddress          Flags Mask Iface
192.168.1.1       ether   00:20:78:CF:3D:66  C          eth0
192.168.1.101     ether   00:40:D0:08:6A:72  C          eth0
```

-*d* Host

Sometimes it is necessary to delete the arp entry of a host to troubleshoot networking problems where address resolution is not working correctly, such as when two nodes are misconfigured with the same IP address or where a network interface card might seem to be misbehaving. The -d entry can be used to remove specific entries. The -d is followed by the host, which can be the IP address or the hostname of the node. To remove speedy's MAC address from the arp cache, the following is typed:

```
[root@lefty /root]#arp -d speedy
```

And to see that it has been removed:

```
[root@lefty /root]# arp
Address              HWtype  HWaddress          Flags Mask Iface
192.168.1.1          ether   00:20:78:CF:3D:66  C          eth0
```

Oftentimes when troubleshooting ARP-related problems, there is a need to clear the complete ARP cache. The following script, darpcache, uses the -d parameter to parse through the cache and remove all entries:

```
#!/bin/bash
# darpcache
# This script deletes all arp entries from the arp cache

for host in `arp -n | awk '{print $1}' | grep -v Address`
        do
                echo "Deleted entry for host:  $host"
                arp -d $host+
        done
```

It's output looks similar to this:

```
[root@lefty /root]# ./darpcache
Deleted entry for host:  192.168.1.1
Deleted entry for host:  192.168.1.101
```

A related protocol, RARP, works similarly to ARP; however, its purpose is to allow a host to determine its IP address by broadcasting its MAC address as an RARP request. A node then responds with the mapped IP address. The RARP protocol has all but been replaced with dynamic host control protocol (DHCP) for several reasons, including RARP's tendency to be statically mapped on a particular node and DHCP's ability to provide additional information beyond the IP address (including DNS configuration like name servers and domain suffixes). DHCP is also widely supported on non-UNIX systems.

RARP support must be configured in the Linux kernel, and the RARP table is managed using the rarp command.

traceroute

traceroute is likely only second to the ping command as the most often used network troubleshooting tool. traceroute shows the path between the source (the Linux node where the command is executed) and the destination.

traceroute, unlike ping, does not rely on the routers in the path responding to a particular path but rather assembles a UDP packet with the destination address—but with the time-to-live bits set to 1 for the first packet that is sent. traceroute then sends the packet, and the first router on the way to the destination accepts the packet and decrements the time-to-live. Because the time-to-live was 1, the time-to-live is now zero, which triggers the first router in the path to send back an ICMP time exceeded message and drop the packet. traceroute prints the source address of the ICMP message for the user, increments its internal counter that is setting the time-to-live, and sends out the second packet.

The first router decrements the time-to-live from 2 to 1, and the second router decrements the time-to-live from 1 to zero and returns the ICMP message timer exceeded. traceroute then prints the second router's IP address based on the source address of the ICMP message and continues to the final destination. The final destination does not have a service listening to that port, so it returns an ICMP port unreachable. When traceroute receives this message, it prints the final address and exits.

Now that traceroute has been explained, a closer look at traceroute's options will show some of the more advanced uses of traceroute.

–*d*

To turn on additional debugging with traceroute, use the -d parameter. The additional information, especially if it applies to networks under internal administration control, might help in determining network problems. For example, the following output with the -d option implies that there is possibly a routing problem (network unreachable) or an interface problem through which the network should be reachable:

```
[root@lefty /root]# traceroute -d host.anydomain.com
traceroute to host.anydomain.com (192.168.100.100), 30 hops max, 38 byte packets
traceroute: sendto: Network is unreachable
 1 traceroute: wrote host.anydomain.com 38 chars, ret=-1
```

–*f ttl*

The -f parameter followed by the time-to-live tells traceroute to start the time to counter at ttl, effectively not reporting ttl −1 hops. This is useful when tracerouting through a firewall that will not respond to a traceroute but will allow the request through. It is also useful when the first few hops are known.

−*F*

The do not fragment (-F) option tells traceroute to set the do not fragment bit so that any routers along the path should not forward the UDP packet if it will be forwarded out an interface that has an MTU larger than the UDP packet sent by the traceroute. This can be useful to troubleshoot problems related to MTU or MTU discovery.

−*i* Interface

On multi-homed systems, there is sometimes the need to specify which interface to use for the traceroute command. By using the -i parameter, traceroute will use the specified interface—and therefore the IP address of the specified interface—as the source address for the traceroute.

−*I*

As described earlier, traceroute uses UDP packets targeted at high ports; however, the -I tells UDP to use ICMP echo request packets as opposed to UDP. This might be useful should a firewall not allow UDP but allow ICMP echo requests. This also makes the traceroute function more like the Microsoft version of tracert, which is the tool that serves the same purpose as traceroute on Microsoft Windows.

Except for using ICMP packets, traceroute functions the same—the ttl is still set appropriately to ensure the same behavior from the transit routers. A key difference is the final destination—it might actually reply to the echo request with an echo reply.

−*n*

The -n parameter turns off name resolution with traceroute. Generally this is used to speed up the operation of traceroute—especially if the name server is not reachable due to the network problem being analyzed. By using -n, each hop along the way does not have to be looked up, so the user need not wait on the traceroute's resolution to time out before continuing.

−*m* Maximum Hops

The -m option tells traceroute to stop after maximum hops are reached:

```
[root@lefty /root]# traceroute -m 3 host.somedomain.com
traceroute to host.somedomain.com (192.168.50.50), 3 hops max, 38 byte packets
 1  gw4.isp1.net (192.168.14.2)  39.331 ms  33.990 ms  51.079 ms
 2  router3.isp2.net(10.1.1.254)  25.888 ms  31.675 ms  25.988 ms
    router5.isp2.net(10.5.5.254)  25.296 ms  26.012 ms  26.335 ms
```

The -m can be combined with the -f to further limit the output and routers reported:

```
[root@lefty /root]# traceroute -f 2 -m 3 host.somedomain.com
traceroute to host.somedomain.com (192.168.50.50), 3 hops max, 38 byte packets
 2  router3.isp2.net(10.1.1.254)  22.888 ms  32.675 ms  27.887 ms
 3  router5.isp2.net(10.5.5.254)  25.186 ms  26.122 ms  26.322 ms
```

tcpdump, covered later, will give a complete breakdown of a traceroute during execution.

-t tos

The -t tos parameter allows the type of service bits to be specified in the IP packet. This parameter is growing in popularity as voice-over packet technologies are growing. Many voice-over deployments rely on the tos bits, or more specifically the DIFF-SERV implementation of the bits, to ensure bandwidth requirements are met. However, outside these next generation networks the -t parameter has very little use.

traceroute Gotchas

traceroute is a very useful tool and can be used to quickly locate network trouble spots; however, it should not be soley relied upon given that its behavior can be affected by network conditions. Following are a few items to be aware.

Asymmetrical Routes

Most complex networks include multiple routes to destinations; so some network conditions (peering policies, asymmetrical network outages, routes flapping, or plain old misconfiguration) will mean that the ICMP message returned to traceroute does not take the same path as the initial UDP packet and so the message might never be returned to traceroute.

Network Security

If traceroute is used through secure areas, the UDP traffic might possibly not be allowed through a firewall because UDP is often frowned upon (for good reason). And even if UDP is allowed through, the particular packet may not be allowed if the firewall is configured to allow only specific traffic through.

netstat

netstat, short for network statistics, is a command for displaying network information on the local node. The most common use of netstat is to display the route table:

```
[root@lefty /root]# netstat -r
Kernel IP routing table
Destination     Gateway         Genmask         Flags MSS Window  irtt Iface
lefty           *               255.255.255.255 UH    0 0           0 eth0
192.168.1.0     *               255.255.255.0   U     0 0           0 eth0
127.0.0.0       *               255.0.0.0       U     0 0           0 lo
default         192.168.1.1     0.0.0.0         UG    0 0           0 eth0
```

There is much more to netstat than simply printing the routing table. In fact, most of netstat's output shows network connections on the local node.

-a

The -a, or "all" parameter tells netstat to print all open sockets on the local node. This includes any connections initiated from the local node or daemons listening to particular ports.

```
[root@lefty /root]# netstat -a
Active Internet connections (servers and established)
Proto Recv-Q Send-Q Local Address          Foreign Address         State
tcp        0    138 lefty:telnet           192.168.1.102:1062      ESTABLISHED
tcp        0      0 *:www                  *:*                     LISTEN
tcp        0      0 *:smtp                 *:*                     LISTEN
tcp        0      0 *:printer              *:*                     LISTEN
tcp        0      0 *:linuxconf            *:*                     LISTEN
tcp        0      0 *:finger               *:*                     LISTEN
tcp        0      0 *:login                *:*                     LISTEN
tcp        0      0 *:shell                *:*                     LISTEN
tcp        0      0 *:telnet               *:*                     LISTEN
tcp        0      0 *:ftp                  *:*                     LISTEN
tcp        0      0 *:auth                 *:*                     LISTEN
tcp        0      0 *:980                  *:*                     LISTEN
tcp        0      0 *:1024                 *:*                     LISTEN
tcp        0      0 *:sunrpc               *:*                     LISTEN
udp        0      0 *:ntalk                *:*
udp        0      0 *:talk                 *:*
udp        0      0 *:978                  *:*
udp        0      0 *:1024                 *:*
udp        0      0 *:sunrpc               *:*
raw        0      0 *:icmp                 *:*                     7
raw        0      0 *:tcp                  *:*                     7
Active UNIX domain sockets (servers and established)
Proto RefCnt Flags       Type       State         I-Node Path
unix  0      [ ACC ]     STREAM     LISTENING     474    /dev/printer
unix  0      [ ACC ]     STREAM     LISTENING     573    /tmp/.font-unix/fs-1
unix  7      [ ]         DGRAM                    380    /dev/log
unix  0      [ ACC ]     STREAM     LISTENING     531    /dev/gpmctl
unix  0      [ ]         DGRAM                    13679
unix  0      [ ]         DGRAM                    843
unix  0      [ ]         DGRAM                    576
unix  0      [ ]         DGRAM                    518
unix  0      [ ]         DGRAM                    468
unix  0      [ ]         DGRAM                    402
unix  0      [ ]         DGRAM                    390
```

Line 3 of the `netstat -a` output is the column heading. The first column, `proto`, determines the protocol that is listening on the particular port. The `proto` is actually the socket method used to access the port, which will either be tcp, udp, or raw. The `Recv-Q` is the number of packets received by the kernel but that have not yet been read by the daemon listening to the port. The `Send-Q` is the number of packets pending acknowledgement by the remote host.

The `Local Address` is made up of the local node's IP address and the logical name of the port. In the preceding example, the first entry shows that the connection is a telnet session. If the IP address is shown by an `*`, then the daemon is listening to all connected interfaces, which implies the daemon is in listen mode.

The `Foreign Address` is made up of the remote node's IP address and the port it is connected to. In the `telnet` entry given earlier, the remote host is the client using the `telnet` protocol on its port 1062. (The local node is running the `telnet` daemon running on port 23.)

The `State` column applies only to TCP connections and reports the state the connection is in: `CLOSING`, `CLOSED`, `CLOSE_WAIT`, `ESTABLISHED`, `FIN_WAIT1`, `FIN_WAIT2`, `LAST_ACK`, `LISTEN`, `SYN_SENT`, `SYN_RECV`, `TIME_WAIT`.

With the `-a` parameter, `netstat` displays a second table with the UNIX domain socket connections, which are accessed directly through a device driver as opposed to a listening daemon.

-l

To determine which ports are listening on the Linux node, use the `-l` parameter. The output is similar to the `-a` with the exception of not showing outbound connections initiated by users.

-p

The `-p` option will show which processes own or are listening to the specific port. This parameter, combined with the `-l`, acts like a network aware ps command:

```
[root@lefty /root]# netstat -pl
(Not all processes could be identified, non-owned process info
 will not be shown, you would have to be root to see it all.)
Active Internet connections (only servers)
Proto Recv-Q Send-Q Local Address        Foreign Address        State
PID/Program name
tcp        0      0 *:www                *:*                    LISTEN
602/httpd
tcp        0      0 *:smtp               *:*                    LISTEN
571/sendmail: accep
tcp        0      0 *:printer            *:*                    LISTEN
527/lpd
tcp        0      0 *:linuxconf          *:*                    LISTEN
513/inetd
```

```
tcp         0      0 *:finger              *:*                    LISTEN
513/inetd
tcp         0      0 *:login               *:*                    LISTEN
513/inetd
tcp         0      0 *:shell               *:*                    LISTEN
513/inetd
tcp         0      0 *:telnet              *:*                    LISTEN
513/inetd
tcp         0      0 *:ftp                 *:*                    LISTEN
513/inetd
tcp         0      0 *:auth                *:*                    LISTEN
463/identd
tcp         0      0 *:978                 *:*                    LISTEN
375/rpc.statd
tcp         0      0 *:1024                *:*                    LISTEN
-
tcp         0      0 *:sunrpc              *:*                    LISTEN
350/portmap
udp         0      0 *:ntalk               *:*
513/inetd
udp         0      0 *:talk                *:*
513/inetd
udp         0      0 *:976                 *:*
375/rpc.statd
udp         0      0 *:1024                *:*
-
udp         0      0 *:sunrpc              *:*
350/portmap
raw         0      0 *:icmp                *:*        .           7
-
raw         0      0 *:tcp                 *:*                    7
-
Active UNIX domain sockets (only servers)
Proto RefCnt Flags       Type      State       I-Node PID/Program name    Path
unix  0      [ ACC ]     STREAM    LISTENING   470    527/lpd
/dev/printer
unix  0      [ ACC ]     STREAM    LISTENING   570    645/xfs
/tmp/.font-unix/fs-1
unix  0      [ ACC ]     STREAM    LISTENING   527    586/gpm
/dev/gpmctl
```

There are a few lesser-used parameters for `netstat`, but they are used seldom and often overlap the information shown. For those reasons, they've not been covered here.

tcpdump

All of the tools covered thus far in this chapter are most likely included in whichever Linux distribution you choose. tcpdump, although very popular, might not be included but should be the first thing installed after system installation. tcpdump is available at http://www.tcpdump.org/ and requires libpcap, also available at http://www.tcpdump.org, to operate. tcpdump is a small footprint protocol analyzer that should be placed on any Linux hosts acting as routers or performing other centralized services where troubleshooting should be infrequent but must be performed in a timely fashion when it is needed.

> **Sniffers on Routers**
>
> Some security professionals frown on the practice of placing sniffers on routers given that the sniffer will provide an easy means of additional hacking should the router be compromised. Of course, once a router is compromised, the sniffer can be installed by the hacker. In any case, consider your security needs and requirements before placing a sniffer on a router.

If tcpdump is started without any command-line parameters, it will place all connected interfaces into promiscuous mode and dump all packets the Linux node sees to stdout, which is typically the terminal. Besides a quick view to ensure the node is seeing network traffic, tcpdump without parameters usually creates too much output to be of much use; and because it is going to stdout, the output storage is limited to the terminal's buffer. tcpdump, with the correct parameters, can turn screens of network traffic into useful chunks of data that can be analyzed and often lead to problem resolution.

–I Interface

To limit which packets tcpdump matches on, the -I interface can be used to tell tcpdump to only examine packets from a particular interface. For example, to only examine packets on eth1, use:

```
[root@lefty /root]# tcpdump -i eth1
Kernel filter, protocol ALL, datagram packet socket
tcpdump: listening on eth1
```

Before examining tcpdump parameters and output, let's dissect the basic line of a tcpdump output:

```
11:22:53.138977 < 192.168.1.101.1041 > 192.168.1.254.telnet: . 0:0(0) ack 288 win
➡7479 (DF)
```

The first field in the tcpdump output is the time stamp with an additional sequence number added after the seconds. Following the time stamp is the > symbol, which signifies the direction of the packet in relation to the Linux node where tcpdump is running. < signifies incoming and > outgoing. Next is the source address of the packet followed by the port number (1041). The > is a placeholder between the source and destination. The destination is followed by the port number (`telnet` here) xxx, followed by the window size. The (`DF`) signifies that the do not fragment bit is set, so routers between the source and destination should not fragment the IP datagram into smaller frames during transmission.

—n

Like the `arp -n` parameter, `tcpdump` also uses the `-n` to not perform name resolution on the names. Generally, `-n` should be used because using name resolution creates an additional load on the node and network as `tcpdump` tries to resolve IP addresses it is examining. Here is an example of using `-i` with the `-n` parameter.

```
[root@lefty /root]# tcpdump -i eth0 -n
Kernel filter, protocol ALL, datagram packet socket
tcpdump: listening on eth0
11:22:52.739123 < 192.168.1.101.1041 > 192.168.1.254.telnet: . 3768648:3768648(0)
ack 2572562729 win 7766 (DF)
11:22:52.739231 > 192.168.1.254.telnet > 192.168.1.101.1041: P 1:82(81) ack 0 win
32120 (DF)
11:22:52.939102 < 192.168.1.101.1041 > 192.168.1.254.telnet: . 0:0(0) ack 82 win
7685 (DF)
11:22:52.939142 > 192.168.1.254.telnet > 192.168.1.101.1041: P 82:288(206) ack 0
win 32120 (DF)
11:22:53.138977 < 192.168.1.101.1041 > 192.168.1.254.telnet: . 0:0(0) ack 288 win
7479 (DF)
11:22:53.139013 > 192.168.1.254.telnet > 192.168.1.101.1041: P 288:477(189) ack0
win 32120 (DF)
6 packets received by filter
```

—q

`-q`, or quiet mode, tells `tcpdump` to just print the Layer 4 (tcp, udp, or ICMP) protocol and port number or name. Here is a tcp (`telnet`) example:

```
[root@lefty /root]# tcpdump -i eth0 -nq
Kernel filter, protocol ALL, datagram packet socket
tcpdump: listening on eth0
11:26:39.114679 < 192.168.1.101.1041 > 192.168.1.254.telnet: tcp 0 (DF)
11:26:39.114788 > 192.168.1.254.telnet > 192.168.1.101.1041: tcp 81 (DF)
11:26:39.314634 < 192.168.1.101.1041 > 192.168.1.254.telnet: tcp 0 (DF)
11:26:39.314674 > 192.168.1.254.telnet > 192.168.1.101.1041: tcp 147 (DF)

4 packets received by filter
```

And here is an ICMP (`ping`) example using the `-q` in addition to other parameters:

```
[root@lefty /root]# tcpdump -i eth0 -nq
Kernel filter, protocol ALL, datagram packet socket
tcpdump: listening on eth0
11:27:59.459644 < 192.168.1.101 > 192.168.1.254: icmp: echo request
11:27:59.459708 > 192.168.1.254 > 192.168.1.101: icmp: echo reply

2 packets received by filter
```

–t

The -t parameter instructs tcpdump to *not* print the timestamp on its output.

–x

The -x parameter will cause tcpdump to print the packets out in hexadecimal.

–w Filename

When a tcpdump output needs to be saved, the -w can be used to save the file in libpcap format, which saves space, as well as put the file in a format that can be read by many other network analyzers. The files created by tcpdump can grow quickly, so disk space should be monitored closely when saving the file.

–r Filename

Files created with the -w option can be read by tcpdump, and further analysis can be performed on the packet. If the original tcpdump was a tcpdump -w with no filters, then the tcpdump -r can use filters to refine the output to exactly what is needed:

```
tcpdump -r savedfile -n host 192.168.1.101
11:39:52.498409 eth0 < 192.168.1.101.1041 > 192.168.1.254.telnet: . 3768803:3768
803(0) ack 2572567146 win 7781 (DF)
11:39:52.498518 eth0 > 192.168.1.254.telnet > 192.168.1.101.1041: P 1:89(88) ack 0
win 32120 (DF)
11:39:52.698395 eth0 < 192.168.1.101.1041 > 192.168.1.254.telnet: . 0:0(0) ack 89
win 7693 (DF)
```

–v

The -v (for verbose) tells tcpdump to print the time-to-live information as well as the type of service. Notice the difference between the output that follows with the -v parameter and the same command without the -v in the -r example given;

```
[root@lefty /root]# tcpdump -r savedfile -n -v host 192.168.1.101
11:39:52.498409 eth0 < 192.168.1.101.1041 > 192.168.1.254.telnet: . 3768803:3768
803(0) ack 2572567146 win 7781 (DF) (ttl 128, id 37383)
11:39:52.498518 eth0 > 192.168.1.254.telnet > 192.168.1.101.1041: P 1:89(88) ack 0
win 32120 (DF) (ttl 64, id 21483)
11:39:52.698395 eth0 < 192.168.1.101.1041 > 192.168.1.254.telnet: . 0:0(0) ack 89
win 7693 (DF) (ttl 128, id 37639)
```

tcpdump Expressions

tcpdump uses the concept of expressions to define which packets to display. The expression follows any command-line parameters that are passed to tcpdump. An expression is made up of a qualifier followed by an ID.

The qualifier is either an IP type (host, network or port), the direction (source or destination), or protocol. This may seem very confusing, but a few examples will clarify `tcpdump`'s use tremendously. If you examine the last `tcpdump` output, you will notice that the `tcpdump` already made use of the expression host 192.168.1.101, which tells `tcpdump` to print all packets that have the address 192.168.1.101 in either the source or destination fields.

To tell `tcpdump` to only print packets from 192.168.1.254, the `src` qualifier is used:

```
tcpdump -n -v src 192.168.1.254
```

Or to display only packets destined for 192.168.1.254:

```
tcpdump -n -v dst 192.168.1.254
```

To further limit the output to not only a destination of 192.168.1.101, but to also limit the output to DNS (udp or TCP port 53), the following can be used:

```
tcpdump -n -v dst 192.168.1.254 and port 53
```

`tcpdump` does not require the integer port number but can interpret the logical name for the service (protocol) as defined by the Internet Assigned Numbers Authority (`http://www.isi.edu/in-notes/iana/assignments/port-numbers`) Table 9.7 lists some common services. The file `/etc/services`, located on Linux (and UNIX) hosts' also lists the ports and their logical names.

Table 9.7 **Common Protocols Ports and Logical Names**

Application	Application Protocol	Layer 4 Protocol	Port (Assigned Number)	tcpdump Logical Port Name
Email	Simple Mail Transport Protocol (SMTP)	TCP	25	`smtp`
Email	Post Office Protocol version 3	TCP	110	`pop-3`
File Download	File Transfer Protocol (ftp)	UDP UDP	20 (data) 21 (command)	`ftp` `ftp-data`
Name Resolution	Domain Name System	TCP/UDP	53	`domain`
Name Resolution (Microsoft)	NetBios	UDP TCP	137 137	`netbios-ns`

continues

Table 9.7 **Continued**

Application	Application Protocol	Layer 4 Protocol	Port (Assigned Number)	tcpdump Logical Port Name
Network Management	Simple Network Management Protocol (snmp)	UDP UDP	161 162 (traps)	snmp snmp-trap
Network Time	Network Time Protocol (ntp)	UDP TCP (rarely implemented)	123	ntp
Remote Access	Telnet	TCP	23	telnet
Routing Protocol	Border Gateway Protocol	UDP TCP	179 179	bgp
System Logging	syslog	UDP	514	syslog
World Wide Web	Hyper Text Transport Protocol (http)	TCP UDP (rarely implemented)	80 80	www

This means the aforementioned:

```
tcpdump -n -v dst 192.168.1.101 and port 53
```

can also be entered as

```
tcpdump -n -v dst 192.168.1.101 and port domain
```

And if this command is run and someone attempts to contact the web server at http://www.newriders.com/, a name resolution attempt would be printed:

```
[root@lefty /root]# tcpdump -n -v dst 192.168.1.254 and port domain
Kernel filter, protocol ALL, datagram packet socket
tcpdump: listening on all devices
10:36:31.504218 eth0 < 10.1.1.1.domain > 192.168.1.254.1026: 1552 2/12/12
www.newriders.com. CNAME newriders.com., newriders.com. A 63.69.110.220 (465) (DF)
(ttl 250, id 31400)
```

In addition to this modifier, tcpdump also supports the modifiers, not and or. A very useful application of the not modifier is to not print packets that are being created through the remote access session to the Linux node. Assuming telnet, the following tcpdump will print out all packets to and from the host except telnet:

```
tcpdump host 192.168.1.254 and not port 23
```

Using and, or, and not and the common expressions shown in Table 9.8, it is possible to troubleshoot most network problems and to filter exactly what needs to be analyzed.

Table 9.8 *tcpdump* **Expressions**

`dst`	`host`	`tcpdump` examines the IP packet and determines if there is a match.	The *host* is the IP address or name of the node being monitored. If the name resolves to multiple IP addresses, `tcpdump` checks for each address.
`dst host`	`host`	Same as above.	Same as above.
`src host`	`host`	The source bits are examined to determine a match.	
`src host`	`host`	The source bits are examined to determine a match.	
`host`	`host`	`tcpdump` examines the source and destination bits.	
`ip | arp | rarp host`	`host`	`tcpdump` determines if the packet is of type IP, ARP, or RARP and if the source or destination bits match *host*.	
`gateway`	`host`	`tcpdump` examines the MAC address of the packets	
`dst | src`	`net`	`tcpdump` examines the destination or source bits (depending on `dst` or `src`) and determines if the address is within the address range defined by net.	`net` can be either a network defined in `/etc/networks` or a network address such as 192.168.1.0 or a network mask with the prefix notation used: 192.168.1.0/24.
`net`	`net`	`tcpdump` determines if the source or destination falls within the address range defined by `net`.	

continues

Table 9.8 **Continued**

`[tcp	udp] port`	Determines if the TCP or UDP destination port numbers equal `port`. If either `tcp` or `udp` from (`[tcp | udp]`) are specified, the match will check for the protocol specified.	`port` can be an integer or logical name. See Table 9.8.
`[tcp	udp] port src port`	Determines if the TCP or UDP destination port numbers equal `port`. If `tcp` or `udp` is specified, the match will include the protocol.	
`[tcp	udp] port port`	Determines if the TCP or UDP port source or destination port equal `port`. If `tcp` or `udp` is included, the match will include the protocol.	
`ip broadcast`	Determines if the destination address is set to all 1s or zeroes.	The `netmask` is used to determine the appropriate broadcast address.

tcpdump Example

As mentioned in the `traceroute` section, the `traceroute` command deserves closer examination, and `tcpdump` is the perfect tool to see the command in action. For this example assume three nodes: the source (192.168.1.254), the first router (10.1.1.254), and the final destination router (10.2.2.254).

For this example, we will use ICMP as opposed to UDP to send the `traceroute` to the destination router:

```
[root@lefty /root]# traceroute -In 10.2.2.254
```

To capture the output, we will turn off name resolution to avoid further traffic creation and turn on the verbose flag. Below is the output of the traceroute command with the output lines numbered for easy reference.

```
[root@lefty /root]# tcpdump -nv
1  11:56:57.885796 eth0 > 192.168.1.254 > 10.2.2.254: icmp: echo request [ttl 1]
➡(id 34072)
2  11:56:57.949353 eth0 < 10.1.1.254 > 192.168.1.254: icmp: time exceeded in-
➡transit (ttl 64, id 11798)
3  11:56:57.949738 eth0 > 192.168.1.254 > 10.2.2.254: icmp: echo request [ttl 1]
➡(id 34073)
4  11:56:57.984039 eth0 < 10.1.1.254 > 192.168.1.254: icmp: time exceeded in-
➡transit (ttl 64, id 11804)
5  11:56:57.984272 eth0 > 192.168.1.254 > 10.2.2.254: icmp: echo request [ttl 1]
➡(id 34074)
6  11:56:58.017169 eth0 < 10.1.1.254 > 192.168.1.254: icmp: time exceeded in-
➡transit (ttl 64, id 11810)
7  11:56:58.017459 eth0 > 192.168.1.254 > 10.2.2.254: icmp: echo request (ttl 2,
➡id 34075)
8  11:56:58.043489 eth0 < 10.2.2.254 > 192.168.1.254: icmp: echo reply (ttl 254,
➡id 34075)
9  11:56:58.043740 eth0 > 192.168.1.254 > 10.2.2.254: icmp: echo request (ttl 2,
➡id 34076)
10  11:56:58.068649 eth0 < 10.2.2.254 > 192.168.1.254: icmp: echo reply (ttl 254,
➡id 34076)
11  11:56:58.068873 eth0 > 192.168.1.254 > 10.2.2.254: icmp: echo request (ttl 2,
➡id 34077)
12  11:56:58.094390 eth0 < 10.2.2.254 > 192.168.1.254: icmp: echo reply (ttl 254,
➡id 34077)
34 packets received by filter
```

As can be seen in line 1, lefty (192.168.1.254) has sent out three echo requests with the ttl set to 1 to destination 10.2.2.254. The first router 10.1.1.254 decrements the ttl to 0 and then sends back the ICMP: time exceeded message to each of the echo requests as seen in lines 2, 4, and 6. traceroute then increments the ttl 2, which makes it to the destination and the destination then replies (lines 8, 10, and 12).

Summary

In this chapter, the Linux commands for displaying and configuring Linux nodes have been covered. The common uses of ifconfig, route, ping, traceroute, arp, netstat, and tcpdump have been covered. ifconfig is used to configure and show configuration options for network interface cards. route is used to add and display routing entries on the Linux node.

ping and traceroute are troubleshooting tools used to determine and localize network connectivity issues. And finally, tcpdump is a general-purpose, freely available protocol analyzer available for Linux, definitely recommended for Linux network nodes.

10

Planning Basic Router Layout and Function

NOW THAT WE'VE COVERED SOME of the basics, it's time to do some planning. Specifically, you need to plan how your router is going to fit in with your overall networking scheme. If you're starting from scratch, then it's time to devise a networking scheme so that you can fit a router or routers into that plan.

Introduction to Network Planning

Network planning is not a hard and fast science. There are as many theories about planning networks as there are network admins—maybe more if you count admins with multiple personalities.

We'll try to provide some guidelines that will help you plan your router setup in terms of the rest of your network, but they should be seen as just that—guidelines. Every situation is unique, and you have to decide what works best for you. In other words, your mileage might vary.

Things to Consider

In this section we'll try to cover the most important aspects of network planning so that you can cover all of the bases. Some of these categories overlap a bit. We hope that this section will give you some helpful guidelines to go by while planning your network or integrating a Linux router into your existing network.

Goals

The first thing to consider when planning your network (and where your router(s) fit into that plan) is your overall goals for your network.

Are you just devising a small home LAN that's going to serve for two or three computers sharing a dial-up connection, DSL, or cable modem? Or is this going to be a WAN joining LANs in three different states and providing a VPN for your company's various remote offices and road warriors dialing up from their hotel rooms to check email and transmit sales figures?

As you can see, the answers to those questions will start to shape your planning and dictate the type of protocols you'll need to support as well as the hardware that will be needed to support it. (It will also determine which chapters you'll need to read thoroughly and which ones, if any, you can skim!)

Resources

The next question is: What resources do you have to fall back on? This will provide a clear picture of what you have to work with while trying to achieve your goals and how aggressive you can be in terms of future-proofing your setup and providing redundancy.

For instance, can you afford to deploy redundant systems? For corporate setups, we strongly recommend that you take the time to build a back-up system for each mission-critical system. This is particularly true if you have small remote offices without dedicated technical staff. Should you suffer a hardware failure, you can simply have someone swap out the dead or malfunctioning system with a backup and proactively reduce your downtime from hours or days to a few minutes. Almost anybody can be trained to swap out a standard system.

A Word About Reliability

We're not trying to convey the message that Linux is unreliable. Quite the contrary...many folks have Linux systems with uptime measuring in years. That's right—years. However, you'll probably be building your system with standard PC components that have mechanical parts, and eventually those parts will fail. Note that we didn't say they might fail—they will fail. It's only a matter of when and how prepared you'll be when it does happen.

You can protect yourself somewhat by buying decent components, but even the cream of the crop can suffer unexpected failure. Even a Rolls Royce can get a flat tire.

Another question is whether you'll be buying new systems or if you're going to be digging through the company's computer "bone yard" to scrape together parts for your soon-to-be router. If your needs are small, there's quite a lot to be said for recycling old hardware and repurposing it with Linux. Actually, we rather like the fact that Linux allows you to reclaim hardware that might have otherwise gone to the junkyard.

Maybe your situation allows you to purchase one new system to build your router, but you can build a backup system from old parts to pinch-hit in the event the primary system fails.

Budget Concerns

In an ideal situation, you have unlimited spending authority, don't have to justify your hardware purchases, and your budget rivals Bill Gates's yearly income. Of course, in an ideal situation you're independently wealthy and building Linux routers just for the sheer joy of it.

More than likely you'll have a fixed amount of money to spend on your routing project and a fixed amount of time as well. Don't skimp on hardware or time spent up front, only to have to spend more money later or, even worse, more time fixing bugs or issues that could have been solved up front.

Growth

Is your network going to be growing (or shrinking!) in the foreseeable future? If you can reasonably expect that your network is going to undergo significant growth in the next six months to a year, you might want to plan your router as if the growth had already occurred.

For instance, if you know your company plans to open its first remote office in a few months, now is the time to start planning for a WAN and budgeting for equipment for the remote office. Life will be much easier if you can set up and test equipment weeks or months in advance and just plug it in the day before employees start turning up at the new office.

Dealing with ISPs and the Phone Company

It's a nightmare to show up at a new office planning to get to work only to find out that the T1 that was supposed to be installed a week ago is going to take another month. Even worse is what happens when 20 employees try to share a dial-up connection to send and receive email and do work on a remote server.

This does happen, particularly when admins think they can have a T1 installed at a location as quickly as they can get residential phone service. Order your connectivity at least a month ahead of time and confirm the order at least a week before the turn-on date. Don't schedule installation the same day that workers will be arriving and expecting to get to work, either. That's a recipe for disaster.

If you're reading this and shaking your head in disbelief that we feel it necessary to point these things out, you're lucky. Some of us have worked with admins and CTOs who didn't understand the importance of preplanning when dealing with phone companies—and lived to tell the tale.

Security Planning

Security is a major concern when planning your network and router configuration. You need to ask yourself how paranoid you need to be when planning and what steps you can take to ensure maximum security on your network.

Note that we didn't say, "ask yourself if you need to be paranoid," because a touch of paranoia is absolutely necessary to protect your data. Even if you're just planning a home network, odds are there's data on your computer that you'd rather not give the world access to. Security is absolutely critical when planning for a corporate network where crackers might seek to steal credit card information or competitors might try to discover corporate secrets. (Public companies also can open themselves up to lawsuits if they can't prove due diligence when it comes to computer security.)

Admins for schools and universities need to be particularly vigilant—there's no security risk like talented computer geeks with too much time on their hands. We only wish that we were being too dramatic when we suggest that security is a major issue.

Remember also that security isn't just an "us against them" proposition. Sometimes it's "us against us" as well. While it would be nice to believe that none of your company's employees would do anything malicious, and that might be true, you can't go on that assumption. There are degrees of attacks. For instance, while maybe none of your fellow employees would ever do damage to your systems or attempt to "root" one of your servers, they might be inclined to try to browse systems in your payroll department to find out how much other folks in the company are making. Or maybe they want to read the bosses' email to see if they've been mentioned, or vice versa.

By setting up subnets in your office between departments, it's possible to cut off unwanted traffic between departments if necessary. If you'll be working with other companies inside your network, you'll want to look into how to set up your Extranet and configuring a DMZ. If your budget allows, it might be a good idea to bring in a security consultant to help evaluate your security measures or even help plan and implement security for your network. Even some of the most talented system admins don't have the background or depth of understanding of security that they need. Whatever your security needs, it's best to plan proactively instead of reacting.

Ease of Administration

Another consideration is the ease of administering your network. What can you do to make life easier for yourself and other admins or network staff? Whatever policies you decide on while planning your network, you'll want to commit them to writing and revisit them periodically to see how effective they've been. (Okay, not so necessary for home networking. We hope that you don't feel it necessary to distribute printed network policies to Rover and the kids. If you start thinking about giving the dog its own subnet, it's time to put down the book, back away slowly, and spend some time in the "Big Blue Room.")

For large networks, you might wish to plan so that you can delegate authority over subnets to other admins and spread the workload out equally—or by department or some other scheme that will keep things sane.

You'll also want to plan to automate as much as possible and set up notification systems to alert you to any failure in the network. This brings us back to redundancy. Having redundant systems reduces a situation from a "drop everything" emergency to a "fix as time allows" situation.

Router Choice, Placement, and Functionality

Before you embark upon the task of actually building your Linux router, you need to decide what functionality you need from your router or routers. Will you be setting up just a plain vanilla router, or are you going to need a VPN or Extranet configuration too? Should those tasks be combined or deployed on separate machines?

Mixing and Matching Protocols

Considering you've invested in this title and have read this far, we're assuming that you have decided to go ahead and utilize Linux for at least some of your routing needs.

There's no reason why you couldn't utilize Linux for some routing tasks and a Cisco or other proprietary router for others. However, we can't begin to cover all the possibilities of using Linux routers with any/all of the other potential router hardware and/or software. Suffice it to say that Linux works and plays well with other operating systems and network devices. If you want to mix and match, you could have little trouble getting Linux to cooperate.

Edge and Access

When we talk about an edge router, we're not referring to the guitarist from U2. The term, "edge router," refers to a specific kind of router used to route packets between one or several LANs and an Asynchronous Transfer Mode (ATM) network or in Frame Relay.

Support for ATM on Linux is not quite as mature as some other forms of networking. You'll want to do some research to be sure the equipment that you want to use is supported under Linux and plan a little extra time to work out the kinks if you're going to be using a Linux router as an edge router.

Security Zones (DMZ and Extranets)

In this section, we'll touch on some very specialized situations that will pose security and configuration challenges while you are planning your network. Naturally, your router will play an important role in dealing with these challenges.

We've already mentioned using subnets as part of the overall security strategy. In some cases you might wish to extend your network, or parts of it, to other companies. Perhaps you've got a supplier that accesses a database so you can speed up the supply chain, or you're sharing your product information automatically with resellers who simply pluck data from your database and create a dynamic catalog of your products.

You might want to allow your developers and developers from another company to collaborate on a project, necessitating access to one another's networks.

Opening up your network to other companies creates new opportunities and allows business to be done faster than ever before. It also creates new and interesting security headaches, or at least concerns, for system administrators and networking professionals.

What is a DMZ?

Geeks really love to give things TLAs (Three Letter Acronyms), but in the case of the DMZ, networking geeks simply appropriated a term already in use. DMZ is short for demilitarized zone, a term that came into use during the Korean War.

In networking parlance, a DMZ is usually one host that acts as a buffer between the router and the internal network. It provides an extra hurdle for anyone attempting to break into your network because even if they're successful in overcoming the security on your router/firewall, they have to get through another host before they actually reach your network.

Particularly cautious admins will not only maintain a DMZ, but also set up a "honeypot" as well. A *honeypot* is a computer that's deliberately set up to be noticed by intruders and usually has one or more intentional security flaws so crackers will be enticed by an easy target and be lured away from vital machines. Honeypots are also usually outfitted with intrusion detection systems, so admins will know when their network has attracted unwanted attention. With any luck, a honeypot will also allow a skilled admin to trace the attacker so that they can be identified and possibly prosecuted. While that's a bit of a detour from the main topic, we thought it was worth mentioning.

Single Purpose or Multipurpose Routers

Single purpose routers are just that—routers that handle routing and only routing. At one time, choosing whether to allow your router to handle other tasks was pretty much a moot point. Routers were hardware appliances with limited scope, and you bought a router that handled routing and that was that.

With Linux, routing is just one little piece of the pie. You could conceivably set up one machine that handles file, print, and web serving in addition to being a firewall and router. If you're a college student with a Linux computer in your dorm room, this might be an acceptable practice.

On the other hand, we think it's probably best to separate functions as much as possible in a production environment. It's great that Linux is capable of doing so many different tasks, and we don't hesitate to recommend using Linux for all of those tasks—just not all on the same machine!

For instance, it's tempting to set up a router that is also a firewall, and many networks are configured that way. However, if budget allows, we'd recommend that you set up one box as a router, and another as a dedicated firewall. That's not to say you shouldn't configure a firewall on the router itself, but we recommend a separate hardened firewall as well.

It's possible, for example, to set up a DMZ on a machine by using three network cards and configuring everything in software. This is fine for very small networks or networks with minimal security needs. However, for most purposes we don't recommend it. Hardware is (relatively) cheap, Linux is free, and recovering from a break-in is expensive. You do the math.

Effective Router Management Through Managed Routing Tables

One of the challenges for many organizations is effectively managing routers, especially the size of routing tables.

Due to the urgency and immediacy of many network changes to support the enterprise, network configuration and especially network tables become inefficient. As routing tables grow in size and networks are created to meet the need without a lot of thought for the long-term effects multiple changes will have on the efficiency of a network or the complexities created for network administrators.

There are several strategies, both operational and technical, that can ensure routing configurations are kept orderly and routing tables do not become larger than necessary.

Operational Considerations for Router Configuration Efficiency

Network administrators using good operational practices is the best method to ensure smooth network operations and to ensure routers are configured optimally.

Software Control and Version Dependency Requirements

Regardless of the platform used, newer versions of software are released for routers, and Linux is no exception (with some releases happening weekly or daily). The newer versions often fix bugs and add new features; however, newer software can also bring new bugs and interoperability issues. Therefore, it is important that you not get caught up into the "upgrade it because it is available" strategy.

New software should be tracked, and release notes should always be read with the following in mind:

- Does it fix any problems the organization is having?
- Does it identify any problems that relate to our environment but that we are not aware of?

- Does it add new features that are needed by the organization now or in the near future?
- Does it fix any security holes?
- Does it increase performance significantly?

If you answered "yes" to any of the these questions, a software upgrade should then be considered for your router systems.

Should you determine that the software is worth considering for an upgrade, you should investigate if there are any known interoperability issues with equipment in your environment. Issues of interoperability with the current software also should be investigated because upgrades must often be performed in phases.

Technical Considerations for Router Efficiency

The most common technical consideration for effective router efficiency is the routing table or more specifically, the routing table size. A minimized routing table ensures efficiency in routing decisions because a smaller routing table speeds routing decisions. A minimized routing table also ensures efficiency in administration given that a smaller routing table is easier to troubleshoot by network administrators.

Routing Tables in Static Routing Networks

Networks that use static routes will tend to be very efficient networks during the early stages of the network but will tend to become inefficient as changes are made to solve the specific network requirement without consideration of the complete network. The following tips, when applied to the complete network, will ensure networking tables maintain the minimum size necessary to support the network.

Effective Use of Default Route

Probably the most underused feature among experienced and inexperienced network administrators is the use of the default route. While it is well understood that the default route is the route of last resort, many administrators are in the habit of creating routes on all routers when a new network is brought into service. This is typically unnecessary in most static route-based networks due to their simplicity and tendency to route towards the core of the network or a central router, which is in the patch for the new network.

Consider the network in Figure 10.1. When network 10.1.40.0/24 is brought online, many network administrators will tend to create routing entries for 10.1.40.0/24 at sites B, C, and D. However, because sites B, C, and D must use site A for transport to 10.1.40.0/24 and there is a pre-existing default route, adding a routing entry for 10.1.40.0/24 is an unnecessary routing entry.

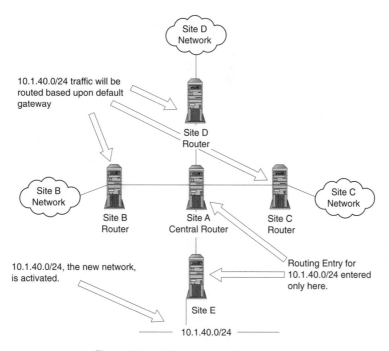

Figure 10.1   Effective use of default route.

In fact, at sites B, C, and D, the routing tables of the gateways to the central site, A, only need routing entries for local networks and a default route pointing back to the central site.

Effective Use of Supernetting and Variable Length Subnetting

In networks where remote sites also have gateways to the Internet, such as those shown in Figure 10.2, the default gateway cannot be used whenever the new network, 10.128.1.0/24, is brought into service. However, because the network administrators have chosen to use the RFC 1918 address range 10.0.0.0/8 for the complete network, the routing entry for the supernet 10.0.0.0/8 at the gateway for site B includes the new network 10.128.1.0/24.

In addition, the routing entry at site A for the network 10.128.0.0/24 can be changed to a supernet to include the new network 10.128.1.0/24. The new supernet routing entry would be 10.128.0.0/23, which saves a routing entry at site A for site B.

This example has made effective use of a feature that was created with the support of variable length subnetting—the use of routing entries that summarize the "rest" of the network for edge routers, even though, technically, the entry does not point to a particular network (10.0.0.0/8) in this case.

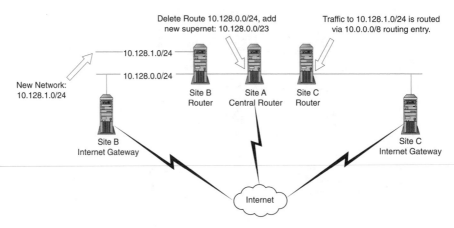

Figure 10.2   Effective use of supernetting.

The use of variable length subnetting also can, however, prove troublesome when not used effectively.

Avoiding Ineffective Usage of Variable Length Subnetting

Variable length subnetting can be used to manage IP address space in a fashion such that a minimum of IP addresses are used for each network; however, with multiple networks masks used in a network, this often adds unnecessary complexity to the network.

In a static route network, generally not more than one or two netmasks should be necessary: a netmask, often 255.255.255.0 for the local area networks, and 255.255.255.252 for transit networks, which are usually point-to-point links. However, even a separate netmask for the transit networks is not necessary given that the 10.0.0.0/8 offers more than enough address space for most networks—especially any networks using static routing.

Universal Use of Transit Networks

Whichever netmask is used for transit networks, the netmask should be used universally. In addition, most routers support the concept of unnumbered interfaces for point-to-point links. This means that the link between the two sites does not receive an IP address for the link. Should unnumbered interfaces be used, they should also be used universally if possible.

Routing Tables in Dynamic Routing Networks

As in static route networks, avoid the ineffective use of variable length subnetting. Supporting numerous subnet masks adds even more complexity to dynamic environments given that these networks already tend to be larger than their static route counterparts. Transit networks also should use the same guidelines just covered for static route networks.

Route Summarization

Route summarization performs a similar function to that which static route supernetting provides—it combines multiple subnet routes into one entry. Route summarization is a step more versatile because the routing protocol is still aware of specific network outages through routing advertisements.

Figure 10.3 shows that router A has used route summarization for 10.0.0.0/8 through interface A1. (Assuming equal weights, the network can be summarized through A2 as well, but it would not be used until a failure occurs because it is an additional hop.) Router B can also summarize the route.

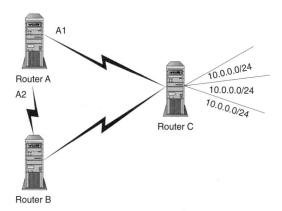

Figure 10.3   Network management system.

Avoiding Multiple Protocol Support

Supporting multiple dynamic routing protocols on the same network should be avoided. Multiple protocol support is usually the result of corporate acquisitions or failed upgrades from an older metric-based protocol to a link state protocol such as open shortest path first (OSPF).

Supporting multiple protocols requires not only an understanding of the protocols involved, but also how they interoperate on routers that support both protocols, which will typically be vendor specific. It must be understood which protocol takes priority on the routers that support both protocols, which entries are further propagated by the "other" protocol, and how to troubleshoot the interaction of the two protocols.

Special Case Routing Functions

As covered in Chapter 7, "Kernel Support Tools", adding additional functions to Internet gateways can add additional value to a Linux router and, indeed, often gives Linux an edge over traditional routers as Internet access gateways.

There are additional considerations, or special cases, that also arise when planning and deploying networks that you should be aware of.

IP Version 6 Support

Chapter 4, "IPv 4 and IPv 6 Addressing," covers the innards of addressing networks. Organizations choosing to support IPv6 will need phase-in methodologies to support both versions of the Internet protocol.

RFC 1933, "Transition Mechanisms for IPv6 Hosts and Routers," defines two methods for transitioning to IPv6: dual IP layer and IPv6 over IPv4 tunneling.

Dual IP layer is very similar to dual stacks to support multiple protocols. For example, many workstations and PCs supported both IP and Novell's IPX during Novell's popularity in the 1990s.

Dual stacks is a host-based solution, that is, the host can communicate with both IP version 6 and version 4 nodes, which provides a very broad base of interoperability capability.

Many organizations wish to deploy specific IPv6 networks as opposed to a dual stack approach. Therefore, RFC 1933 also defined tunneling of IPv6 over IPv4 networks. Tunneling of IP version 6 over version 4 is similar to other tunneling technology. An example of the tunneling is shown in Figure 10.4.

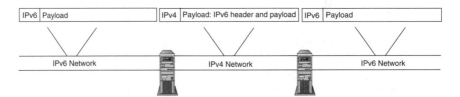

Figure 10.4   IP version 6 over IP version 4.

Node A and B both have IP version 6 and IP version 4 interfaces. For traffic flowing from A to B, A encapsulates the IPv6 packet received on interface A1 into a version 4 packet and routes it out interface A2. Router B then accepts the IPv4 packet on interface B1, strips the IPv4 header from the packet, and routes it out interface B2 as an IP version 6 packet.

Multihoming

Multihoming, for most system administrators, describes connecting a host or network to multiple networks. A router, by definition, is multihomed. In this chapter, multihoming refers to actually connecting to the Internet via at least 2 upstream providers.

Administrative Considerations

Internet service providers' policies on multihoming vary greatly—from very little concern on how you implement multihoming (these ISPs will tend to use filtering very strongly on the edge of the network to ensure your network is not affecting the core network) to a very detailed list of dos and don'ts. This chapter covers the technical aspects of multihoming, but do consult with the ISPs of choice on their policies and recommendations.

Simple Multihoming

The simplest form of multihoming is shown in Figure 10.5.

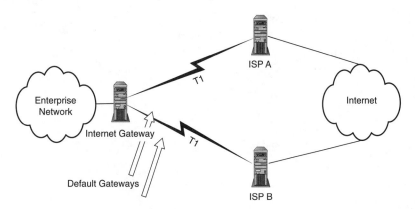

Figure 10.5   Simple multihoming.

In Figure 10.5, the enterprise is connected to ISP A and ISP B via T1 connections. On the router, penguin, two default routes with equal weights are pointed to each ISP A and B creating a load balance between the two ISPs.

The major advantage to this solution is simplicity and a total bandwidth for Internet connectivity of 3Mbps. The major disadvantage of this solution is that 50% of traffic destined to ISP A for outsourced services such as WWW, DNS, or even email, will travel through ISP B. Static routes for the ISP's networks can be entered to create a hybrid Simple Multihoming network; however, the ISPs also have many customers where traffic should go through a particular link (assuming the link is in service). Therefore, a more efficient method is often needed.

BGP Multihoming

By using BGP with both providers, the edge router(s) can determine the best path to both ISP providers' customers. This can be implemented in several ways. Should the provider only advertise customer networks with customers, then a direct BGP implementation is straightforward. Should the provider advertise all routes, a filtering mechanism is required at the edge of the provider's network or on the customer premise.

Filtering is preferred over simply adding entries for the providers' networks given that adding entries does not take failures into consideration. Consider the network shown in Figure 10.6. With the static entry, the connection will fail because all the traffic is going out link A1. However, if router A knew about the failure through a routing update, then the router will use link A2, and the traffic will arrive through ISP B.

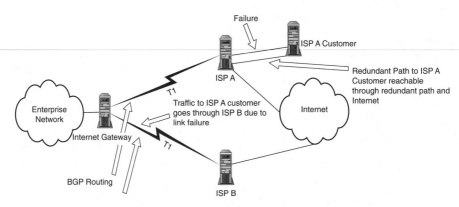

Figure 10.6 Link failure bypass.

Challenges of Multihoming

Due to the wide spread acceptance of CIDR by ISPs, ISPs are resistant to advertising networks not within their CIDR domain. Multihoming, by nature, creates the situation where an ISP needs to advertise another provider's CIDR portion within its network. Even if the ISP is willing to advertise the route for the other provider's address space within its domain, routers outside the domain will not know that both ISPs have a path to the network.

Due to the large number of Internet attacks that make use of spoofed addresses, ISPs also will filter out packets that have source addresses not belonging to their CIDR. This, then, also should be considered when designing the access network for multihoming.

NAT could be used to ensure all packets through a particular ISP use the address space assigned by that ISP as the source address. This will add complexity to the network; however, most networks use NAT already, so it is a question of the specific network requirements and implementation on how much additional complexity is added.

Summary

This chapter covered some of the basic considerations for planning your routing setup from connectivity to security. While this is not a concrete blueprint for router planning, it gives a good overview of the necessary considerations for router planning.

This chapter also covered practices for ensuring effective routing table sizes, special case routing functions such as IPv6 support, and connecting to two or more ISPs through multihoming.

11

Linux Routing Basics

IN THIS CHAPTER, AS THE TITLE suggests, we'll take a look at some of the basics of routing with Linux. We'll also discuss some basics of common network configurations. This includes pre-planning for your network.

As you'll see, it all sounds a lot more difficult in theory than it is in practice.

LAN Routing Basics

In this section, we'll look at what a network admin will need to know to set up a local area network. Setting up a LAN with Linux is very simple these days. We can recall a time when the tools weren't quite as mature as they are today, but Linux has come a long way in the last three or four years. Linux has always been very good at networking, but the set-up and configuration tools have gotten better over time.

Linux's routing capabilities, however, have really come to the forefront in the 2.4.x kernel series. A lot of the more advanced capabilities aren't necessary for simple LANs, though you might find the Netfilter framework makes life a lot easier in some ways.

Setting up the One-Part LAN

Setting up a one-part LAN is pretty easy, whether you have a router/gateway between one computer and the Internet or a router/gateway that sits between 100 computers and the Internet. As long as you don't want to break your LAN into subnets, then your configuration is the same no matter how many clients live behind your router.

For simple LANs, all you'll need to do is set up a box with IP Masquerading or possibly NAT. (For a full discussion on the differences between IP Masquerading and NAT see Chapter 14, "Security and NAT Issues."

For a simple one-part LAN that's using IP Masquerading through a single router/gateway, there's not a whole lot to setting up routing at all. Simply setting up IP Masq and IP Forwarding is all that it takes; the kernel does the rest automatically. Again, all that is covered in Chapter 14.

Static or Dynamic IP Addresses

One of the first issues you'll have to deal with is whether to set up static or dynamic IPs for your hosts. If you have a very small LAN, fewer than 20 computers, then using static IP addresses won't be too big a chore. As long as there aren't too many hosts on your network, using static IPs is easier than setting up DHCP. If you can remember the names and IP addresses of every computer in your network, there's no reason to fuss with DHCP.

On the other hand, if you find yourself adding new hosts to the network on a regular basis or have more than 20 or 30 machines, you'd probably save yourself some headaches by configuring a DHCP server. This is especially true if more than one person sets up new machines. Murphy's Law will rear its ugly head if multiple folks are assigning static IPs at the same time. You can use your router as the DHCP server or use an old 486 or Pentium computer dedicated just to serving DHCP.

Some applications perform authentication using IP addresses. This is true of NFS, printing, mail transfer, and NAT to name a few. If DHCP is improperly configured, it can cause major problems with printing, file sharing, and other tasks.

You can mix and match, though. If you have a few work areas for telecommuters who pay an occasional visit to the office, for instance, you can have DHCP set up for "visiting" computers while other hosts on the network have static IPs. In fact, in just about any office setting it's probably a good idea to plan for the occasional visitor with a laptop who is going to need to plug it in to check email and whatnot.

Setting up DHCP is uniformly easy on client computers, whether you're using Linux, Windows, MacOS, or one of the BSDs. We won't go into setting up a DHCP server or client here given that most distros provide their own interfaces for configuring a DHCP service. Suffice it to say that it's relatively easy.

Another benefit of DHCP is the fact that you can "recycle" IP addresses. By that we mean that you can use DHCP to maximize your available IP addresses by requiring machines to "lease" the IP addresses and put the IP addresses back in the pool after a set amount of time. This way, when a visiting manager plugs in his laptop and uses an IP address while in the office, it will be reclaimed after they leave for another machine to use.

Don't Make Your Router a Moving Target

Just in case this isn't obvious, you don't want to allocate a router's IP address dynamically. For instance, if you're going to use a private Class C network, give your router an IP such as 192.168.1.1—one that's easy to remember while setting up new hosts. Things like routers, firewalls, mail servers, or NFS servers, should pretty much always have the same IP address.

Setting up a LAN with Subnets

If you're dealing with subnets in your LAN, things are going to get a little more complicated, but not to worry—it's still not that bad.

Considering that we've already covered the gory details of subnet mask math in Chapter 4, "IPv4 and IPv6 Addressing," we won't boggle your mind with it again here. (Okay, it's actually not that hard, but anything that smacks of math makes some of our heads spin…)

We will, however, cover the differences between a single-sized subnet and a variable-sized subnet and reasons why you might want to work with subnets on your LAN. You'll definitely want to have read through Chapter 4 if you don't already have a strong grasp of IP addressing schemes.

IPv6

Because IPv6 is so rarely implemented, we're not going to spend any time on discussing IPv6 subnetting here. Considering the abundance of IPv6 addresses, it might never be necessary to consider subnetting IPv6 addresses anyway—even if IPv6 does become commonly used.

Why Subnet?

Subnets are created for a number of reasons. Generally, subnets on a network exist because of physical and geographical logistics, for the purpose of segregating internal networks or making the most of the IP address scheme.

We've already covered the physical and geographical logistics of networking earlier in the book; however, segregating networks for security is kind of a new topic. Protecting your data internally is just as important as protecting your data from outside threats. You wouldn't leave the HR department's personnel files unlocked in common hallways, would you? Of course not. So it sometimes makes sense to segregate your office's LAN by department and use your router/firewall as a barrier to keep prying eyes from data they shouldn't see. For instance, you might wish to create subnets on your network to separate your finance department from the rest of the office. Using `ipchains` or `iptables` you can set up rules that will filter certain types of traffic between subnets and possibly log any attempts that may raise eyebrows.

Note that two (or more) subnets can still share common resources. For instance, if you have a subnet for your finance department and a subnet for your graphic arts department, they could still share a networked color laser printer. Both `ipchains` and `iptables` allow you to set up access by source IP, destination IP, port, and protocol. The configuration options are nearly limitless, and once you've worked with the tools for a while, you'll find that they're very flexible and easy to use. We'll talk more about both `ipchains` and `iptables` in Chapter 14.

Performance is one good reason to segregate into subnets. Let's say you have a LAN with 100 clients. Because of the way that Ethernet works, if all 100 machines are on the same network, all traffic is essentially broadcast to all machines. This creates a high rate of collisions and slows network performance. By subnetting the network into, say, four equal subnets, you'll drastically reduce the amount of network traffic being seen by each machine and boost network performance.

Subnets also allow segregation of your network to simplify administration issues. Each subnet, or group of subnets, can be administered by an admin or group of admins separately from other subnets. This simplifies administration issues in larger organizations where responsibility might occasionally be unclear.

For the purpose of examples in this chapter, we'll look at subnetting a private Class C network. It is, however, also possible to subnet Class A or B networks—whether you're using some of the private IP address ranges set aside in the RFCs or using a real range of IPs.

Single-Size Subnets

Single-size subnets exist when you divide up an IP range into equal-sized subnets. For instance, if you take a Class C network and divide it into four equal subnets, you would have four subnets that could each handle 62 hosts. In some cases you might want to split the network up into equal parts but reserve one subnet for future growth.

With a Class C addressing scheme you can have a network that consists of anywhere from 4 to 64 equal subnets. Though why anyone would want to administer 64 subnets with 2 hosts each is beyond us! But if you're really weird or have really special needs (or both....), the option is there.

If you use a Class B addressing scheme you can split your network into anywhere from 4 equal subnets to, get this, 16,384 subnets. If you feel the need to administer 16,384 equal subnets of 2 hosts apiece, we advise that you seek professional help. More than likely, a Class C internal addressing scheme will be plenty for almost any corporation.

Variable-Sized Subnets

A variable-sized subnet is used when you need to break an address range into subnets of different sizes. For instance, in the previous example we divvied up a Class C range of IPs into eight subnets of equal size—that is, each subnet has an equal number of IP addresses. But, what if you need more IP addresses in the IT department's subnet than in the Finance department's subnet? You have all those extra servers, workstations and whatnot in that department, but only three people in Finance.

In this case, you would assign each subnet a different subnet mask that would depend on the number of hosts needed on each network. The subnet number would be varied to give as much or as little room necessary for hosts.

Stub Network

When two variable-sized subnets are created, the subnet with fewer hosts is referred to as the "stub network."

WAN Routing Basics

As you can imagine, setting up a wide area network is a bit trickier than setting up a LAN. For one thing, when you set up a LAN everything is more or less under your control. (Barring Murphy's Law, of course.) When you're constructing a WAN, there are factors that are outside your control.

Choosing the External Connection Type

When setting up your WAN, you want to try to pick the connection type that befits your bandwidth and uptime needs as well as your budget.

In some cases, your options might be chosen for you. Depending on where you're attempting to get connectivity, you may have the opportunity to choose from dial-up, DSL, ISDN, cable modem, T1, high-speed satellite dish, or carrier pigeon. In other cases, your options could be limited to only one or two types of connectivity.

You should be able to get a dial-up connection virtually anywhere, though only a masochist would voluntarily choose to put a WAN together on a 56K connection these days unless that was his only option. (Granted, back in "the day" 56K would have seemed awfully sweet.) Lets face it—dial-up connectivity is a solution for road warriors and other intermittent connections only. As a temporary VPN for your staff attending trade shows, it's livable but not as a permanent option. If any other type of connectivity is available to your locations, take it.

The next step up from dial-up, ISDN, also is widely available. If ISDN is the only option available, it is probably suitable for small offices and home offices. However, the price to bandwidth ratio for ISDN is much worse than DSL or cable modem connections. In most major cities, DSL and cable modem connections are available for both home and business use.

Chapter 12, "Network Hardware Components, Technology, and Solutions," covers hardware types in detail and discusses how to deal with whatever connection type(s) you have.

WANPIPE

One WAN package for Linux is the WANPIPE package. To utilize this package you'll need a supported card, and you'll also need to compile support for WAN Router and WAN Interfaces in the Linux kernel. (See Chapter 13, "Building a Routing Kernel," for a walk-through on kernel compilation.)

If you need the WANPIPE package, you can download it from the Sangoma FTP server `ftp://ftp.sangoma.com/linux/current_wanpipe/`. This directory also includes a README that might contain information newer than what we have as of this writing. Follow the instructions in the `README.install`, and you should be ready to go. If you're a Debian GNU/Linux user, it's even easier. Simply run:

```
apt-get update
apt-get install wanpipe
```

as root, and `apt-get` will download and install the package for you automatically, assuming that you have a valid download site in `/etc/apt/sources.list` for the packages. Note that packages in the Debian GNU/Linux "stable" release are usually not the most recent packages, so if there's a brand-new feature that you need, you might need to install the version from testing or unstable.

The `wanpipe` program calls the `wanconfig` program, which loads a configuration file with the proper options for your WAN card. The `/etc/wanpipe/wanpipe1.conf` configuration file is a symlink to the `/etc/wanpipe/router.conf` file, which contains all of the information about your WAN device or devices, the definitions for your WAN interfaces, and a hardware and physical interface section.

The usage of the `wanpipe` is very simple; the only difficult thing might be to get your configuration file set up correctly. Because there are so many options for the configuration file, we won't try to delve into them here. However, the Sangoma folks maintain a mailing list for WANPIPE, and the odds are if you pop into the list and detail your setup, someone on the list will be able to give you the information you need.

To start your WAN devices after you've gotten the configuration file set up, simply issue the command:

```
wanpipe start
```

which will start all of the devices that are listed in your configuration file. If you need to shut down the WAN interfaces then use:

```
wanpipe stop
```

As you might have guessed, it's also possible to stop or start individual devices, by using:

```
wanpipe start ¦ stop wanpipe#
```

where the "#" is the number of the interface. The device numbering starts at 1, and you are allowed up to 16 devices, which should be more than enough under normal circumstances.

VPN Routing Basics

Typically, VPNs are set up through a firewall rather than a router. However, because we're using Linux we've got the flexibility to combine the two. Alternatively, you could still use Linux for the router and firewall/VPN but build them on separate boxes for security purposes. Whatever you want to do, Linux is flexible enough for you to do it.

A VPN is an alternative to expensive leased lines that are closed to other network traffic. By making use of the Internet as a bridge between networks, companies can save a lot of money and still be secure by utilizing a VPN.

A Little More About VPNs

As you probably already know, VPN stands for Virtual Private Network. Because the Internet is hideously insecure, you wouldn't want to transmit any important data over the Internet unencrypted. For folks doing commerce, we have HTTPS. For people who just want to run a shell or X sessions, there's SSH. But what if you want to join two far-flung networks together securely and share all the common resources across the Internet? That's where VPNs come in.

The metaphor most often used to describe the method of connecting two networks securely is a tunnel. You think of the communications taking place between the two networks as being inside a few layers of outer coating. You're still using TCP/IP to transmit your data, but instead of unencrypted data being transmitted, the data is encrypted so that even if a potential attacker can intercept your packets—something you have no control over on an unsecured shared network—they shouldn't be able to make any sense out of the packets themselves. Your data is (theoretically) safe from prying eyes, and your network is safe from intruders.

So it's considered a private network even though the transmissions take place over a public network. It's not always as convenient as a WAN, but VPNs can prove a very useful substitute where budget and resource constraints make WANs impractical or when time and mobility are factors. For instance, you might wish to implement a VPN to allow Linux-based Point-of-Sale terminals to operate over a dial-up to interact with a central credit-card processing machine for your company while doing sales at trade shows.

One of the most common protocols for VPNs is the Point-to-Point Tunneling Protocol. As the name suggests, PPTP is based on the Point-to-Point Protocol. There are several implementations of PPTP for Linux that are interoperable with other operating systems such as Windows (and Linux, of course!) that you can utilize to create your own VPN. We cover VPNs extensively in Chapter 8, "Kernel 2.4.x Routing Daemons."

Summary

In this chapter we've covered some of the basics of using Linux as a router in normal-case scenarios. For the most part, using Linux as a router in normal LAN and WAN situations is a piece of cake because most of the work is done by the kernel and software automatically.

One of the things that Linux excels at is networking, so it's nearly a no-brainer to pick Linux as the glue for your network even if the rest of your LAN or WAN consists of Windows, Mac, or other types of machines. Linux is kind of the great "uniter" of operating systems.

In later chapters we'll cover more difficult routing tasks such as load balancing and VPNs in greater detail, which are tasks that used to be the domain of expensive hardware routers only.

12

Network Hardware Components, Technology, and Solutions

NETWORKS, INTERNETWORKS, AND THE INTERNET are all made up of hosts, nodes, routers, and telecommunication facilities. This chapter examines telecommunication technology that makes up the framework that most networks are built upon. Telecommunication facilities and infrastructure traditionally were owned and operated by AT&T, which was broken up (the parts after the breakup were known as "Baby Bells") by the US government. The term telephone company or telco is used loosely in this chapter to mean any organization that provides the services we cover in this chapter.

Analog Communications and Modems

The modem is the most common method for remote and home users to connect to corporate networks and the Internet. Modems modulate the digital signal from the PC into an analog signal that can be sent over the phone line. The modem also demodulates the analog signal received from the telephone network to a digital signal that can be understood by the computer.

Modems provide connection speeds up to 56kbps under ideal situations, but typical speeds are 33.6 to 44kbps. The 56kbps standard requires very clean connection (very little interference) and only one analog to digital conversion. Due to power regulations in the US, 53kbps is the maximum download speed with an upload speed of 33kbps.

A common misconception created by the use of modems is that the telephone network is analog given that the modem is converting the computer's digital signal to an analog signal. This is not the case. The analog signal sent over the copper wire from the customer premises to the telephone company is converted to a digital 64kbps signal.

This 64kbps signal is referred to as a DS0 that is then combined (multiplexed) with 23 other DS0s into a 1.54Mbps DS1. The DS1 is often referred to as a T1 or "trunk." The T1 is typically multiplexed with other traffic to be transported via a DS3/T3 (672 DS0s) or higher connection. Figure 12.1 shows how a connection between two modems would operate. Such a network was often used with electronic bulletin board systems in the 1980s and was the basis of worldwide store-and-forward type networks such as Fido. Modem to modem connections are seldom used except by system administrators; however, even this application of modem–to–modem communication is often a second choice to terminal servers. Terminal servers are covered later in this chapter in the "Terminal Servers" section.

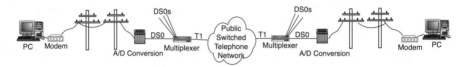

Figure 12.1   Modem connections through a telecommunications network.

The modulation used by the modem must match that of the far end and determines the speed of communication, typically represented in bits per second (bps). Table 12.1 lists some of the common speeds, the modulation standard, and where use of the modulation is likely. In the past, modulation protocols determined interoperability; however, wider support of protocols and improved protocol negotiation allows most modems to have a common protocol that can be used. Additionally, remote access servers, which are covered later, also support a wide base of modulation protocols and error correction protocols.

Table 12.1   **Common Modem Speeds, Standards Body, and Deployment Area**

Modem Speed	Standards Body	Deployment Area
300	Bell 103	US
	CCITT V.21	Outside the US
1200	Bell 212A	US
	CCITT V.22	Outside the US
	CCITT V.23	Europe
2400	CCITT V.22bis	International
9600	CCITT V.32	International

Modem Speed	Standards Body	Deployment Area
14400	CCITT V.32bis	International
28,800	CCITT V.34	International
33,600	CCITT V.34	International
56,000★	ITU V.90	International

★This is maximum download speed (and which is really limited to 53kbps). Upload is typically 33kbps.

Internal or External Modem

Internal modems are very popular for PC distributors; internals often cost 50% less than their external counterparts because the modem manufacturer does not have to provide housing for FCC shielding requirements (the PC cover does this) or a power supply (the PC provides the voltage). The major disadvantage of internal modems is their lack of lights, which can be used for troubleshooting. Additionally the modem cannot be easily transported between two PCs.

A relatively late entry to the internal modem market is the so-called WinModem. WinModems rely on the PC's internal CPU to provide most of the logic normally provided by the modem's hardware including error correction and flow control, which means WinModems typically impact system performance more than the regular internal modem. In addition, these modems can usually only be used on Windows operating systems, and we do not recommend their use. However, there is quit a bit of development effort going into the support of WinModems on Linux. For current development check the LinModem web site at `http://www.linmodems.org/`.

The WinModem is based on an earlier vendor's attempts at similar engineering; however, the more universal support of Windows will likely ensure some success of these modems.

Internal modems are available with the ISA 16-bit interface and PCI 32-bit interface. ISA modems are widely supported under Linux; whereas PCI (non-WinModems) depend on the modem used. The 2.4 kernel has wider support for PCI, but a posting to USENET is recommended before purchasing a PCI modem to determine the latest development.

External modems connect to the PC's serial port using a DB-25 or DB-9 connector. The DB-25 and DB-9 connectors are shown in Figure 12.2, and the pin outs of the modem's port are shown in Tables 12.2 and 12.3. Most modems use female connectors.

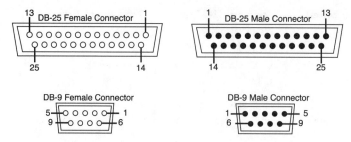

Figure 12.2 DB-25 and DB-9 connectors.

Table 12.2 **DB-25 Pin Outs**

Pin	Description
1	Protective Ground
2	Transmit Data (TD)
3	Receive Data (RD)
4	Request to Send (RTS)
5	Clear to Send (CTS)
6	Data Set Ready (DSR)
7	Signal Ground
8	Primary Carrier Detect (CD)
20	Data Terminal Ready (DR)
22	Ring Indicator (RI)

Table 12.3 **DB-9 Pin Outs**

Pin	Description
1	Carrier Detect (CD)
2	Receive Data (RD)
3	Transmit Data (TD)
5	Signal Ground
6	Data Set Ready (DSR)
7	Request to Send(RTS)
8	Clear to Send (CTS)

Whether the modem is internal or external, it will use a Universal Asynchronous Receiver-Transmitter (UART). In the past it was important to ensure that the serial card or the internal modem had a 16550 UART, which was an improvement on the earlier 8250 UART. The 16550 has a 16-byte buffer that allows 15 more bytes to be stored than the 8250. This allows smoother operation and a smoother experience in multitasking environments. Ensuring a 16550 is present is no longer as important as it was—serial card and modem manufacturers use the 16550 or a compatible UART as a minimum.

Hayes AT Commands

Communications software also must be in place to use the modem for communications with other systems. Early modem vendors included terminal software that could use a proprietary protocol to communicate with the vendor's software. Hayes Microcomputer created a command set where all commands started with the mnemonic AT and then the command for the modem. The Hayes command language became known as the *AT command set*, and many vendors emulated the command set creating the defacto standard *Hayes compatible*. Practically all modems on the market are now Hayes compatible.

AT commands are used for all communications with the modem and range in function from dial commands, to hardware flow control, to waiting on a dial tone before dialing. Special features of a modem also can be used without requiring modification of the AT command set through the use of registers, which are similar to variables in other languages, with the exception that the registers are stored in nonvolatile memory and are stored across modem resets.

Most communications software has preconfigured AT commands documented for optimal use; however, AT commands can be helpful in troubleshooting communications problems. Table 12.4 shows some of the more useful commands. Remember, all commands start with the AT before the command shown.

Table 12.4 **Common Hayes AT Commands**

Command	Meaning
A	Answer the incoming call.
D nnn-nnn-nnnn	Dial the telephone number *nnn-nnn-nnnn*. The D command takes additional parameters with P and T being the most common, which are used to dial using pulse or tones. DL is useful for dialing the last number again.
En	Echo to the terminal program where if $n=0$ then turn off local echo, and if $n=1$ turn on echo.
H	Hang up the current connection.
Xn	Extended error code handling. X3 is very useful for ignoring the requirement for dial tone, which might be the case if the modem is going through a private branch exchange (PBX).
Z	Reset the modem.

Terminal Communications Software

Networking applications have killed most users' needs for communications software; however, system administrators often need terminal software to connect to the console of PCs, modems, routers, and other network devices. Most distributions of Linux include the communications application, minicomm, which looks similar to an early DOS application by the name of Telix. However, there are many Linux communication packages available, with Seyon and pcomm being other favorites. The IBLIO Linux archive maintains a list of Linux communication programs at `http://www.ibiblio.org/pub/Linux/apps/serialcomm/`.

Other Uses of Analog Communications

The remaining portions of this chapter cover digital-based communications; however, we should point out some of the important roles that analog communications still provide. While the modem, as an individual piece of hardware, is not necessarily used in these applications, the technology present in modems is used in terminal servers and remote access servers.

Terminal Servers

Modem-to-modem connections are seldom used except by network administrators who require connections to remote systems that have dedicated modems for remote management. (Most remote connections from a modem are to a remote access server, which we cover shortly.)

However, even this modem-to-modem application is being phased out by terminal servers. A terminal server is a special-purpose remote access device that has multiple serial ports that can be terminated directly on systems to be remotely managed or even modems for dial connectivity. For example, the terminal server shown in Figure 12.3 can be used to access the Linux system, `righty`. This is ideal for situations where it is unclear if an outage is caused by a system or the network. In this particular case, the administrator has an "out-of-band" method of accessing righty and can telnet to the terminal server and then access `righty` via the serial connection. Should telnet to the terminal server not be possible due to a common network failure with the Linux server, the administrator can also dial in to the terminal server and then access the Linux server through the terminal server.

The major advantage of terminal servers over dedicated modems is consolidation of resources and a central point for security, which avoids back doors left by employees "forgetting" about modems connected to the network. Administration is also typically easier because the terminals server connection can make use of the console connection on most routers and a simple serial connection on UNIX hosts; this means no vendor-specific modem configuration requirements.

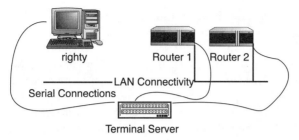

Figure 12.3   Terminal server.

Linux can act as a terminal server, but the typical two serial ports found on most PC hardware is inadequate, so a multi-serial card is required for most deployments. (The Linux Terminal Server Project [`http://www.ltsp.org/index.php`] should not be confused with a Linux based terminal server, this project covers using diskless Linux workstations.)

Remote Access Servers/Network Access Servers

Remote access servers, also known as *network access servers* as the name implies, provide remote users access to networks. The remote access is provided through dial-up connections such as asynchronous modems or ISDN. Figure 12.4 shows a typical corporate remote access server with one T1 providing 24 dial-in channels for access.

Remote access servers can provide analog, as well as integrated digital services network (ISDN) access, through the primary rate interface, which is discussed later.

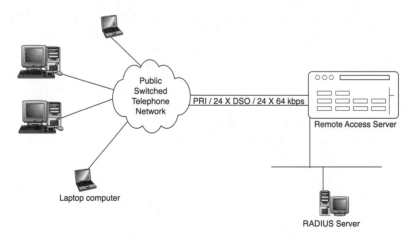

Figure 12.4   Corporate remote access server.

Remote access servers provide support for multiple protocols, with IP being a favorite, although IPX is also found in legacy Novell environments. Although the remote access server provides protocol, interface, and security policy, the remote access server does not typically store user-specific information locally, but rather the user specific-information such as authentication, packet filtering, and protocols available to the user, are determined through a remote access server protocol such as Remote Access Dial In User Service (RADIUS) as defined in RFC 2058. Linux makes an ideal RADIUS server. Table 12.5 lists some RADIUS servers that run on Linux.

Table 12.5 **RADIUS for Linux**

RADIUS Version	**Organization**	**Source**
Ascend RADIUS version 970224	Lucent	ftp://ftp.ascend.com/pub/Software-Releases/Radius
Cistron Radius Server version 1.6.4	Cistron Telecom	http://www.radius.cistron.nl/
Livingston Radius Server	Lucent	http://www.livingston.com:80/tech/docs/radius/ftp://ftp.livingston.com/pub/radius/

This section has covered traditional remote access, but the recent broadband offerings, such as cable modems and digital subscriber line (DSL), have opened new opportunities for personal and business users. Cable modems and DSL are covered in the next two sections.

Cable Modems

Cable television networks, outside of the public switched telephone network, are likely the most common networks used by home users. This marketing aspect combined with the infrastructure to create broadband cable networks is an excellent combination for data networking applications.

The cable modem is the hardware used to connect to the Internet through the cable provider's network. Traditional cable networks were uni-directional by nature, and data networking is bi-directional; however, cable providers have long needed the capability to transmit upstream information to provide additional services based upon conventional cable technology, such as pay-per-view. The bandwidth and technology designed to provide this upstream channel is what allows cable networks to provide an upstream data path. (The fact that the technology to pump data upstream is not always there in every cable system should not be considered trivial—many cable networks have required upgrades to provide cable network services.) Figure 12.5 shows a cable modem-based network.

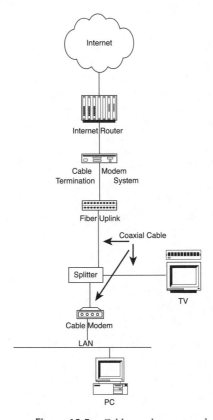

Figure 12.5   Cable modem network.

The cable modem has a LAN connector that is typically an RJ-45 10baseT connector and a "WAN" connector that is connected with a local splitter that feeds the cable modem and the cable–ready television or the set–top box for cable television. The splitter is responsible for feeding a 6Mhz downstream and 2Mhz upstream signal between the cable modem and the cable modem termination system (CMTS).

The cable 6Mhz downstream channel can provide up to 56Mbps. It should be noted that although there is a shared medium to the CMTS, the cable modems do not communicate with each other—traffic must first go through the CMTS. Also note that the CMTS does not provide IP routing capability. The 2Mhz upstream provides up to 3Mbps bandwidth.

Although cable modems use a shared bus, the bandwidth available, consumer acceptance of cable television, and (lack of) availability of other technologies such as DSL will ensure that cable modems are here to stay.

Digital Subscriber Line

DSL, unlike analog services, does not provide a digital to analog conversion, but rather acts as an interface to a digital signal that is carried on the same subscriber line that provides the analog line for the telephone. While digital communications to the customer premises is common for business customers, the "last mile" to private customers has traditionally been analog; however, this is now changing with DSL. Although Asymmetric DSL (ADSL) is the most widely deployed DSL, a brief overview of some of the more common service offerings of DSL is presented as well.

High Data-Rate Digital Subscriber Line (HDSL)

HDSL is a T1 (or E1 in Europe) replacement that allows the use of copper without the necessary repeaters of T1. HDSL supports distances up to 12,000 feet. (For T1, a repeater is normally needed every 6,000 feet.) HDSL uses four wires for transmissions.

HDSL-II

HDSL-II was the next generation of HDSL and offers the same speeds as HDSL but only requires one pair of wires. A single pair of lines requires fewer connections, and single pair wires are often pre-existing in many facilities.

Single-Line Digital Subscriber Line (SDSL)

SDSL, like HDSL and HDSL-II, operates at T1 speeds; however, it only uses one pair of wires. The use of two wires does limit the distances that SDSL can function with distances ranging from 10,000 to 11,000 feet.

Asymmetric Digital Subscriber Line (ADSL)

As the name implies, ADSL does not provide the same speed in both directions as HDSL and SDSL, but rather provides a higher downstream than upstream bandwidth, which makes it ideal for Internet access where the user is downloading much more information than is being uploaded. "Uploaded" data is often simply acknowledgements to the traffic being routed downstream.

As mentioned, ADSL is the most popular form of DSL and is typically used by home and small office users. Also when DSL is mentioned, most consumers are usually referring to ADSL.

ADSL provides bandwidth up to 8.44Mbps with a distance of up to 9,000 feet. Speed offerings, however, vary by service providers and are not uniformly deployed.

Figure 12.6 shows how ADSL is offered by most service providers. An examination of the various elements that make up an ADSL deployment are covered next.

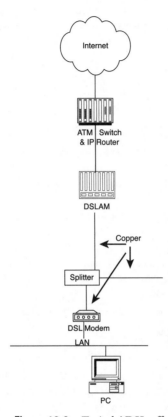

Figure 12.6 Typical ADSL offering.

The DSL Modem

The DSL modem is located at the subscriber's location—typically the residence—and is referred to as customer premises equipment (CPE) by telecommunications technicians. The DSL modem provides a LAN interface that provides a 10Mbps Ethernet connection and a WAN interface that is connected to the splitter, which has split the lower 4khz off to the telephone.

The Digital Subscriber Line Access Multiplexer (DSLAM)

The DSLAM multiplexes the signals from the various DSL subscribers onto the provider's network. Current generation of DSLAMs provide an Asynchronous Transfer Mode (ATM) interface to the service provider's network. Early implementations were typically frame relay interfaces (covered later). Some DSL proponents expect IP to become the interface of choice in next generation DSLAMS, but market reality and current deployments will likely encourage vendors to provide multiple interfaces and let the service provider choose.

Data Networking with Routers

Until the push of broadband technology in the last several years, the router was the most common hardware used to connect remote sites requiring multiple user support. Routers are known for their Layer 3 routing capability and multiple physical interface support.

This book covers routing with Linux in detail. However, much of the following covers interfaces that can be purchased for both Linux and hardware-based routers.

One of the major advantages of hardware routers over host-based solutions, such as Linux, is their simplicity and dedicated operating system. With a generic operating system, one of the other services can affect the routing functionality. For example the kernel might mistakenly have an unneeded, buggy, IPX stack compiled with the kernel. In addition, there is also the tendency to activate additional services because "the box can do it."

In addition many hardware routers, like Linux routers, provide security functionality such as packet filtering, network address translation, and additional networking functions such as acting as a frame relay access device in a frame relay network. On the high end, core routers also can process many more packets than a PC motherboard...the router's back plane is optimized to route packets quickly.

In addition, hardware routers will typically support a wider range of network interfaces, as was covered earlier.

For these reasons, interaction with routers is likely in most environments...at a minimum the Internet access router provided by the ISP is likely to be a hardware router. Therefore we'll cover some of the more likely facilities used in enterprise networks.

T1 and E1

As covered in the modem section, the T1 is the 1.54Mbps digital facility that is the standard for voice networks. Its proven technology confirmed its effectiveness in customer premises and has become the standard for narrowband digital communications only likely to be offset by the current broadband technologies. HDSL is the natural replacement and is being marketed as the T1 replacement for business connectivity in some markets.

The T1, a 1.544Mbps link, is made of up 24 64kbps channels referred to as DS0s.

Due to the expense of T1s, U.S. telcos offered a fractional T1 service based upon n X DS0s, and it proved itself very popular for Internet connections and networks requiring point-to-point connections. A T1 or fractional T1 is referred to as a leased line or nailed connection because no dialing or signaling must take place—the connection is always on.

The E1 is the European (and other parts of the world) digital facility that operates at 2.048Mbps. It offers 32 channels of DS0s.

To make use of a T1, the two routers communicating must use the same protocol to communicate. Point-to-Point Protocol (PPP) (covered in Chapter 10, "Planning Router Layout and Function") is a favorite and offers very good interoperability; however, there is some interoperability with HDLC protocol, and if the same types of routers are used, the vendor specific HDLC can be used.

When more than the bandwidth of a T1 or E1 is needed, the next facility available is a DS3, which offers 44.736Mbps. An E3 has 34.368Mbps and is generally not available to customer premises. The expense and exponential increase cannot be justified by most network upgrades; therefore, multiple T1 connections are chosen.

When multiple connections to the same site are used, a protocol that allows the two links to be treated as one must be used. Some routers allow the connections to use load balancing over the connection, which means that each frame that arrives is sent over the connection where the last frame was not sent (as shown in Figure 12.7).

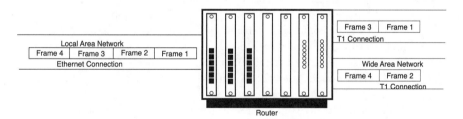

Figure 12.7 Load balancing.

PPP Multilink protocol as defined in RFC 1717 can also be used to combine multiple connections into one logical connection and has the added advantage of increased interoperability likelihood.

Integrated Services Digital Network

ISDN was the first effort to provide digital services to customer premises and the predecessor to ADSL. ISDN provides two interfaces—the basic rate interface (BRI) and the primary rate interface (PRI).

The BRI provides two channels of 64kbps for payload and a signaling channel of 16kbps. The two payload, or bearer channels, are referred to as *B channels*, and the signaling channel is referred to as the *D channel*.

The PRI provides 24 channels for T1 (32 for E1). The most popular use of the PRI is private branch exchanges (PBX), or enterprise telephone switches, which provides such features as voice mail and speed dial. PRI is also very popular for remote access services. The BRI interface has enjoyed widespread use in Europe but has not been widely deployed, especially for voice use, in the United States.

ISDN Uses

The BRI does have some interesting applications for data networking, such as dial–on–demand networks, bandwidth on demand, and dial backup.

Because ISDN is digital, the signaling required to connect is, unlike a modem, very quick. This fact, combined with a total bandwidth of 128kbps for the payload provide network designers additional flexibility in network design.

Dial-on-demand networking avoids the use of a leased line and is transparent to the user or application. By connecting two sites with ISDN, one or both B channels can be dialed when traffic is detected for the remote side, and the channels can be torn down after a certain amount of inactivity. ISDN and dial-on-demand networking is popular in areas where fractional T1 services are not available (mostly Europe) or where the costs of the ISDN are cheaper than a fractional T1. Most service providers bill ISDN based upon usage, so the application is limited in many cases.

ISDN can also be used to create additional bandwidth during peak utilization. For example, a router can be configured to bring up a channel after utilization reaches 98% and should bring the channel back down after it goes back below 95%. The "master" channel can be a leased facility or an ISDN channel.

Probably the most popular use of ISDN in North America is dial backup. The router will use an ISDN connection to connect to the remote site when a network failure is determined. The network failure can be determined based upon a loss of signal on the leased line or by a network event, such as a network routing update announcing the route unavailable.

Frame Relay

The major disadvantage of leased lines for data communications is the requirement for an interface for each leased line. Consider the network shown in Figure 12.8. There is a central site with four remote sites. With leased lines being used, the central router requires four physical interfaces to be used to network the four remote sites. Additionally, each remote site must route traffic through the central site to communicate with another remote site, or an additional leased line must be activated between the two remote sites. This means that for a 4 node network, 10 connections are required to fully mesh the network.

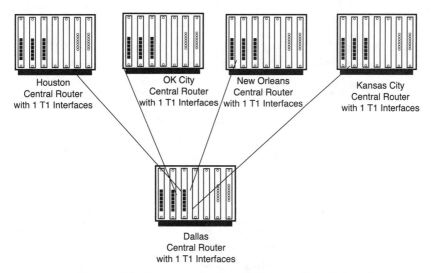

Figure 12.8 Remote networks with Point-to-Point links.

Because leased lines are very expensive and become more expensive as the distance increases, a network technology that allows a more scaleable architecture is needed for building wide area networks. *Frame Relay* is such a networking topology.

Frame Relay networks are Layer 2 networks provided by service providers that allow enterprises to build scaleable WANs without requiring a physical interface per connection or leased lines dedicated to individual sites.

Figure 12.9 shows a typical Frame Relay network as seen by the enterprise customer. It should be noted that the Frame Relay network might or might not provide a complete meshing among the remote sites; typically the customer will have to pay a higher service fee for the full meshing. Should the remote sites not be meshed, traffic will be routed through the central site for Layer 3 routing. Note that the central site in Dallas requires only one T1 interface for connectivity.

Figure 12.10 provides a closer look at Frame Relay as seen by the service provider. The Frame Relay switch (FR switch) provides the actual interfaces to the network. Although the Frame Relay network is a private network for the customer, the FR switch is actually a shared resource providing access to many customers in each of the cities where the service provider has a Frame Relay point of presence (POP).

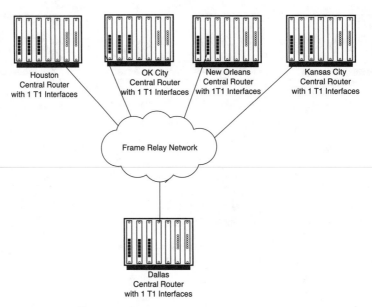

Figure 12.9   Typical Frame Relay network.

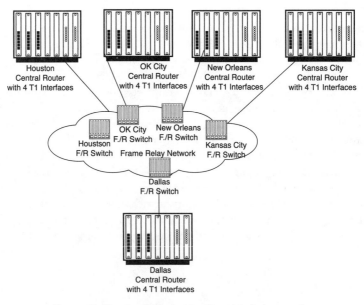

Figure 12.10   Service provider Frame Relay network.

There has not been much Frame Relay development for Linux; however, it is important to know that the technology exists and plays a very important role in many WAN environments. Frame Relay should be considered anytime where multiple site connectivity is needed.

Summary

In this chapter we have examined telecommunication facilities upon which data networks are built. Analog, digital (T1/E1), DSL, cable, and Frame Relay have been covered.

13

Building a Routing Kernel

O<small>NE OF THE MAIN SELLING POINTS</small> of the GNU/Linux operating system is the ability to recompile the Linux kernel on demand. The ability to add needed functionality or to strip out unneeded bits was one of the key reasons that Linux has been so widely adopted. System administrators, software vendors, and power users have flexibility with Linux that they do not have with proprietary operating systems or hardware routing appliances.

Why Build?

If you obtain one of the typical Linux distributions, the odds are that you'll have the ability to enable some routing functions without having to recompile. If routing is just one of the tasks for which you'll be using Linux, using a pre-compiled kernel might be the best way to go. However, if you're going to be doing routing only, you'll also be saddled with many functions that increase the size of the kernel with functions that you don't need—and don't want—in a system dedicated only to routing functions.

For instance, most precompiled kernels come with support for sound, CSLIP, Point-to-Point Protocol (PPP), RAID controllers, and other protocols and devices that you won't need. (Very few routers have need of a sound card, for example.)

In this chapter, we'll look at customizing the Linux kernel for use in routers and some of the specialized Linux distributions created especially for routing.

You might wonder if it's worth the trouble to recompile the Linux kernel if it already has the functionality that you need. The answer is, almost always, yes. Most commercial Linux distributions have kernels that are pretty much one-size-fits-all. They throw in the kitchen sink because that's the best way to make sure that most users will be able to install Linux and get it running right away. This approach is great for getting the system installed quickly but leaves something to be desired in terms of optimization and security.

Even the specialized routing distributions that we'll look at later in the chapter will eventually need to have the kernel patched for upgrades or security updates. The great thing is that Linux, unlike proprietary operating systems (OSs) used in Cisco or other routing hardware, can be modified easily to suit your needs.

Upgrades and Flexibility

To be fair, Cisco routers and other routing appliances usually can be upgraded if a security hole is found or if they have a bug of some kind. However, they do not allow the kind of flexibility and the same level of customization that Linux enjoys. A Linux router is typically capable of more functions than a traditional router—and at a lower cost.

Smaller and Faster

The most obvious benefit of tailoring the kernel to meet your needs and only your needs is that you'll have a kernel that takes up less memory and has better performance.

Admittedly, this is less of a concern today than it was a few years ago—with standard Intel-based hardware reaching speeds of 1.5GHz on a single-processor machine and RAM being priced under $1.00 a megabyte. In some cases, admins are able to buy just a new whitebox computer and set it up as a Linux router without worrying about cost. However, Linux routers are often refurbished computers from the company "boneyard" that don't have the muscle of newer computers. That's okay; you can save your hardware budget for something else and get a few more years of use from that old Pentium "classic" that's been gathering dust.

The Linux kernel isn't the only place to put a standard distro on a diet, however. Presuming you're installing a system from scratch, you'll want to install the bare minimum number of packages and be careful not to include unnecessary software.

Specialized Functionality

The "stock" kernel compiled for most distributions won't include options such as the Netlink socket or Reverse ARP, but it's likely you'll want to use these on your Linux router. The only way to get from there to here, then, is to recompile the kernel with support for these features. (While you're at it, it's a good time to strip out unnecessary features and support for unused devices.) This is probably the most common reason, along with upgrades and security fixes, that folks compile their own kernel.

You'll almost certainly need to recompile the kernel if you want to enable the IPv6 protocols (or if you want to support bridging, the X.25 packet layer or any lesser-used protocols). Again, Linux's support for these protocols really shows the strength of an open operating system. Generally, commercial entities such as Microsoft, Sun, or Novell simply decide what protocols they're going to support, and that's it. The most common options will be supported, and any customers using "exotic" or legacy systems are going to be left out in the cold.

On the other hand, Linus or other kernel developers might not decide to support protocol X, but that doesn't stop anyone else from developing a patch or module to support their protocols and submitting it to the kernel team.

Specialized Hardware

Generally, the kernel is compiled to support the most common hardware. If you have special controller cards or devices that are supported by the Linux kernel but are exotic or rare enough not to be included in the default kernel, you'll need to be able to recompile the kernel to support those devices.

Another situation that's fairly common is adding the latest patch or "experimental" code to the kernel to support a relatively new device or one that hasn't yet been judged stable. For instance in the 2.4.3 Linux kernel, several of the Netfilter and IP Tables modules are still considered experimental, but many users might want to test and possibly deploy this code rather than waiting for it to become "stable."

Wide area network (WAN) router cards are good examples of "specialized" hardware. The average user won't need a WAN router on their workstation or web server, but Linux does support a number of these cards and the ability to perform WAN routing over X.25 or frame relay.

When planning out your router, be certain to make sure that the hardware you want to use is supported under Linux. Hardware support under Linux isn't always guaranteed, though networking hardware—particularly high-end hardware—often does have support. If you're unsure, do a Google search on the Internet with the name of the product and "Linux." Ninety-eight times out of a hundred, this will return useful results from one of the various Linux mailing lists. You also might try the mailing list archives for your Linux distribution or post a message to that list if all else fails. (Unless you like wearing asbestos skivvies, always do your searching before posting to a mailing list. It's not only good Netiquette, it'll keep you from getting flamed by folks who have seen the same question asked 30 times in the same week.)

Security and Bug Fixes

If you have no special case hardware to consider and the added performance of a tweaked kernel doesn't strike you as enough of a reason to learn to "roll your own," then you might want to consider security and bug fixes as reasons to learn how to patch and recompile the kernel.

Regardless of when the distribution you're using was put together, the odds are that there have been bug fixes and security patches released for it. The kernel development team might not speed between major releases, but the minor releases come out at fairly regular intervals. These point releases frequently have important security and bug fixes. Even if your kernel is the latest release when you set up the router, the odds are there will be newer version with a crucial bug fix or security patch released within six months.

In addition, depending on your level of paranoia, you might want to disable loadable kernel modules. This prevents an intruder who has gained access to your system from loading a kernel module that would help them cover their tracks or perform other unwanted activities. Granted, if someone has cracked your router and gained root access, you have problems either way. However, limiting the potential damage is one of the hallmarks of system security. This also prevents a cracker from unloading any kernel security features because they've been compiled as part of the kernel rather than as modules.

Additional Security

If you're going to go to the length of compiling a static kernel, be sure to remove the kernel source and configuration files so that crackers can't guess what you've already compiled if they do get access to your system.

Building the Linux Kernel

Now that we've covered the "Whys," it's time to roll up our sleeves and actually compile a kernel. If you haven't done this before, it's best to do it on a test machine or make a backup of your old kernel just in case. If you use LILO to boot your Linux machine, make a copy of the Linux kernel before compiling a new kernel and make a new entry in your /etc/lilo.conf for the old kernel. It should look something like this:

```
root=/dev/hda2
boot=/dev/hda
install=/boot/boot.b
map=/boot/map
vga=normal
timeout=300
prompt
default=Linux
lba32

image=/vmlinuz
        label=Linux
        read-only
        initrd=/boot/root.bin
        root=/dev/hda2
```

```
image=/vmlinuz.old
        label=Old_Kernel
        read-only
        optional
        root=/dev/hda2
```

Then simply run `lilo` and you'll have a working kernel to fall back on should you make a mistake while compiling the new one.

At the time of this writing, the current version of the Linux kernel is 2.4.3, but most Linux users are still using the 2.2.x kernel series for production machines. While the 2.4.x kernel series has a number of new features and improvements to old features, it will be some time before the 2.4.x kernels become the norm. Of the commercial Linux distributions, only SuSE, Red Hat, and Linux-Mandrake have put out distributions with a 2.4 kernel, and they all feature 2.2 kernels as an option.

In this section we'll walk through obtaining the Linux kernel source and compiling the 2.4.x kernel using the `Menuconfig` tool. While some of the options differ between the 2.2.x and 2.4.x kernels, the process is the same. It might sound intimidating if you've never done it before, but it's actually fairly simple.

The 2.0.x Linux Kernel Series

The final release in the 2.0.x series was released in February 2001 at version 2.0.39. For those who don't follow kernel development, it's customary for the last stable version of the kernel to be maintained while development of the current kernel continues. While many Linux users are enthusiastic about using cutting edge technology, just as many admins are hesitant to make drastic changes in production machines and usually wait for a compelling reason to upgrade.

If you have any routers or systems currently running the 2.0.x series of kernels, it would be a good idea to upgrade to the 2.2.x series if at all possible.

Choosing the Kernel

If you're not locked into the 2.2.x or 2.4.x series, you'll need to decide which series you want to build your router around. Obviously, the 2.2.x series has been more thoroughly tested and is more mature. On the other hand, the 2.4.x series has a slew of performance increases and new features that might be attractive. If you're not reading the book sequentially, you might want to go back and review the chapters that focus on the kernel daemons and Chapter 14, "Security and NAT Issues," which covers the routing "basics" of 2.2 and 2.4.

All things being equal, it probably makes more sense to put time and effort into the latest kernel series. While the 2.4 kernel isn't quite as mature as the 2.2 series, it will enjoy the most concentrated development efforts in the future and already has significant performance increases and more advanced networking features.

Finally, there's no harm trying both kernels if you're unsure. It is free software, after all. If possible, take a few days just to experiment with setting up your router and testing different configurations.

Upgrading from 2.2.x to 2.4.x

Upgrading from the 2.2.x series to the 2.4.x series isn't that difficult, but there is a little prep-work you'll need to do before actually compiling the kernel. There are a few support programs and libraries that will need to be upgraded to the latest version. The latest requirements can be found in the file, /usr/src/linux/Documentation/Changes. You will probably need to upgrade GNU C, GNU Make, binutils, modutils, and e2fsprogs at the very minimum—unless you've been keeping up with the latest versions already.

Obtaining the Source

The first thing to do is to get the source code for the Linux kernel. Most distributions include the most recent source code to the kernel at the time that the distribution was packaged for sale, but that's probably a few versions behind by the time that it lands on your hard drive.

To get the most up-to-date kernel source for either kernel series, go to the Linux Kernel Archives at http://www.kernel.org/. The Kernel Archives have an extensive mirror system, which will likely be faster than grabbing the source from the main archive itself. It's probably best to find the mirror closest to you and bookmark it for later use. Compiling your own kernel is addictive, so you'll want to visit often.

The kernel source is available in gzip or bzip2 format. The bzip2 format shaves several megabytes off of the size of the archive, but not every distribution comes with bzip2 tools by default. It might be worthwhile to grab the bzip2 utilities, though, because some projects offer only bzip2-compressed files. The Netfilter project, for instance, only offers their user-space tools as a bzipped archive.

Getting Bzip2

Bzip2 is faster and generally delivers better compression than GNU Gzip. Because you'll probably need it for uncompressing various projects anyway, you should give it a whirl. The Bzip2 Homepage and source code can be found at http://sources.redhat.com/bzip2/.

After you've downloaded the kernel source, copy it to /usr/src/. You will need to be logged in as the root user to do this and to compile and install the kernel. Before you uncompress the kernel source, run an ls -l in the /usr/src/ directory to see if there's a linux directory or symlink there already. Delete the symlink or directory and then execute tar -zxvf linux-2.x.x.tar.gz to uncompress a tarred and gzipped file. If you downloaded the bzipped kernel source, run bzip2 -d linux-2.x.x.tar.bz2 and tar -xvf linux-2.x.x.tar.

After the source is uncompressed, cd to the linux directory. To make sure that everything is set up correctly, run the make mrproper command:

```
$ cd linux
$ make mrproper
```

And then everything should be configured correctly for the next few steps.

Now comes the fun part, choosing the components of your custom kernel. You have the option of running `make config`, `make menuconfig` or `make xconfig`. Running `make config` will run through all of the possible kernel options one at a time and prompt for a choice of Yes, No, or (sometimes) Module. This can be long and tedious because you'll be prompted for just about every kernel configuration option without being able to switch between questions.

The `make menuconfig` option will bring up an `ncurses`-based menu system at the console that will enable you to configure the various kernel options. If you're running X on this machine, you can use the `make xconfig`, which will bring up a `Tcl/Tk`-based menu interface. Most of the time, the `make menuconfig` is the best way to go given that most Linux routers won't have XFree86 installed.

Before you get to this step, be sure that you know what hardware you need to support. Having all the routing options you need without support for your Ethernet cards or WAN cards wouldn't be very useful! One of the ways to find out what hardware is in your computer without cracking open the case is to `cat` the special files residing in `/proc`. For instance, `cat /proc/pci | less` will give you output containing the name of all of your PCI devices. Running `cat /proc/dma` will show you any Industry Standard Architecture (ISA) devices—if you're still using those. Information about your SCSI devices can be found by running `cat /proc/scsi` and so on.

Here's a snippet of the output from `cat /proc/pci`. As you can see, this machine has an Ethernet card using a LiteOn chip.

```
PCI devices found:
  Bus  0, device  13, function  0:
    Ethernet controller: LiteOn LNE100TX (rev 32).
      Medium devsel.  Fast back-to-back capable.  IRQ 9.  Master Capable.
Latency=32.
      I/O at 0x8800 [0x8801].
      Non-prefetchable 32 bit memory at 0xdd800000 [0xdd800000].
```

If you installed a distribution that does hardware detection for you, it will likely have detected all of your Ethernet cards and such. In that case, you can run `lsmod` and see which kernel modules are already loaded. Armed with that knowledge you should be able to figure out which Ethernet cards and other devices you should compile into the kernel, or as modules.

Keep Extra Cards Handy

By the way, it's probably a good practice to compile support for the most common Ethernet cards or to make sure that you have a stock of extra cards of the same make handy. Ethernet cards are known to go dead from time to time, and it's a lot faster to be able to simply power down the machine and swap a working card into the machine than it is to recompile the kernel to support a new Ethernet card. If you use other specialized WAN cards or whatnot, it's a very good idea to have a spare around in case of emergencies. The cost of duplicate hardware is nowhere near as hard on the budget as a day or two of unplanned downtime due to hardware failure.

Configuring Your Kernel

When configuring your kernel, the number of options might seem overwhelming at first. However, for a routing machine there is a fairly small subset of functions and devices that you'll need to worry about; the rest can safely be disabled. For instance, you're almost certainly not going to need support for telephony or Ham radio in a routing machine.

In this section we'll cover the options that you will want to deal with. We're looking specifically at the 2.4 kernel, but most of these options do apply to the 2.2.x kernel series as well.

By the way, it's worth noting that there might be additional hardware support or functionality in the kernel by the time that you read this. We aren't aware of any planned additions for the kernel at the time of this writing, but that's not to say that it's unlikely.

Code Maturity Level Options

Several of the new networking functions in the Linux kernel are still considered "experimental." Selecting the Prompt for Development and/or Incomplete Code/Drivers option will simply give you the option of selecting these options when configuring the rest of the kernel. Selecting this option, in and of itself, won't add any "experimental" code to your kernel, make it unstable in any way, or increase the size of the compiled kernel. It's probably a good idea to say yes to this option.

Processor Type and Features

This option is mostly specific to Intel-based hardware. You can choose the type of processor that you're using in your router to optimize the kernel for that machine. Note that if you compile a kernel for a specific processor, such as the "PPro/6x86MX Processor Family," it might not boot on other processors. If you choose this option, you might wish to compile a "generic" kernel with the same options in case you have to swap motherboards and processors in the machine at a later date.

If the routing machine is a dual-processor, you also will want to enable symmetric multi-processing (SMP) support in the kernel.

The Math emulation and MTRR (Memory Type Range Register) support shouldn't be necessary for a routing machine. Any recent CPU (486 and up) will already have a math co-processor and won't require math emulation.

Loadable Module Support

As the name implies, selecting this option will allow you to compile module support into the kernel. Naturally, this option is one of the kernel options not available as a module, for obvious reasons.

More than likely you'll want to enable this option. The Set Version Information on all module symbols will allow you to use modules compiled previously. For instance, if you compile kernel version 2.4.3 and then later compile 2.4.4, you will still be able to use the modules that worked with the previous kernel. You will definitely need to enable this option if you use modules compiled from non-kernel sources.

The Kernel Module Loader allows the kernel to `autoload` modules if they're available. If you'll be using `iptables`, you will want to enable this option.

General Setup

This menu item includes Networking support, which must be enabled. For the most part, you can accept the default selections in this section of the kernel configuration.

Networking Options

There is a dizzying array of choices in this section of the kernel configuration. Depending on the network you'll be working with, and the functions the router will handle, you might want to enable IPX, Appletalk, or other networking protocols. This is the section of the kernel that contains all of the possible routing functions that Linux handles. The experimental protocols or functions are clearly marked, but you might wish to try them if you need the functionality.

The `Packet socket` option allows userspace programs such as `tcpdump` to work. You'll probably want to enable this option. You will definitely want to enable TCP/IP networking and IP: advanced routing options.

You also will be able to select advanced routing functions, tunneling, and other networking options in this section.

Network Device Support

The hardware for networking is broken out from the network protocols and functions in its own section. Unless you have exotic hardware, it's likely you'll be able to find support for your Ethernet or other devices here. Again, be sure to purchase any hardware with an eye towards support under Linux.

Compiling the Kernel

After you've finished choosing the options for your kernel, you will run the `make dep` command to ensure that you'll be able to build the kernel properly. Unless `make dep` exits with an error, after it finishes you will want to run `make bzImage` followed by `make modules` and `make modules_install`.

After the kernel has been compiled, you can copy it from `/usr/src/linux/arch/i386/boot/bzImage` to `vmlinuz` or `/boot/vmlinuz`, depending on where your distribution places kernel images. Typically it is under `/boot/vmlinuz`, but Slackware and several other distributions have the kernel image residing in `/vmlinuz`. This is the standard naming convention, but you can call the kernel anything you want, so long as the entry in `/etc/lilo.conf` corresponds with the name of the kernel. If it makes you happier to call the kernel "Bob," feel free.

After you've copied the kernel over, run `lilo`. To try out your new kernel you'll need to reboot the machine. Again, be sure you've got a backup kernel, just in case. Congratulations, you now have a custom Linux kernel!

Special Function Distributions

In addition to the many general-purpose distributions such as Red Hat, Slackware, SuSE, or Debian GNU/Linux, there are hundreds of special purpose Linux distributions.

Some distributions, such as EnGarde Linux or Immunix, focus on security, while others focus on smaller, special needs such as Beowulf clusters or "real time" scheduling. Of particular interest when setting up a router are the Linux routing distributions that take advantage of Linux's networking strengths and add simplified configuration options.

In this section we've highlighted a few of the distributions that are designed especially to power routers. This is by no means a comprehensive list; it's simply a look at some of the most popular routing distributions.

Herding Cats

It might be impossible to provide a complete and comprehensive listing of all Linux distributions—or even all of the distros that focus on one particular task.

There are probably at least a hundred general-purpose and special-purpose English-language distributions floating around right now, enjoying varying degrees of popularity. It's really difficult to guess how many available distros there are in all languages.

Linux Router Project

The Linux Router Project is, not surprisingly, a project to create a Linux distribution specifically for routing.

The project has yielded a Linux distribution that fits on a single floppy, which they refer to as a "micro-distribution." It's pretty amazing how much they've been able to fit on one standard 1.44MB floppy disk. While it comes in a tiny package, the LRP packs quite a punch. According to the Linux Router Project's web site, the LRP (Linux Router Project) distro can be used to make anything from a simple Linux router to a Router/Switch, T1 Bridge, secondary DNS server, and WAN router.

Currently the LRP comes with support for the 2.0 and 2.2 kernels. There are also additional packages that can be downloaded for the Linux Router Project distro that take it beyond a single floppy, such as Perl, Python, BIND, and Wanpipe. In addition, a number of other custom distributions have used the LRP as a starting point and created their own routing or networking distro.

If you want to try a micro-distribution to build your Linux Router, you might want to start with the Linux Router Project. The Project's homepage is at `http://www.linuxrouter.org`.

Zipslack

The ZipSlack distribution, as the name suggests, is based on Slackware Linux and fits on an Iomega Zip disk. Actually, it will fit onto any FAT or FAT32 partition with 100MB of space or more, but it's most popular for systems that have bootable Zip drives.

ZipSlack is primarily aimed at users who want to try Linux but don't want to repartition their drives. However, for networks with modest needs, a PC with a Pentium or better processor, 32MB of RAM, and a Zip drive can make an excellent router and firewall using ZipSlack.

The ZipSlack distribution can be found on the Slackware Linux homepage at `http://www.slackware.com/`.

Embedded Linux

One of the most important computing markets in the near future is going to be the embedded market. This encompasses everything from PDAs, such as the Palm Pilot, to the embedded computing functions in devices such as cars, refrigerators, stereos, set-top boxes for TVs, and a plethora of other devices. Linux was virtually unheard from in the commercial embedded market in 1999 but snared a major portion of the embedded device market in 2000.

Routers, of course, have traditionally been embedded appliances. Linux has opened the door to using traditional PC hardware as a router and is making inroads into the routing appliance market as well.

It isn't just routers, though. Linux is being developed for PDAs, networked cameras that have their own web servers, Network Attached Storage (NAS) devices, and much more. IBM has even developed a watch that runs Linux! It's not as stylish as a Rolex, but it certainly does a lot more.

What is Embedded Linux?

Embedded Linux is a fairly broad term used to describe quite a gamut of Linux solutions. Basically, so-called embedded devices are usually hardware that requires an operating system that is "embedded" on a ROM chip. Unlike PCs, servers, and work-stations, these devices are not easily modified and are designed to handle a limited range of functionality.

Proprietary operating systems, like those produced by Wind River or Cisco, held sway in these devices for a long time. However, some companies looked around for a more flexible and open solutions and found that Linux was just the ticket.

Non-Intel Hardware

One of the reasons Linus Torvalds started developing Linux was to learn about the Intel 386 processor. Originally, no thought was given to the portability of the code or the possibility that Linux might someday run on anything other than the 386.

The majority of folks who run Linux on workstations or servers still use Linux on Intel-based hardware, the original platform that Linux was ported to. However, Linux now runs on the PowerPC, Alpha, SPARC and UltraSPARC, PA-RISC, StrongARM, MIPS, and a number of other processors.

Linux now scales from handheld computers to 64-bit multiprocessor machines. As mentioned previously, IBM has even developed a wristwatch that runs Linux!

Network Processors

One of the recent additions to the networking hardware world is the network processor. Basically, a network processor is like any other CPU, but it's optimized for networking functions. In the past a company such as Cisco would develop its own proprietary processor to use in its routers. Unlike Intel's x86 line, companies didn't have a generic all-purpose processor for network devices like PC manufacturers do.

Any company that wanted to make a router product would have a double-whammy against it trying to enter the market. It would have to either license or develop its own operating system for the router, and it would have to develop its own processor for the machines as well. As you might imagine, this created a rather high barrier of entry into the market, which is one of the reasons Cisco has done so well.

Now companies such as Intel, Motorola, IBM, and Lucent have started manufacturing "generic" CPUs optimized for networking. This means that start-ups or existing companies that want to enter the network device market can purchase "off-the-shelf" processors from one of these companies without the development costs of creating their own.

This has become particularly attractive now that a Free Software operating system with a robust networking stack is available. Companies have at their fingertips the opportunity to enter the lucrative network device market with a much lower cost of entry, and many are already introducing Linux-based network devices for firewalling, routeing, and many other tasks.

Lineo SecureEdge

Lineo, Inc. was originally a division of Caldera Systems, a company that was formed by ex-Novell employees to offer Linux-based solutions.

Lineo is now a company that focuses on embedded systems, real-time OSs, and high availability solutions. They offer several Linux-based solutions, including the Embeddix and uClinux distributions.

The SecureEdge is a customizable network product that utilizes the uClinux distribution and can be configured to use as a router, firewall or even a full-blown web server. This device is just one example of what Embedded Linux can be used for in a commercial setting.

Hard Hat Linux

MontaVista software offers a number of products based around their Hard Hat Linux distribution. Hard Hat Linux is an embedded distribution that runs on a number of processor architectures, including Intel's network processor.

The Hard Hat distribution has been customized with support for Java, Flash file systems, and has a Real Time kernel for applications that require real-time support.

Hard Hat Linux also runs on standard x86 computers, which makes it easier for developers to work on solutions that will eventually be ported to embedded devices.

uClinux

The uClinux distribution is specially designed to work on processors without a Memory Management Unit (MMU). This distribution is derived from the 2.0.x kernel series, and the kernel and tools can fit in less than 900KB of memory. Lineo makes some devices for uClinux, and it runs on a wide range of processors such as the Motorola Dragonball, ETRAX, Intel i960, and several others. The distribution has also been ported to the Cisco 2500, 3000, and 4000 router series.

If you're interested in this distribution, you can visit the uClinux project's homepage at `http://www.uclinux.org/`.

Summary

In this chapter we've looked at how to compile the Linux kernel and customize it to remove unneeded functionality for use as a dedicated routing machine.

We've also looked at some of the existing single-purpose Linux distributions developed for routing and networking, both commercial and non-commercial.

Configuring Linux for a router can be as simple as compiling the kernel. Companies looking to develop a commercial routing solution or a routing system for internal deployment can go so far as to create their own distribution using Linux and other Free Software.

14

Security and NAT Issues

IN THIS CHAPTER WE'LL TAKE A BRIEF look at the security issues involved in configuring your own Linux router and how you can use your router to improve your overall network security. This is a pretty big topic, so this chapter will mainly serve as an overview rather than an in-depth study. Some of the concepts in this chapter will go a bit beyond routing, including some basics of creating a firewall with `ipchains` and Netfilter.

One of the pluses of using Linux for your router is that you're also able to enable other networking features you might not typically find in routers. However, that does tend to make the topic of Linux routers just a bit more complicated. In this chapter we'll touch on several topics that could take an entire book to explain. We'll try to give a complete overview without straying too far from the topic at hand. If you need to set up a particularly complicated and comprehensive firewall, for instance, you might want to look into one of the books on Linux firewalls.

It goes without saying that things change pretty quickly in the world of computer security. While we'll attempt to lay down some guidelines in this chapter that will help you to be security-conscious, your router is just one component of your network's security. New attacks are found every day, and patches are usually created just as quickly.

Whatever distribution of Linux you decide to use for your router, be sure that distribution does a good job of announcing security issues and dealing with them. For instance, most Linux distributions maintain a security announcement mailing list, with a web-based archive of security announcements. Whenever a security hole is found, they'll send an announcement with instructions on how to fix the issue (usually with a newer version of the package) or how to minimize exposure if the package has no fix available.

If your router is a single-purpose machine with the bare minimum of services turned on, your exposure is already limited. You also might want to install the Linux Intrusion Detection System (LIDS) or another intrusion detection system just in case and perform a full security audit of your router at least once a month—even if there have been no security announcements and everything seems to be okay.

It also goes without saying that remote management of your router should only be done using encrypted communications, such as Secure Shell (SSH). Transmitting passwords and usernames over Telnet is a very bad idea indeed.

SSH Vulnerabilities

It has recently come to light that even some implementations of the SSH protocol aren't completely immune to packet sniffing. It was long believed that even if SSH-encrypted communications were sniffed, the encryption would prevent a would-be attacker from getting any useful information from the sniffed packets.

Both SSH-1 and SSH-2 might disclose password and username length and possibly the length of shell commands or the actual names of commands used. While it is extremely unlikely that a cracker would be able to get the actual password from a session, it makes using a brute-force password cracking program easier because the attacker would have the actual length of the password.

The OpenSSH implementation of SSH, probably the most popular in the Linux community, addressed this vulnerability with the 2.5.2 release. If you're using a release older that 2.5.2, you should upgrade immediately.

Packet Filtering and Packet Mangling with Your Router

In addition to using your Linux box to perform routing tasks, you might want to set it up to do some other kinds of packet filtering. There are two packages that we'll take a look at in this section: the `ipchains` package and Netfilter/`iptables`.

The `ipchains` package is a little more limited than Netfilter/`iptables`, but if you're using the 2.2.x series of the kernel, then you're limited to `ipchains`—at least until someone backports them to 2.2.x. If you're already well-versed in writing rules for `ipchains` but want to upgrade to the 2.4.x series, you'll be happy to know that there is an `ipchains` compatibility module for 2.4.x.

What is Packet Filtering?

As you're already aware, all this networking and routing stuff relies on information being broken down and transmitted as packets and then reassembled when it reaches its destination.

Different protocols, such as HTTP, FTP, SSH, Telnet, and so on, each have distinctive packet headers so that the client and server computers (or peer computers with programs like Napster) are able to distinguish the purpose of the packets and handle them correctly.

It's also possible for individuals with malicious intentions to attempt to "spoof" packets in some way or to attempt to sniff packets and piece together information from those packets that might enable the cracker to successfully attack a computer. Crackers also might attempt to perform a Denial of Service (DoS) attack or Distributed Denial of Service (DDoS) attack by overloading the computer with certain types of packets or by sending packets that can confuse the target computer.

Packet filtering, then, is the act of examining the packets that pass through a computer and then deciding how to handle them based on things such as protocol, port, source, and/or destination IP address, and possibly examining headers of packets to ensure that they're not packet fragments or harmful in some other way.

With packet filtering it's possible to deny incoming or outgoing (or both) connections of certain types by blocking packets of a certain type or by blocking popular ports. For instance, if you want to disable transfer of mail from an outside machine to machines inside your network, you would want to disable incoming connections from outside your network to port 25 to any computer behind your router/firewall. This is a particularly good idea if you run a mail server that is only designed to allow mail to be sent from the internal network, as many spammers will attempt to find mail servers that aren't properly configured to use as open relays for their spam.

You also might want to perform packet filtering to perform load balancing. For instance, let's say you have a high-traffic web site and you want to spread the load for the site across more than one server. In this instance you'd use NAT to balance the load between the servers.

Any Linux box that is properly configured can perform packet filtering, but for any network connected to the Internet by a router/firewall, it's far easier to spend your time configuring one machine (most likely your router) to filter all of the incoming and outgoing packets. However, if you're using a Linux workstation to connect to the Internet directly, you'll probably want to go ahead and configure at least a minimal firewall on that machine to protect your data from would-be crackers.

What is Packet Mangling?

It might sound painful, but it isn't. To be completely clear, a mangled packet is also a filtered packet, but it's also a packet that has been rewritten in some way.

Introduction to *ipchains*

Every major iteration of the Linux kernel comes with a new mechanism for packet filtering since the 1.1 kernel series. The 2.0 series used the program, `ipfwadm`, to control the filtering rules in the kernel; the 2.2 series introduced the `ipchains` program, which was generally considered an improvement over `ipfwadm`. Currently this is the program with the widest usage.

The majority of Linux boxes are still running the 2.2.x series of Linux kernels, though as the 2.4.x series matures more and more, admins will begin to feel comfortable enough to migrate their servers to the 2.4.x series. (There are still quite a few servers running the 2.0.x series as well, though that kernel series is no longer undergoing active development, and admins are being encouraged to move to the 2.2.x or 2.4.x series.)

Using *ipchains*

To use `ipchains` you'll need to have enabled support in your kernel and have the userspace program compiled. As with most all commercial Linux distributions, this should be done already. If you've never compiled a Linux kernel before, you can refer to Chapter 13, "Building a Routing Kernel."

A Word About "Userspace"

Because we've used the term, *userspace*, a few times in this chapter, it occurred to us that it might be confusing to folks who aren't longtime Linux users and developers.

The kernel developers refer to programs that people actually use and interact with as "userspace" code. Essentially, userspace programs are the programs that actually let you get useful work done while the Linux kernel chugs away in the background unnoticed and underappreciated unless something goes awry.

When both userspace code and kernel features have the same name, as in the case of `ipchains` and `iptables`, it can get a bit confusing for Linux novices.

If you don't have `ipchains` or want to check to be sure that you've got the latest version, you can find the code and HOWTOs at `http://netfilter.gnumonks.org/ipchains/`.

Development of ipchains seems to have slowed dramatically since the release of the 2.4.x kernel. The last release of ipchains at the time of this writing was 1.3.10 on October 5, 2000.

ipchains *Syntax*

Naturally, to muck about with kernel settings, you'll need to be logged in as root. We recommend strongly that if you're experimenting with `ipchains`, you start with a machine that's not crucial to the operation of your company's network—or at least wait until after hours when a boo-boo won't draw the wrath of the entire staff and your boss. If your company is large enough to merit two or more shifts, making after hours work horribly inconvenient or impossible, it should be large enough to spring for a couple of test machines.

The syntax for `ipchains` is pretty simple. The basic command syntax is `ipchains` [-action] *chainname* [options]. You use the `ipchains` command to create, modify, or remove rule chains from the kernel. The rules can get somewhat complex, but they're built up from a combination of simple rules.

The easiest way to demonstrate `ipchains` is by giving a simple example. Before you work on your chains, you probably want to see what chains are already loaded, so you'll run `ipchains` [-L] to see what rules are already in place. If you haven't set any rules, you should see something like this:

```
root@host:/ > ipchains -L
Chain input (policy ACCEPT):
Chain forward (policy ACCEPT):
Chain output (policy ACCEPT):
```

By default `ipchains` [-L] will list all rules. If you want to specify, you'd use something like this:

```
root@host:/ > ipchains -L input
Chain input (policy ACCEPT):
```

Adding a Rule to a Chain

There are three chains that exist by default: `input`, `forward`, and `output`. It will probably come as no surprise that the input chain handles incoming packets, the outgoing chain deals with outgoing packets, and the forward chain deals with packets that come to the router/firewall but are destined to go on to other hosts.

The syntax for adding a rule to a chain is simply `ipchains` [-A] *chainname* options. If you really enjoy typing, you can substitute [—append] for [-A]. Remember, a chain needs to exist before you can add rules to it. If you specify a nonexistent chain, you'll just get an error message.

For the sake of an example, let's say that you want to deny all incoming packets by default and then allow a few desirables. The first step is to define a default rule, like this:

```
root@host:/ >ipchains -P input REJECT
```

This creates a default rule that will reject all incoming packets. This is a bit extreme, so let's add a rule that will allow some traffic through, as follows:

```
root@host:/ >ipchains -A input -i eth0 -s 10.0.0.0/24 -j ACCEPT
```

The `-s 10.0.0.0/24` argument tells `ipchains` to accept (`-j ACCEPT`) any incoming packets from the internal (`10.0.0.0`) network with a subnet of 255.255.255.0 going anywhere. If you wanted, you could specify destination addresses as well with the `-d` option. Sometimes it's easier to say which IP addresses should not match a rule. In that case you would use `-s ! 10.0.0.0/24`, using the "!" expression.

The `-j` option tells `ipchains` to "jump" to a rule, or basically to go ahead and make a decision about any packet that matches this rule. In this case, we're telling `ipchains` to accept those packets. By the way, you have the choice of `ACCEPT`, `DENY`, `REJECT`, `MASQ`, `REDIRECT`, or `RETURN` for any target packets that match a given rule. See the `ipchains` man page for full details.

Chain Names and Case Sensitivity

It's worth pointing out that the names of your rule chains or tables are case sensitive, like most things in the *NIX world. When using the 2.2.x series, the default chains are "input, forward, output." When using the 2.4.x series, the defaults become "INPUT, FORWARD, OUTPUT."

Flushing a Chain

If you've created a set of rules for a chain and you want to get rid of them, simply "flush" the chain using the -f option. For example, if you wanted to get rid of all the input rules, you'd type `ipchains -f input`.

This will completely reset the rule chain. If, however, you only want to drop one rule from a chain, you would use the drop (-D) option instead. The rules in each chain are numbered, so if you wanted to drop the first rule from a chain, you would issue `ipchains -D input 1`. Remember, to check which rules you have set already, you can use `ipchains -L` or `ipchains -L` *chainname*.

Starting from 1

Folks who are new to Linux and/or programming will probably find the practice of beginning at 1 to be fairly straightforward. However, it's unusual for a numbering scheme to begin at 1 for anything related to the Linux kernel internals. Usually any numbering scheme begins at 0 and goes from there. For instance, if you have a multi-processor system, they will be numbered CPU0, CPU1, and so forth.

Saving and Restoring Your Configuration

After fiddling with `ipchains` all day, you've finally gotten exactly the setup you want. Congratulations! Now it's time to make sure that you'll be able to restore your golden configuration in the event you have to reboot or your system loses power. Remember, the rules you set up with `ipchains` don't become permanent; they need to be restored any time the computer restarts.

This is very easy, though. The authors of `ipchains` have included two scripts, `ipchains-save` and `ipchains-restore`, to make your life very easy. When your setup is exactly as you like it, run `ipchains-save > router_config`. This will save your current rules in a file called `router_config` that you can reload by using `ipchains-restore router_config`.

For More on *ipchains*

While this hasn't been an exhaustive look at `ipchains`, it should get you started with the basics. If you're interested in doing comprehensive firewall setups, you might want to look into *Linux Firewalls* by Robert L. Ziegler, also published by New Riders. (Yes, we'd recommend it even if this book weren't published by New Riders…it's just a coincidence.) It covers using `ipchains` to create firewalls in great detail.

Introduction to Netfilter and *iptables*

The distinction between Netfilter and `iptables` seems to get blurred quite a bit. Netfilter is actually a set of "hooks" in the Linux kernel's network protocol stacks that allow various modules to work with network packets. As a packet travels through the stack, Netfilter can allow a module to drop a packet, forward it on, queue it for a program outside the kernel, or change it in some way.

The `iptables` program is a userspace program that is used to add rules to the network tables. Technically, it should be possible to interact with the Netfilter framework using a program other than `iptables`.

The Netfilter framework and `iptables` are direct descendants of `ipchains`, which means that `iptables` has quite a bit in common with `ipchains`. For the most part, they share the same syntax and options, with only a few minor changes.

Netfilter is more than just another name for `iptables`. Netfilter also supports NAT, the `ipchains`, and `ipfwadm` modules used for backwards-compatibility and the connection-tracking system.

Differences Between 2.2.x and 2.4.x

How much packet filtering, IP Masquerading, and NAT have changed between the 2.2.x series and the 2.4.x series depends on your point of view. There have been quite a few changes under the hood, and new capabilities have been added that allow stateful filtering and other functionality that make Linux a force to be reckoned with for routing.

However, the differences between `ipchains` and `iptables` syntax aren't very drastic at all. There are some changes, but anyone who's been doing work with `ipchains` should have no problem getting up to speed with `iptables`.

Using *iptables*

As with `ipchains`, you'll need to have the proper kernel modules compiled/enabled and have the `iptables` program installed as well. If you don't have `iptables`, you can download it from the Netfilter project homepage at `http://netfilter.gnumonks.org`.

Most Current Version

Even if your distribution comes with `iptables` already installed, you should probably check to see that you have the latest version. As of this writing, the current version is 1.2.2. If you have a version earlier than 1.2.1a, your version has a security weakness in the `ip_conntrack_ftp` module. It's hard to overstress the importance of keeping up with the most current version of tools like `iptables`. Sometimes updates are released to fix minor bugs or add features, but many updates are security-related or address serious bugs that could cause problems down the road. Spending a few hours a month checking for and installing updates could save you days in cleaning up after a cracker—or weeks looking for a new job after a script kiddie "owns" your system.

iptables *Syntax*

Did you read through the section on iptables? Well, if you did, then you already have a good feel for using iptables. You use iptables to add, modify, or flush rules from the tables of IP packet filtering rules in the Linux kernel.

Chains, Rules, Tables...What's Going on Here?

All the talk about rules, chains, and tables can get kind of confusing if you don't know what's going on. Actually, even if you do know what's going on, it can get a bit murky at times.

Starting from the smallest building block, a *rule* is a way of describing criteria for matching a packet and what is to be done with that packet. If the packet matches, it fits a rule. A packet that matches one or more rules is called a *target*.

A *chain* is a collection of rules that match a set of packets or targets. And, finally, a *table* is a collection of chains. In the 2.4.x kernels, you have a filter table that contains INPUT, OUTPUT, and FORWARD chains by default, nat, and mangle.

Inspecting The Chains

Before we add any rules to the chains, it's probably a good idea to take a gander at the existing chains to see if there are any rules already lurking about. Even if you haven't been working with iptables, some distros might slip a few rules in the startup files.

To view the exiting rules, type:

```
iptables -L
```

and you should see something like this:

```
root@host: >
Chain INPUT (policy ACCEPT)
target     prot opt source               destination     Chain FORWARD (policy
➥ACCEPT)
target     prot opt source               destination        Chain OUTPUT (policy
➥ACCEPT)
target     prot opt source               destination
```

Even though there are no rules currently in place, you'll notice that the output from iptables is a bit more verbose than ipchains.

After you've put added rules to some of the existing chains or added chains of your own, you might want to view only that chain. In that case, simply specify the name of the chain you'd like to view, like this:

```
root@host: >iptables -L CHAINNAME
```

Adding a Rule to a Chain

To add a rule to one of the existing chains, you will use the append (-A) command and specify the chain to which you want to append the rule. You also will need to specify a source (-s), destination (-d), protocol (-p), and the action (-j) you want taken on the target packet.

All of this is easier done than said. To illustrate, here's a simple example that will block any `telnet` connection coming in from outside the local network:

```
root@host: >iptables -A INPUT -s ! 10.0.0.0 -p tcp —destination-port telnet -j
➥REJECT
```

This example will reject (`-j REJECT`) any packets attempting to establish a `telnet` connection, unless they're being made from inside the local network. Because using `telnet` is a bad idea these days anyway, you can keep your users from making outgoing `telnet` connections as well with the following:

```
root@host: >iptables -A OUTPUT -p tcp —destination-port telnet -j REJECT
```

Creating a New Chain

If you'd like to specify a chain other than `INPUT`, `OUTPUT`, or `FORWARD`, you can create a custom chain. This one is easy—simply decide what name you'd like to use for the new chain (up to 31 characters) and use the new chain (`-N`) option.

```
root@host: >iptables -N NEW_CHAIN_NAME
```

Now if you run the `iptables -L` command, you'll see something like this:

```
root@aesir:~ > iptables -L
Chain INPUT (policy ACCEPT)
target     prot opt source              destination

Chain FORWARD (policy ACCEPT)
target     prot opt source              destination

Chain OUTPUT (policy ACCEPT)
target     prot opt source              destination

Chain NEW_CHAIN_NAME (0 references)
target     prot opt source              destination
```

As you can see, when you create a new chain, it has no default rules, unlike the default chains.

Flushing a Rule

As with `iptables`, flushing a chain requires using the `-F`. To flush the `OUTPUT` chain, for instance, you would type **iptables -F OUTPUT**. This will get rid of all rules that have been set in that chain.

For More on *iptables*

This has been a fairly brisk overview of `iptables`. If you want to learn more about them, the man page contains a fairly extensive description of the use of `iptables`. The Netfilter home page also has several well-written HOWTOs by the primary author of Netfilter, Rusty Russell. Even if you're not going to use Netfilter or `iptables` extensively, they're worth reading. How can you pass up documentation by an author who claims, "My pet hamster dressed up in a penguin suit and appeared to me in a dream, telling me to write documentation for random stuff and include lots of obscenities." (We haven't found any obscenities yet, but they're very well written and amusing in spots.) You'll find them under "Rusty's Remarkably Unreliable Guides" (`http://netfilter.samba.org/unreliable-guides/`).

IP Masquerading

In many cases, you'll want to use a router to perform IP Masquerading. Typically IP Masquerading is used to connect a private network with "illegal" IP addresses to the outside world. This is particularly true when your location only has one public IP address through a dial-up line, DSL, cable modem, or whatever.

All of the traffic from one or more computers routed through a machine with a direct interface to the Net appears to come solely through that machine. The practical upshot of this, of course, is that a number of computers can share one connection to the Internet. This is cheaper and causes less of a security risk. Assume you have a computer behind your router/firewall with all of your credit card numbers and Aunt Grizzelda's world-famous, top-secret chocolate chip cookie recipe. Before evil crackers can plunder your valuable information, they'll have to fight their way through the firewall/router and then figure out your internal network and then fight their way through any security you have on internal hosts.

Because the Linux kernel is doing some pretty complicated stuff under the hood, people often assume that setting up IP Masquerading is going to be a long and painful process. In this section we'll show you how to set up IP Masquerading in a few easy steps so you can get on with important things, like going through the User Friendly archives one more time.

Quick and Dirty IP Masquerading with *ipchains*

Setting up IP Masquerading with `ipchains` can be done in a jiffy, provided you've already got everything enabled and compiled. (And, naturally, that you have two interfaces—one that interfaces with your LAN and the other that interfaces with your connection.)

For IP Masquerading to work, you need to enable IP Forwarding. Again, this is easier than it sounds. Just type:

```
echo 1 > /proc/sys/net/ipv4/ip_forward
```

This doesn't return any result if you type it in correctly. To be sure that you've enabled IP Forwarding, enter:

```
cat /proc/sys/net/ipv4/ip_forward
```

and it should return a result of "1," which in this case is kernel-speak for "true" or "yep, I'll forward them packets now boss!"

We're not quite done yet, though. Now we need to enable a rule to allow forwarding in the `forward` chain. By default we don't want to allow just any packets to be forwarded, so we'll set up a rule that doesn't allow forwarding.

```
ipchains -P forward DENY
```

This will deny packet forwarding through your router/firewall. But we want to allow some forwarding, specifically through the interface that's connected to the Net. The second Ethernet interface is often used for the outside connection, so we'll use `eth1` as the example.

```
ipchains -A forward -i eth1 -j MASQ
```

Do a quick `ipchains -L forward` to make sure everything is entered correctly, and you're in business. That's all there is to setting up simple IP Masquerading with `ipchains`. Granted, you'll probably want to set up some firewall rules to block nasty cracking attempts, but we'll let you season to taste.

Quick and Dirty IP Masquerading with *iptables*

In the 2.4.x series, IP Masquerading isn't much more difficult. However, IP Masquerading has moved from the `forward` chain to the `nat` chain. This makes sense because IP Masquerading is actually just simplified Network Address Translation.

To set up IP Masquerading with `iptables`, you'll also need to be sure that the `iptable_nat` module is loaded. A quick reminder—you do need to be logged in as root to do this. To load the module, use the `modprobe` command.

```
modprobe iptable_nat
```

Be sure to add the `nat` chain to the kernel tables.

```
iptables -N nat
```

The kernel won't return any messages as long as the operation is successful, so if you want to be really sure that you've been successful, use `lsmod` to check and see what kernel modules are loaded.

Just like with the 2.2.x kernel, we need to enable IP Forwarding, as follows:

```
echo 1 > /proc/sys/net/ipv4/ip_forward
```

And now we can use `iptables` to set the appropriate rule in the `nat` chain to perform IP Masquerading.

```
iptables -t nat -A POSTROUTING -o eth1 -j MASQUERADE
```

The main difference here is that the Netfilter framework handles packets differently than in the 2.2.x kernel. Basically, this operation will take place after all other (potential) operations on the packets have taken place. This makes sense, as it's really difficult to work with a packet after it has been forwarded.

Network Address Translation (NAT)

We've already looked at one form of NAT, IP Masquerading. That's the simplest form of NAT and will take care of a lot of situations where you're just trying to use one connection for a number of computers.

Now we'll take a quick look at doing full-blown NAT, in case you've got a more complicated setup that calls for it.

What's the Difference Between NAT and IP Masquerading?

To the casual observer, there might be some confusion between NAT and IP Masquerading. However, there are some distinctive differences that will help you to know which one you'll want to use.

Actually, IP Masquerading is a form of NAT. In some instances you have a group of computers that you want to share one public IP address. In this case, you'll want to use IP Masquerading to make those computers share that precious IP address. This is basically a stripped-down version of NAT.

On the other hand, let's say you have several valid IPs, but they're dynamic IP addresses. In this case, you'd use NAT on your router to allow each computer to use one of the public IP addresses, without actually being directly connected to the Internet and without having to configure dynamic IPs at the host level. Each machine could have its own internal network static IP while using NAT to have a public IP address of its own.

In most scenarios, you'll be able to stick with IP Masquerading. However, if you need the full functionality of NAT, you've got it at your fingertips.

Setting up NAT with *iptables*

As mentioned earlier in the section on IP Masquerading, you'll need to load the `iptable_nat` module.

A Quick Note on Module Names

If you've ever gone poking through the directories where your modules are stored or watched your computer as it boots, you've probably noticed that all modules end with a *.o extension. For instance, the `iptable_nat` module filename is actually `iptable_nat.o`. However, you only need to tell modprobe or insmod to load `iptable_nat`. We only bring this up because, occasionally, folks get confused and try to load `iptable_nat.o` and get frustrated when the program says "Can't locate module iptable_nat.o" when they know that they've got that module. It's an easy mistake to make, and we see it on the newsgroups occasionally, so we thought we'd mention it.

Source NAT

The first type of NAT we'll look at is Source NAT, or changing the source address of a packet before it heads out into the world. If you've already gone through the section on IP Masquerading earlier in this chapter, then you've gotten a taste of Source NAT.

IP Masquerading is a limited type of Source NAT that maps multiple addresses to one address. It's also possible to map source addresses to public addresses on a one-to-one basis or to map to one of several source addresses.

Let's say you have a range of public IP addresses from 1.2.3.4 to 1.2.3.10 (yes, we know those aren't legal) and you want to enable the router to change the source addresses to one of those addresses. Note that this will happen after any other packet mangling so that the last step in the packet's traversal of the kernel is having the source address changed.

To achieve Source NAT, you will specify a packet and then jump to the target of the rule—in this case Source NAT (-j SNAT). Here's what the command would look like:

```
iptables -t nat -A POSTROUTING -o eth1 -j SNAT —to 1.2.3.4-1.2.3.10
```

When specifying the range of addresses you want to use, simply indicate a range using a dash like this ——*to 1.2.3.4-1.2.3.10.* Wasn't that easy?

Destination NAT

The flip side of all this is Destination NAT, or rewriting the destination of incoming packets. This is done before any other packet mangling, so that you can set rules based on internal hosts and incoming packets that have been DNAT'ed will match the right rules.

To perform Destination NAT, you set up rules that will match incoming packets and rewrite them so they'll travel wherever you'd like to send them. Here's a simple example:

```
iptables -t nat -A PREROUTING -i eth0 -j DNAT —to 10.0.0.4-10.0.0.14
```

This will rewrite packets coming in through the first Ethernet interface to one of the internal machines with an IP address of 10.0.0.4 to 10.0.0.14.

You also can set the rule to match incoming ports, so if you only wanted to perform DNAT on incoming HTTP requests, for instance, you could set a rule that matches incoming packets headed for port 80.

```
iptables -P ACCEPT nat
iptables -t nat -A PREROUTING -i eth0 -p tcp —destination-port 80 -j DNAT —to
➥10.0.0.13
```

Assuming that 10.0.0.13 is your web server behind the router/firewall, all HTTP requests would be sent to it. This also can be useful to direct HTTP requests to one machine, HTTPS to another, and so forth. This allows you to spread services across a number of machines while the outside world interacts with them seamlessly.

Summary

In this chapter we've looked at several tools that can be used to enhance security on your network and perform various types of packet filtering and mangling in the 2.2.x and 2.4.x series of Linux kernels.

15

Monitoring, Analyzing, and Controlling Network Traffic

THIS CHAPTER COVERS THE MONITORING, ANALYZING, and quality of service (QoS) support available to the Linux network operating system. The tools covered in this chapter are open source and freely available to Linux network administrators. Most tools available for network monitoring support various node types, from Linux servers and routers to high-end core routers and switches.

Monitoring and Analysis Tools

Linux, like most versions of Unix, is known for its well-rounded command set for real-time troubleshooting and monitoring. A good knowledge of the commands covered in Chapter 7, "Kernel Support Tools," combined with the network analysis tools covered here will ensure that you administer better operating networks.

Network monitoring and analysis tools should not only be useful to the network administrator, but also to network operations center technicians and management.

Simple Network Management Protocol Overview (SNMP)

SNMP was designed to provide an open protocol and means to configure, manage, and monitor network nodes. SNMP is used generically to refer to one of the three commonly used versions: 1, 2, and 3. Versions 1 and 2 are widely supported with version 3 support increasing. The SNMP Internet Engineering Task Force approved version 3 as a draft standard in March 1999.

SNMP Topology

SNMP defines a topology referred to as a *network management system*. The network management system includes the manager that interacts with the network management station and network nodes. The management system is used to manage and monitor nodes that are referred to as *managed devices*.

The managed device then includes the SNMP application stack, the agent in SNMP terminology (which acts as the interface to the managed devices' objects), and the UDP and IP layers of the protocol stack. Figure 15.1 shows the logical view of a network management system.

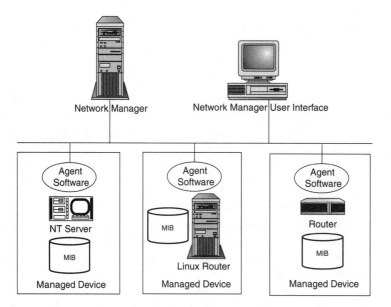

Figure 15.1 Network management system.

SNMP messages between the manager and agent identify the objects that are being managed using a management information base (MIB), with the current and most widely deployed MIB being version 2, known as MIB-II. It is defined in RFC 1213,

"Management Information Base for Network Management of TCP/IP-based internets: MIB-II." The MIB is a tree structure used to identify the data (statistics, counters, interface status, and so on) that is being used by the network node. Figure 15.2 shows the MIB tree for MIB-II.

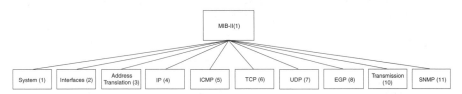

Figure 15.2   MIB-II.

Notice that each leaf, which is referred to as an *SNMP object*, is identified by its location in the MIB tree. Therefore, eth0 on a Linux node can be identified as:

```
.iso.org.dod.internet.mgmt.mib-2.interfaces.ifTable.ifEntry.ifIndex.2
```

eth0 also can be identified using the object ID equivalent of the one just listed. Here part of the tree is shown using the object IDs:

```
.1.3.6.1.2.1.2.ifTable.ifEntry.ifIndex.2
```

When using MIB-II, most SNMP packages enable the user to specify only within the MIB-II tree, so:

```
.iso.org.dod.internet.mgmt.mib-2.interfaces.eth0
```

also can be identified as:

```
interfaces.ifTable.ifEntry.ifIndex.2
```

SNMP Communication

SNMP defines five message types for communicating between the manager and agent: get, get next, set, response, and trap.

The GET, GET NEXT, and SET commands are all issued from the manager to the agent. The GET command is used to poll the specific value of a specific object within the agent's MIB structure. The GET NEXT tells the agent to poll the next value within the MIB structure. The SET is used by the manager to tell the agent to set a particular object's value to the value transmitted by the manager.

The RESPONSE message is an agent that manages communication and is sent in response to the GET, GET NEXT, and SET commands.

The TRAP message is the only SNMP messaging initiated by the agent and is used to send an alarm message to the manager. For example, should an interface lose physical connectivity, the agent typically sends a TRAP message with the appropriate object identification (OID) identified in the TRAP message.

Use of these commands using Linux command-line tools is covered in the next section.

SNMP Authentication

Because SNMP can be used to monitor and manage network nodes, some means of security is required to ensure that network nodes cannot easily be compromised.

SNMP defines two access levels of security: public and private. The public level is granted read-only access to the node, and the private is given full control of the node (read and write). Unfortunately, these levels are passed in clear text.

SNMP Security

The SNMP Internet Engineering Task Force did seek to improve the security with version 2 of the protocol, but the members could not agree on the security requirements, which caused two spin-offs of version 2 with some of the security requirement left to be created: V2u and V2c. The version 3 working group is trying to fix this weakness with a standards track specification (see `http://www.ietf.org/html.charters/snmpv3-charter.html`).

SNMP on Linux

SNMP for Linux was previously supported by two packages: `ucd-snmp` and the CMU SNMP project. Although both of these packages are still available on the Internet, SNMP development for Linux has moved to the NET-SNMP package.

NET-SNMP

The NET-SNMP package available at `http://net-snmp.sourceforge.net/` is the SNMP package known earlier as the ucd-snmp package. The current distribution, 4.2.1, is still referred to as the ucd-snmp package, but all future distributions will be named using the new name. The NET-SNMP package provides an SNMP agent for Linux, an SNMP library, and SNMP command-line tools for issuing SNMP commands and traps.

In addition to supporting the standard MIB-II, the NET-SNMP agent also directly supports monitoring disk usage, as well as provides support to ensure processes are running. The agent will send a trap to the management station when disk usage becomes low or a particular process has stopped executing. The agent also can make use of scripts to add further capabilities to the trap functionality.

The following section provides a brief overview of the installation of NET-SNMP.

Installation   To install the NET-SNMP distribution, download the current version of the package as pointed to in the download section of `http://net-snmp.sourceforge.net/`. At the time of publication of this book, version 4.2.1 is the current version. Place the downloaded distribution in the appropriate place where source files are kept on your Linux system. For this example we use `/usr/src/`.

The installation should be performed as the root user.

Unzip the tarball distribution:

```
[root@lefty src]# gunzip ucd-snmp-4.2.1.tar.gz
```

And untar the tarball:

```
[root@lefty src]# tar xvf ucd-snmp-4.2.1.tar
```

Now move into the directory created by untarring the distribution:

```
[root@lefty src]# cd ucd-snmp-4.2.1
```

At a minimum, read through the README and INSTALL files for any last minute changes to the installation procedures. The FAQ and NEWS files are also worth taking a look at.

Execute the configure script, which will query your system for various settings— such as which C compiler to use, what libraries are present, and so on:

```
[root@lefty ucd-snmp-4.2.1]# ./configure
```

The configure script also will prompt for the name of the contact for the SNMP agent. This is the information the Linux node will return should it be queried via SNMP as soon as the agent is running.

After prompting for the contact name, the configure script will prompt for the geographic location of the Linux node and then the log directory location, which can be customized (or the default of /var/log/snmpd.log can be used).

Finally, the configure script will prompt for the configuration directory. /var/ucd is the default location.

At this point the configure script will create a makefile, so that the make command can be run:

```
[root@lefty ucd-snmp-4.2.1]# make
```

To ensure permissions are set correctly, execute:

```
[root@lefty ucd-snmp-4.2.1]# umask 022
```

And then have make install the distribution in the appropriate locations:

```
[root@lefty ucd-snmp-4.2.1]# make install
```

This will install the distribution into the /usr/local/ directory structure. For this chapter, RedHat 6.1 was used for installation; however, the installation instructions apply to most current distributions. RedHat's root account has the /usr/local/bin/ and /usr/local/sbin/ in its path, so if your distribution does not have these directories in your path, there are three workarounds:

- Add /usr/local/bin/ and /usr/local/sbin/ to the root account. This might not be desirable depending on what other programs are located in these directories and how tight the security is on the box and within the directories.

- Use absolute path names when executing the programs. For some advanced features this could require additional parameters to tell the particular SNMP program where to find particular programs.

- Install the NET-SNMP package in its own directory and set the path accordingly.

Log out of the root account and log back in. (This will return root's umask setting back to its original setting.) Then log back in as root.

Should SNMPv3 support be needed, OpenSSL (`http://www.openssl.org/`) will need to be installed if it is not already present.

The NET-SNMP agent runs as a daemon and is appropriately named `snmpd`. `snmpd` uses a configuration file to determine community access strings and trap settings as is expected of an `snmp` agent. In addition, the `snmpd` also allows advanced configuration settings such as limiting particular community strings to particular object identifications and limiting manager queries to particular IP addressees.

Before starting `snmpd`, create the `snmpd` configuration file: `/usr/local/share/snmp/snmpd.conf` with the following entries:

```
#
# snmpd.conf
# example
#

# Access Control Setup

# rwcommunity: a SNMPv1/SNMPv2c read-write access community name
#    arguments:  community [default¦hostname¦network/bits] [oid]

rwcommunity  fullaccess

# rocommunity: a SNMPv1/SNMPv2c read-only access community name
#arguments:  community [default¦hostname¦network/bits] [oid]

rocommunity  readaccess
```

This is a simple and straightforward snmpd.conf file with only the community strings defined. NET-SNMP uses the field name `rwcommunity` as the private community string, which is defined as `fullaccess` in this example.

`rocommunity` is the public, read-only, community string, defined as `readaccess` in this example.

Should `snmpd` be started without the community strings defined, then anyone can query the box via `snmp`, leaving the box vulnerable to attacks.

Now `snmpd` can be started:

```
[root@lefty /root]# snmpd
```

Assuming all has gone well, the daemon should start and begin listening for requests. The daemon also will create an entry in the log file:

```
[root@lefty /root]# cat /var/log/snmpd.log
UCD-SNMP version 4.2.1
```

To get a closer look at how the agent works, we will take a look at the `snmp` tools that come with NET-SNMP. The command-line tools are not typical managers but rather provide the functionality of the particular messages supported by managers: GET, GET NEXT, and SET.

NET-SNMP Manager Commands   The NET-SNMP command-line utilities are
`snmpget`, `snmpgetnext`, and `snmpset` and correspond with `GET`, `GET NEXT`, and `SET`. These
commands are very useful for network troubleshooting, network management system
troubleshooting, and getting a better understanding of SNMP. Additionally, there is the
`snmpwalk` command, which uses the `GET NEXT` message to retrieve all variables under a
specific object identification. The examples that follow use the NET-SNMP tools with
the `snmpd` daemon that was installed with the package and started earlier.

- `snmpget agent communitystring object-id.` The `snmpget` command will query
  the designated agent for the specific object-id using the community string specified. (For users of earlier versions of the command-line utilities, notice that the
  format community, `string@agent,` is no longer used.)

To get the system uptime, `snmpget` can be used:

```
[root@lefty /root]# snmpget 192.168.1.254 readaccess system.sysUpTime.0
system.sysUpTime.0 = Timeticks: (76980) 0:12:49.80
```

The `snmpd` agent supports most of the complete MIB-II standard, so there is all sorts
of useful information that can be gathered for later analysis or used to check up on a
system.

For example, the `icmp` branch keeps track of icmp traffic. So to determine how
many pings (using ICMP-echo) have been received by the host, the following command can be used:

```
[root@lefty /root]# snmpget 192.168.1.254 readaccess icmp.icmpInEchos.0
icmp.icmpInEchos.0 = Counter32: 43
```

This shows that the system has received 43 ping packets.

While `snmpget` cannot replace a well-designed network management system, it does
add a tremendous amount of analysis power to an existing network management system, as well as adding flexibility to existing automation tools that monitor system
activity.

- `snmpgetnext agent communitystring object-id.` The `snmpgetnext` can be used
  to get the next object in the MIB tree as such:
  ```
  [root@lefty /root]# snmpgetnext 192.168.1.254 readaccess icmp.icmpInEchos.0
  icmp.icmpInEchoReps.0 = Counter32: 3
  ```

  This returns the number of ICMP echo responses the system has received.
  `snmpgetnext` functionality is limited to the next entry; whereas, the `snmpwalk` is
  much more useful.

- `snmpwalk agent communitystring object-id.` `snmpwalk` will use `SNMP GET NEXT`
  commands until all the variables under the current object identifier are
  retrieved. This can be useful for creating tables or even finding specific object
  identifiers when you are not sure of the exact name. For example, the following
  `snmpwalk` reports all `icmp` information maintained:
  ```
  [root@lefty /root]# snmpwalk 192.168.1.254 readaccess icmp
  icmp.icmpInMsgs.0 = Counter32: 12
  icmp.icmpInErrors.0 = Counter32: 0
  icmp.icmpInDestUnreachs.0 = Counter32: 6
  ```

```
icmp.icmpInTimeExcds.0 = Counter32: 0
icmp.icmpInParmProbs.0 = Counter32: 0
icmp.icmpInSrcQuenchs.0 = Counter32: 0
icmp.icmpInRedirects.0 = Counter32: 0
icmp.icmpInEchos.0 = Counter32: 3
icmp.icmpInEchoReps.0 = Counter32: 3
icmp.icmpInTimestamps.0 = Counter32: 0
icmp.icmpInTimestampReps.0 = Counter32: 0
icmp.icmpInAddrMasks.0 = Counter32: 0
icmp.icmpInAddrMaskReps.0 = Counter32: 0
icmp.icmpOutMsgs.0 = Counter32: 9
icmp.icmpOutErrors.0 = Counter32: 0
icmp.icmpOutDestUnreachs.0 = Counter32: 6
icmp.icmpOutTimeExcds.0 = Counter32: 0
icmp.icmpOutParmProbs.0 = Counter32: 0
icmp.icmpOutSrcQuenchs.0 = Counter32: 0
icmp.icmpOutRedirects.0 = Counter32: 0
icmp.icmpOutEchos.0 = Counter32: 0
icmp.icmpOutEchoReps.0 = Counter32: 3
icmp.icmpOutTimestamps.0 = Counter32: 0
icmp.icmpOutTimestampReps.0 = Counter32: 0
icmp.icmpOutAddrMasks.0 = Counter32: 0
icmp.icmpOutAddrMaskReps.0 = Counter32: 0
```

Here is an snmpwalk that shows all the data that makes up the IP routing table:

```
[root@lefty /root]# snmpwalk 192.168.1.254 readaccess ip.ipRouteTable
ip.ipRouteTable.ipRouteEntry.ipRouteDest.0.0.0.0 = IpAddress: 0.0.0.0
ip.ipRouteTable.ipRouteEntry.ipRouteDest.127.0.0.0 = IpAddress: 127.0.0.0
ip.ipRouteTable.ipRouteEntry.ipRouteDest.192.168.1.0 = IpAddress: 192.168.1.0
ip.ipRouteTable.ipRouteEntry.ipRouteDest.192.168.1.254 = IpAddress: 192.168.1.25
4
ip.ipRouteTable.ipRouteEntry.ipRouteIfIndex.0.0.0.0 = 2
ip.ipRouteTable.ipRouteEntry.ipRouteIfIndex.127.0.0.0 = 3
ip.ipRouteTable.ipRouteEntry.ipRouteIfIndex.192.168.1.0 = 2
ip.ipRouteTable.ipRouteEntry.ipRouteIfIndex.192.168.1.254 = 2
ip.ipRouteTable.ipRouteEntry.ipRouteMetric1.0.0.0.0 = 1
ip.ipRouteTable.ipRouteEntry.ipRouteMetric1.127.0.0.0 = 0
ip.ipRouteTable.ipRouteEntry.ipRouteMetric1.192.168.1.0 = 0
ip.ipRouteTable.ipRouteEntry.ipRouteMetric1.192.168.1.254 = 0
ip.ipRouteTable.ipRouteEntry.ipRouteNextHop.0.0.0.0 = IpAddress: 192.168.1.1
ip.ipRouteTable.ipRouteEntry.ipRouteNextHop.127.0.0.0 = IpAddress: 0.0.0.0
ip.ipRouteTable.ipRouteEntry.ipRouteNextHop.192.168.1.0 = IpAddress: 0.0.0.0
ip.ipRouteTable.ipRouteEntry.ipRouteNextHop.192.168.1.254 = IpAddress: 0.0.0.0
ip.ipRouteTable.ipRouteEntry.ipRouteType.0.0.0.0 = indirect(4)
ip.ipRouteTable.ipRouteEntry.ipRouteType.127.0.0.0 = direct(3)
ip.ipRouteTable.ipRouteEntry.ipRouteType.192.168.1.0 = direct(3)
ip.ipRouteTable.ipRouteEntry.ipRouteType.192.168.1.254 = direct(3)
ip.ipRouteTable.ipRouteEntry.ipRouteProto.0.0.0.0 = local(2)
ip.ipRouteTable.ipRouteEntry.ipRouteProto.127.0.0.0 = local(2)
ip.ipRouteTable.ipRouteEntry.ipRouteProto.192.168.1.0 = local(2)
ip.ipRouteTable.ipRouteEntry.ipRouteProto.192.168.1.254 = local(2)
```

```
ip.ipRouteTable.ipRouteEntry.ipRouteMask.0.0.0.0 = IpAddress: 0.0.0.0
ip.ipRouteTable.ipRouteEntry.ipRouteMask.127.0.0.0 = IpAddress: 255.0.0.0
ip.ipRouteTable.ipRouteEntry.ipRouteMask.192.168.1.0 = IpAddress: 255.255.255.0
ip.ipRouteTable.ipRouteEntry.ipRouteMask.192.168.1.254 = IpAddress: 255.255.255.
255
ip.ipRouteTable.ipRouteEntry.ipRouteInfo.0.0.0.0 = OID: .ccitt.zeroDotZero
ip.ipRouteTable.ipRouteEntry.ipRouteInfo.127.0.0.0 = OID: .ccitt.zeroDotZero
ip.ipRouteTable.ipRouteEntry.ipRouteInfo.192.168.1.0 = OID: .ccitt.zeroDotZero
ip.ipRouteTable.ipRouteEntry.ipRouteInfo.192.168.1.254 = OID: .ccitt.zeroDotZero
[root@lefty /root]# snmpwalk 192.168.1.254 readaccess ip.ipRouteTable
ip.ipRouteTable.ipRouteEntry.ipRouteDest.0.0.0.0 = IpAddress: 0.0.0.0
ip.ipRouteTable.ipRouteEntry.ipRouteDest.127.0.0.0 = IpAddress: 127.0.0.0
ip.ipRouteTable.ipRouteEntry.ipRouteDest.192.168.1.0 = IpAddress: 192.168.1.0
ip.ipRouteTable.ipRouteEntry.ipRouteDest.192.168.1.254 = IpAddress: 192.168.1.25
4
ip.ipRouteTable.ipRouteEntry.ipRouteIfIndex.0.0.0.0 = 2
ip.ipRouteTable.ipRouteEntry.ipRouteIfIndex.127.0.0.0 = 3
ip.ipRouteTable.ipRouteEntry.ipRouteIfIndex.192.168.1.0 = 2
ip.ipRouteTable.ipRouteEntry.ipRouteIfIndex.192.168.1.254 = 2
ip.ipRouteTable.ipRouteEntry.ipRouteMetric1.0.0.0.0 = 1
ip.ipRouteTable.ipRouteEntry.ipRouteMetric1.127.0.0.0 = 0
ip.ipRouteTable.ipRouteEntry.ipRouteMetric1.192.168.1.0 = 0
ip.ipRouteTable.ipRouteEntry.ipRouteMetric1.192.168.1.254 = 0
ip.ipRouteTable.ipRouteEntry.ipRouteNextHop.0.0.0.0 = IpAddress: 192.168.1.1
ip.ipRouteTable.ipRouteEntry.ipRouteNextHop.127.0.0.0 = IpAddress: 0.0.0.0
ip.ipRouteTable.ipRouteEntry.ipRouteNextHop.192.168.1.0 = IpAddress: 0.0.0.0
ip.ipRouteTable.ipRouteEntry.ipRouteNextHop.192.168.1.254 = IpAddress: 0.0.0.0
ip.ipRouteTable.ipRouteEntry.ipRouteType.0.0.0.0 = indirect(4)
ip.ipRouteTable.ipRouteEntry.ipRouteType.127.0.0.0 = direct(3)
ip.ipRouteTable.ipRouteEntry.ipRouteType.192.168.1.0 = direct(3)
ip.ipRouteTable.ipRouteEntry.ipRouteType.192.168.1.254 = direct(3)
ip.ipRouteTable.ipRouteEntry.ipRouteProto.0.0.0.0 = local(2)
ip.ipRouteTable.ipRouteEntry.ipRouteProto.127.0.0.0 = local(2)
ip.ipRouteTable.ipRouteEntry.ipRouteProto.192.168.1.0 = local(2)
ip.ipRouteTable.ipRouteEntry.ipRouteProto.192.168.1.254 = local(2)
ip.ipRouteTable.ipRouteEntry.ipRouteMask.0.0.0.0 = IpAddress: 0.0.0.0
ip.ipRouteTable.ipRouteEntry.ipRouteMask.127.0.0.0 = IpAddress: 255.0.0.0
ip.ipRouteTable.ipRouteEntry.ipRouteMask.192.168.1.0 = IpAddress: 255.255.255.0
ip.ipRouteTable.ipRouteEntry.ipRouteMask.192.168.1.254 = IpAddress: 255.255.255.
255
ip.ipRouteTable.ipRouteEntry.ipRouteInfo.0.0.0.0 = OID: .ccitt.zeroDotZero
ip.ipRouteTable.ipRouteEntry.ipRouteInfo.127.0.0.0 = OID: .ccitt.zeroDotZero
ip.ipRouteTable.ipRouteEntry.ipRouteInfo.192.168.1.0 = OID: .ccitt.zeroDotZero
ip.ipRouteTable.ipRouteEntry.ipRouteInfo.192.168.1.254 = OID: .ccitt.zeroDotZero
```

- snmpset agent privatecommunitytstring object-id type value. The snmpset
  uses the SNMP SET message to set objects values to a particular value. For example, to change the system contact, the following snmpset command can be used:

  ```
  [root@lefty apps]# snmpset 192.168.1.254 fullaccess system.sysContact.0 s
  root@testme.net
  ```

In the preceding example, the s is the type of value being assigned, which must match the type supported by the object. The s stands for "string." The types supported by the snmpset command are listed in Table 15.1.

Table 15.1 *snmpset* **Type Abbreviations and Meanings**

Type Abbreviation	Meaning
a	IP Address in xxx.xxx.xxx.xxx format
b	Bits
d	Decimal
i	Integer
n	Null Object
o	Object Identifier
s	String
t	Time Ticks
u	Unsigned
x	Hexadecimal

The snmpset command requires "private" access to the SNMP agent because actual configuration is being changed. Although a change has been accepted by an SNMP agent, the change may not be saved across a reboot. For example, the NET-SNMP package, like many Unix SNMP packages, has very little support for making permanent changes via SNMP. The previous example showing the change of system contact will be lost during the next restart of snmpd or a system reboot. Router and other network elements' support of SNMP support varies, so a thorough investigation and testing on a nonproduction system is highly recommended.

Multi–Router Traffic Grapher (MRTG)

MRTG is likely the most popular open source network analysis tool. MRTG uses SNMP get commands to query a router's interfaces traffic statistics. The results of the get command are then recorded, and the traffic statistics are used to graph the network statistics, which will show trends such as high and low utilization periods, averages, and changes in network patterns.

Specifically, MRTG measures the number of packets sent in and out of an interface, the average number of in and out packets, and the current in and out packets.

MRTG is available for most versions of Unix including Linux. (There is also a Windows version.) MRTG is available at http://www.mrtg.org/, which is a pointer to the original MRTG site at http://people.ee.ethz.ch/~oetiker/webtools/mrtg/. MRTG makes use of the NET-SNMP package covered in the previous section, so NET-SNMP should be installed and configured before installing MRTG.

Parts of MRTG are written in Perl, so Perl also must be installed on the system. Version 5.05 or later is recommended. Several graphics libraries also are required for MRTG to function correctly, but their installation is beyond the scope of this chapter. Refer to the `doc/unix-guide.txt` document (in the MRTG source directory covered shortly) for the exact requirements.

MRTG Installation

MRTG should be downloaded from `http://people.ee.ethz.ch/~oetiker/webtools/mrtg/pub/` and placed in the appropriate directory. For this example, `/usr/src/` is used. The current version of MRTG at the time of publication is 2.9.12, which is used here.

After downloading the MRTG package, follow these steps.

1. Log in as root and move into the directory where the package was downloaded:

```
[root@lefty /root]# cd /usr/src
```

2. Unzip the distribution:

```
[root@lefty src]# gunzip mrtg-2.9.12.tar.gz
```

4. Untar the tarball:

```
tar xvf mrtg-2.9.12.tar
```

5. This will create the MRTG source tree. Move into the source tree:

```
[root@lefty src]# cd mrtg-2.9.12
```

6. Execute the configure script:

```
[root@lefty mrtg-2.9.12]# ./configure
```

7. Execute the make command:

```
[root@lefty mrtg-2.9.12]# make
```

8. Finally, execute the make install:

```
[root@lefty mrtg-2.9.12]# make install
```

This will create the installation directory structure, `/usr/local/mrtg-2/`, and move all the binaries and appropriate files into the directory. Move into the directory structure:

```
[root@lefty mrtg-2.9.12]# cd /usr/local/mrtg-2/
```

MRTG needs a directory that is accessible to the web server. A common directory location for HTML documents for the Apache Web Server on Linux is `/home/httpd/html/`, so the MRTG files can be placed in a subdirectory:

```
[root@lefty mrtg-2]# mkdir /home/httpd/html/mrtg
```

Be sure to use an appropriate directory based upon the web server's configuration. A configuration directory for MRTG also should be created:

```
[root@lefty mrtg-2]# mkdir cfg
```

MRTG Configuration

Now MRTG can be configured using the `cfgmaker` script:

```
[root@lefty mrtg-2]# bin/cfgmaker --global 'WorkDir: /home/httpd/html/mrtg' --
output /usr/local/mrtg-2/cfg/mrtg.cfg readaccess@192.168.1.254
```

The `-global` option with the parameter `WorkDir` tells `cfgmaker` which directory structure to use in the config file, `mrtg.cfg`, which will be used by the MRTG program, `mrtg`, to store the files created. The `-output` parameter tells `cfgmaker` where to write the configuration information to—in this case `/usr/local/mrtg-2/cfg/mrtg.cfg`. The final parameter is the public community string and agent being queried.

After the `cfgmaker` script completes, there will be an `mrtg.cfg` file in `/usr/local/mrtg-2/cfg/`, which can be used with the `mrtg` program to test the setup:

```
[root@lefty mrtg-2]# /usr/local/mrtg-2/bin/mrtg /usr/local/mrtg-2/cfg/mrtg.cfg
Rateup WARNING: /usr/local/mrtg-2/bin/rateup could not read the primary log file
➥for 192.168.1.254_2
Rateup WARNING: /usr/local/mrtg-2/bin/rateup The backup log file for
➥192.168.1.254_2 was invalid as well
Rateup WARNING: /usr/local/mrtg-2/bin/rateup Can't remove 192.168.1.254_2.old
➥updating log file
Rateup WARNING: /usr/local/mrtg-2/bin/rateup Can't rename 192.168.1.254_2.log to
➥192.168.1.254_2.old updating log file
```

The warnings just shown are normal for the first time `mrtg` is run given that no log files exist. Run the command again:

```
[root@lefty mrtg-2]# /usr/local/mrtg-2/bin/mrtg /usr/local/mrtg-2/cfg/mrtg.cfg
Rateup WARNING: /usr/local/mrtg-2/bin/rateup Can't remove 192.168.1.254_2.old
➥updating log file
```

There is only one warning this time. After a third run, the warnings are now cleaned up:

```
[root@lefty mrtg-2]# /usr/local/mrtg-2/bin/mrtg /usr/local/mrtg-2/cfg/mrtg.cfg
```

After the three previous executions, MRTG has created some data that can be viewed. By pointing a web browser to the web server's `mrtg` directory (`http://192.168.1.254/mrtg/`), data similar to Figure 15.3 should be seen. (If the graphs are being created but no data is being mapped, then execute the `mrtg` command just listed several more times.)

The data is still in somewhat raw format, so click the `.html` file in the `mrtg` directory to see the graphic representation of the interface. In this example the file is `192.168.1.254_2.html`. The 192.168.1.254 is the interface's IP address, and the 2 is the interface's index (the loopback is number 1). The graphic representation should be similar to that shown in Figure 15.4.

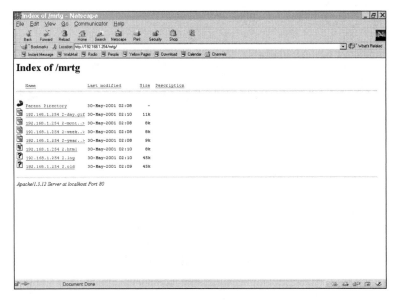

Figure 15.3 MRTG web directory.

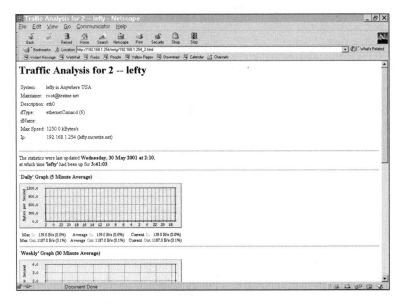

Figure 15.4 MRTG interface statistics.

Now the system must be configured to run mrtg on a regular basis. Use crontab with the -e option to make mrtg run every five minutes:

```
[root@lefty mrtg-2]# crontab -e
```

and add the following entry:

```
0,5,10,15,20,25,30,35,40,45,50,55 * * * * /usr/local/mrtg-2/bin/mrtg
/usr/local/mrtg-2/cfg/mrtg.cfg
```

Additional routers and nodes can be added to the mrtg.cfg with the following command:

```
[root@lefty mrtg-2]# bin/cfgmaker —global 'WorkDir: /home/httpd/html/mrtg'
readaccess@192.168.1.254 >>/usr/local/mrtg-2/cfg/mrtg.cfg
```

As mentioned, the data is still in a somewhat raw format. MRTG includes a tool called indexmaker that will create an index page that links to all the nodes being monitored. To create an index for this example, the following command is used:

```
[root@lefty mrtg-2]# bin/indexmaker /usr/local/mrtg-2/cfg/mrtg.cfg
>/home/httpd/html/mrtg/index.html
```

Permissions and Ownership Issues With the *index.html* File

The index.html file's permissions and ownership might need to be manually set to make the file readable by the owner of the web server process.

This creates the index.html with URLs pointing to all the nodes via a graphic summary—as shown in Figure 15.5.

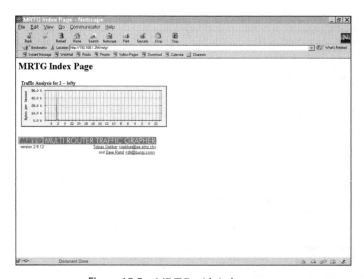

Figure 15.5 MRTG with index page.

After a new node has been added using `cfgmaker`, be sure to run the `indexmaker` again. After `mrtg` has been configured with the nodes to monitor and given time to collect the statistical information, the index page will resemble Figure 15.6.

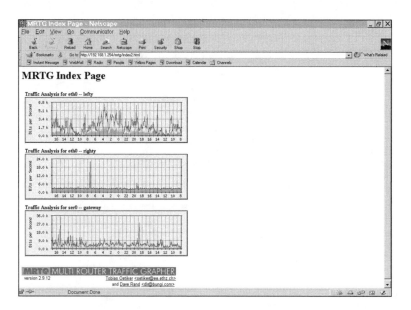

Figure 15.6 MRTG with Populated Index.

IPTraf

`IPTraf` is a network monitoring tool that is geared towards real-time monitoring of network traffic. Unlike a sniffer, such as `tcpdump`, `IPTraf` reports the statistics of the traffic as seen by the Linux network driver. Like a sniffer, `IPTraf` requires the interface to be placed in promiscuous mode; consequently, the program should be run as the root user.

`IPTraf` installation is very simple and straightforward consisting of unzipping, untarring, and running the setup script, so it will not be covered here.

`IPTraf` is installed to the `/usr/local/bin/` directory, so if `/usr/local/bin/` is not in your path, then the complete filename `/usr/local/bin/iptraf` will need to be executed to start the program.

Getting Around *IPTraf*

IPTraf is menu driven; therefore, it proves itself almost immediately valuable to most network administrators. Figure 15.7, shows IPTraf's Main menu. The cursor keys can be used to navigate the window, or each menu also has a short cut key (highlighted) associated with it.

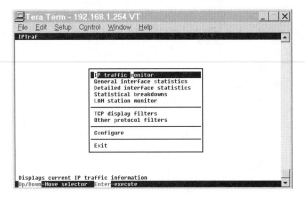

Figure 15.7   IPTraf Main menu.

A closer look at each of the functions supported by IPTraf follows.

IP Traffic Monitor

The IP traffic monitor allows monitoring of IP traffic on a specific interface or on all interfaces recognized by the Linux kernel. Figure 15.8 shows an example of the IP traffic monitor.

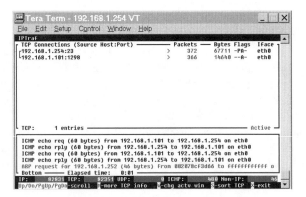

Figure 15.8   IP traffic monitor screen.

The top portion of the IP traffic monitor reports TCP connections. Figure 15.8 shows a telnet connection (port 23) between 192.168.1.254 and 192.168.1.101. The IPTraf output also shows that station 192.168.1.254 has sent 372 packets over the TCP connection and 192.168.1.101 has sent 366.

The flags column reports how the flags were set in the last TCP packet as defined in RFC 793, "Transmission Control Protocol Darpa Internet Program Protocol Specification." Table 15.2 summarizes the TCP flags.

Table 15.2 **IP Traffic Monitor TCP Flags**

IP Traffic Monitor Abbreviation	TCP Abbreviation	Meaning
A	ACK	Acknowledgment
P	PSH	Push all data to queue
U	URG	Packet is marked urgent
S	SYN	Synchronization during handshaking.

IPTraf also will report resets with RST, unacknowledged FINs with DONE, and a properly closed connection with CLOSED. The packet and window size of each of the connections also can be viewed by pressing the m (more) key.

The bottom window in IP traffic monitor shows the most recent non-TCP traffic. In Figure 15.8, this was ICMP-echo requests (pings) and an address resolution protocol (ARP) request.

The bottom of the screen contains two lines. The first line is a real-time view of the packet count for IP, TCP, UDP, ICMP and non-IP traffic.

The second line is the menu for IP traffic monitor. The up and down arrows let you scroll through information when more than one screen is available. The w key switches between the top TCP window and the bottom, all other traffic window.

As mentioned, the m key will report the packet and window size of the TCP connections.

The s key allows the TCP connections to be sorted either using the packet or byte count, which will result in the same ordering; however, the command is useful because the IP traffic monitor does not sort in real time. With the sort command, the connections with the most traffic will "float" to the top of the list.

The x key is used to return to IPTraf's main window.

General Interface Statistics

The General Interface Statistics screen gives a simple breakdown of traffic for all interfaces as shown in Figure 15.9. The counters include IP packets, non-IP (such as IPX), and bad IP, which are packets that can be identified by the IP header, but something in the header is not compliant with the IP protocol.

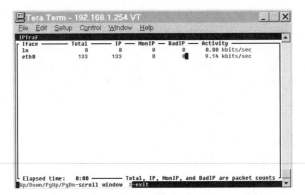

Figure 15.9 General Interface Statistics screen.

Specific Interface Statistics

The Specific Interface Statistics allows the administrator to examine the IP statistics related to a particular configured interface. Figure 15.10 shows the statistics for eth0.

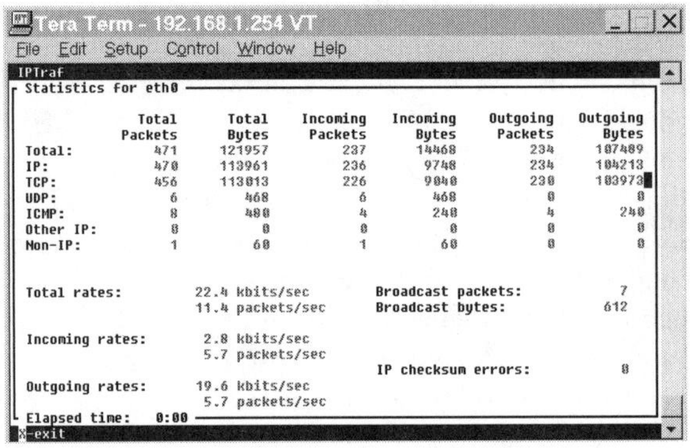

Figure 15.10 Specific Interface Statistics for eth0.

In addition to the breakdown of the types of IP packets, the lower portion of the screen also shows the throughput—both inbound and outbound. The specific interface statistics can be useful for quickly identifying possible problems when troubleshooting a network problem. Refer back to Figure 15.10, and you'll notice the number of ICMP packets is very high when compared to the total number of packets. A ping flood caused this.

Statistical Breakdown

The Statistical Breakdown screen reports the number of packets received by two criteria, either the packet sizes on a particular interface or the TCP/UDP port of a particular interface. The statistical breakdown by packet size is shown in Figure 15.11 and by TCP/UDP port in Figure 15.12.

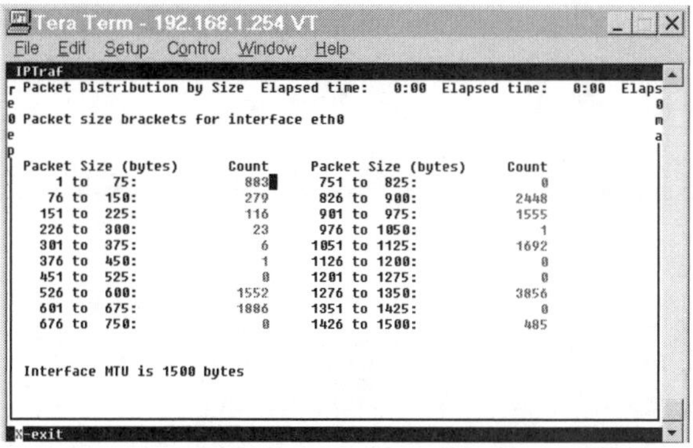

Figure 15.11 Statistical Breakdown—packet size.

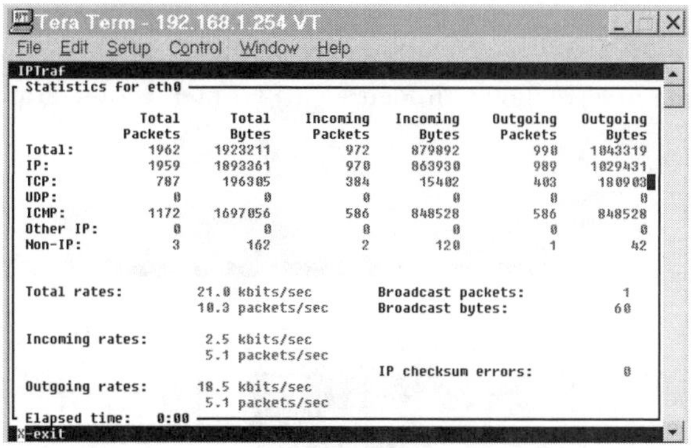

Figure 15.12 Statistical Breakdown—TCP/UDP port.

LAN Station Monitor

The LAN Station Monitor reports statistics based upon the Layer 2 address, or with Ethernet, the MAC address. Its use is limited, but it can be used in conjunction with other tools such as a sniffer to locate Layer 2 related problems. The LAN Station Monitor is shown in Figure 15.13.

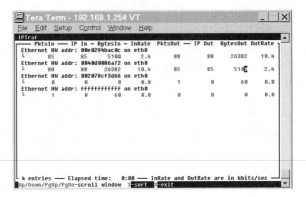

Figure 15.13 LAN Station Monitor screen.

TCP Filter and Other Filters

While examining statistics, it is often useful to examine only certain traffic. The TCP Filters and Other Filters menu allow you to define which traffic should or should not be displayed. The TCP filters apply only to TCP traffic. Should other types of traffic be filtered, the Other Filters option should be chosen.

Creating a filter is straightforward—with only a couple of necessary steps.

After choosing TCP Filter, select Define New Filter, which will prompt for a description of the filter as shown in Figure 15.14. Enter **Telnet Traffic Only** into the description.

Figure 15.14 TCP filter specifying filtering of Telnet Traffic Only.

After entering the description, the screen shown in Figure 15.15 will prompt for IP addresses and ports. The first and second fields are simply the source and destination address in either order. The wildcard mask is actually the `netmask` that will determine how many addresses are included in the range.

Because we are only filtering for `telnet`, 0.0.0.0 is entered in the address and wild-card fields. Telnet's port number, 23, is entered in the Port Number field. Be sure to use the Tab key to move from field to field—the Enter key will create the entry.

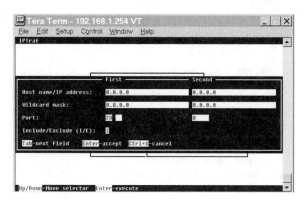

Figure 15.15   TCP filter, IP addresses, and Ports Entry screen.

After pressing Enter, the filter function allows you to enter additional addresses and ports. Press CTRL-X to exit out of the Define TCP filter.

Before using the filter with any of `IPTraf`'s functions, the filter must be applied. The filter is applied using the Apply Filter within the TCP filter section. After Apply Filter is chosen, a list of TCP filters is shown. Select the appropriate filter using the cursor keys and pressing Return on the correct entry. Exit out of the TCP Filter section and then choose the appropriate `IPTraf` function that should be used with the filter applied. Figure 15.16 shows the filter being used with the IP Traffic Monitor.

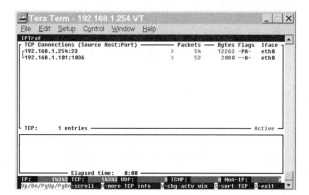

Figure 15.16   IP Traffic Monitor with TCP filter.

Should the protocol being examined not be TCP, the Other Filters item should be chosen at the Main menu. Other filters are created similarly to the TCP and follow the same guidelines with addresses and ports.

In addition to covering monitoring and analyzing of network resources, we need to take it the next step and address quality of service issues. This topic is tackled in the next section.

Quality of Service (QoS)

Bandwidth in data networks, although a limited resource, is generally designed and used in a best effort method: Any retransmissions are in the best case taken care of by the application, or in the case of TCP, by the protocol itself. However, the commercialization of the Internet and applications requiring near real-time network support has driven the need for guaranteeing bandwidth better than best effort.

For example, many organizations require that incoming web requests be given priority over most other traffic—a possible customer that is visiting the web site should not have a "slow" connection to the web server due to email that can wait without the application being affected.

Another application requiring better than best effort routing is a voice application. Voice-over technology and the whole convergence market has created additional pressure on IP technology to support improve QoS support.

There are four common methods used to apply policy to IP traffic: source and/or destination address, source or destination port, service bits in the IP address, and a mixture of the three methods. When bits in the IP address are used, the bits are referred to as *Type of Service Bits* if the methods described in RFC 791 (or 1349, which modified the original RFC 791 spec) are used. If the bits are used with the methods described by the Differentiated Services working group (`http://www.ietf.org/html.charters/diffserv-charter.html`), the bits are referred to as *DS bits*.

If the IP address, UDP, or TCP port is used, the traffic policing is referred to as a *class of service*. Some implementations of QoS policing also allow interface-based policies, which also are considered class of service.

Type of Service: RFC 791 and 795

IP's original method to provide for traffic is the IP type of service (TOS) field in the IP header which is covered in RFC 791, "Internet Protocol Darpa Internet Program Protocol Specification," and RFC 795, "Service Mappings."

The TOS field is eight bits made up of three bits that define precedence, one bit delay, one bit throughput, and one bit for reliability. The remaining two bits were reserved for future use and are set to zero.

Linux Support of TOS

Linux supports setting the TOS bits using filtering under all three packet filtering methods: `ipfwadm`, `ipchains`, and `netfilter`.

Additionally, Linux also can use the appropriate ICMP error messages when a type of service was requested that it should not forward—the network unreachable for the specified IP type-of-service and host unreachable for specified IP type-of-service. Their use, however, should likely just be used within the same autonomous system given that many networks filter out many of the ICMP message types. (Some organizations filter ICMP exclusively.)

Examples of Setting the TOS Bits

The complexity of implementing TOS on Linux is determined by the network design and engineering required in the core network, which will vary depending on the systems supported and complexity. Configuring Linux to set the TOS on packets traversing the Linux router is quite simple after a package that supports configuring the TOS is installed such as `ipfwadm`, `ipchains`, or `netfilter`.

Example with *ipchains*

Giving priority to web traffic was mentioned at the beginning the this section on QoS, so here is an example of setting the IP TOS for web traffic using `ipchains`:

```
/sbin/ipchains -A output -p tcp -d 0/0 80 -j 0x10
```

Table 15.3 lists the various values and type of services based upon RFC 1349, "Type of Service in the Internet Protocol Suite" (paragraph 4). The Linux implementation also includes the Must Be Zero bit following the four bits assigned to the TOS for a total of five bits. This is likely one of the most common errors and troubleshooting tasks Linux administrators face when integrating a Linux router into an existing network with TOS support.

As another example, ftp, on the other hand, might need more of an emphasis on reliability, so the following `ipchains` command would be more appropriate for ftp.

```
/sbin/ipchains -A output -p tcp -d 0/0 21 -j 0x04
```

In Table 15.3 the mnemonics for the various services also are defined. The mnemonic can be used instead of the hexadecimal. For example, this `ipchains` command is interpreted the same as the preceding command.

```
/sbin/ipchains -A output -p tcp -d 0/0 21 -j Maximize-Reliability
```

Table 15.3 **RFC 1349 TOS Settings**

Mnemonic	Hex Value	Binary Value from RFC 1349	Binary Plus Must Be Zero Bit	Decimal
Normal-Service	0x00	0000	00000	0
Minimize-Cost	0x02	0001	00010	2
Maximize-Reliability	0x04	0010	00100	4
Maximize-Throughput	0x08	0100	01000	8
Minimize-Delay	0x10	1000	10000	16

ipchains also can inspect the TOS bit to determine what the TOS bit should be mapped to by the packet filter. The parameter for matching this is the -m parameter:

```
/sbin/ipchains -A output -p tcp -d 0/0 21 -m 0x00 -j Maximize-Reliability
/sbin/ipchains -A output -p tcp -d 0/0 21 -m 0x02 -j Maximize-Reliability
```

Should an ftp session connect to the Linux node and the TOS bits set to 0000 or 0001 (remember the 0001 + 0 binary must be zero bit.), the TOS will be changed to 0x04. If the TOS bits have a 0x08 or 0x10 value then no change will be made to the packet with these rules.

DIFFSERV

As mentioned, DIFFSERV is one of the IETF's current endeavors to improve quality of service on IP networks—by adding new definition to the interpretation of the TOS bits. The DIFFSERV groundwork has been added to the 2.4 kernel, but the applications to effectively use DIFFSERV are still in development and documentation is very scarce. However, further development of DIFFSERV is likely, (check http://diffserv.sourceforge.net/) so the Linux DIFFSERV is likely the best place to learn of new developments, as well as subscribe to mailing lists covering the Linux implementation of DIFFSERV.

Of course Linux can act as an edge device to a DIFFSERV domain and set the TOS bits according to how the DIFFSERV access router expects to see the bits, which it interprets as DS bits.

Summary

This chapter has covered two very important topics: network analysis and quality of service. It started with several tools for network analysis (NET-SNMP, MRTG, and IPTraf) that should play a very important role in network support and analysis. Network analysis provides a look into the network and helps define what the network performs and what it can likely perform in the future. Providing QoS is currently one of the most challenging aspects of networking requiring both analysis and an understanding of the QoS concepts covered here.

III

Appendixes

Linux Routing Resources

THIS APPENDIX CONTAINS POINTERS TO the many routing resources out there for the Linux administrator. While special care has been taken to choose mostly stable links, do remember that URL's are transient.

Linux Routing Daemons

We've talked about many routing daemons throughout this book, and there are more we didn't have room to cover. Table A.1 contains the most complete list of multi-protocol routing daemons available for Linux users that we could pull together, listed by homepage. The key for this table is

- **y.** Feature is supported in at least one version of this program.
- **n.** Feature is not supported in any version of this program.
- **p.** Support might or might not be implemented yet, but it is currently under development.

As usual, the focus here is specifically on the Internet Protocol (IP).

Table A.1   **Multi-Protocol Linux Routing Daemons and Their Niches**

Name	Homepage	Unicast	Multicast	IPv4	IPv6
bird	http://bird.network.cz/	y	n	y	y
gated	http://www.gated.org/	y	y	y	y
mrtd	http://www.mrtd.net/	y	y	y	y
zebra	http://www.zebra.org/	y	p	y	y

Table A.2 contains the most complete list of single-protocol Linux routing daemons we could pull together.

Table A.2   **Single-Protocol Linux Routing Daemons and Their Niches**

Name	Home	Protocol
mrouted	ftp://parcftp.xerox.com/pub/net-research/ipmulti/	DVMRP
pimd	ftp://catarina.usc.edu/pub/pim/pimd/	PIM-SM
pimd-dense	http://antc.uoregon.edu/PIMDM/pimd-dense.html	PIM-DM
routed	Comes with all major Linux distributions.	RIP-2

Linux Routing and Traffic Management Tools

Network administrators always seem to know yet one more statistic to help determine cost and use efficiency data for network connections, security of data, and more. There is a wealth of networking tools out there for the Linux world. Specifically, this section focuses on tools used in conjunction with routing.

Table A.3 contains a list of programs we thought you might find useful in your search to automate your job as efficiently as possible.

Table A.3   **Linux Tools Used in Conjunction with Routing**

Name	Home	Description
CIPE	http://sites.inka.de/sites/bigred/devel/cipe.html	The Crypto IP Encapsulation (CIPE) project is working on routers that encrypt IP packets for transmission to specific destinations.
Edge Fireplug	http://edge.fireplug.net/	Specialized Linux distribution that turns a machine into essentially a network routing and firewalling appliance.

Name	Home	Description
heartbeat	`http://www.linux-ha.org/download/`	Monitoring tool used for dynamically switching network information according to availability.
IPTraf	`http://cebu.mozcom.com/riker/iptraf/index.html`	IP traffic monitor and statistic generator.
lcrzoex	`http://www.laurentconstantin.com/us/lcrzo/lcrzoex/`	Network testing toolkit.
Linux Router Project	`http://www.linuxrouter.org/`	A Linux micro-distribution that fits on a single floppy, and when booted and configured makes the machine into a router.
MRTG	`http://people.ee.ethz.ch/~oetiker/webtools/mrtg/`	The Multi-Router Grapher (MTRG) accumulates and analyzes data on the fly to show you network performance data.
VisualRoute	`http://www.visualware.com/visualroute/index.html`	Graphically enhanced `traceroute` utility.

Related Resources

Routing is just one piece of the TCP/IP networking puzzle. There are many other aspects that you might or might not be fully comfortable with. Table A.4 lists pointers to resources for many of these networking issues and conundrums.

Table A.4 **Resources for TCP/IP Networking Issues**

Name	Home	Description
IETF Home	`http://www.ietf.org/`	The Internet Engineering Task Force's (IETF) repository for all of its Working Groups and the protocols they are solidifying.
RFC Repository	`http://www.faqs.org/rfcs`	A searchable Request for Comments (RFC) repository.
Stardust	`http://www.stardust.com/`	`Stardust.com` has a series of channels devoted to routing-related technologies, such as multicasting, quality of service, wireless, and IPv6.
Types of DSL	`http://www.efficient.com/tlc/dsltypes.html`	Efficient Networks' breakdown of the various types of Digital Subscriber Lines (DSL) that exist.
USAGI Project	`http://www.linux-ipv6.org/`	Linux IPv6 development news and tools.

Official Reference Documents

There are many reference documents listed throughout this book and many more that never came up in the chapters themselves but are useful for those who are dealing with routing and complex networking in Linux. Table A.5 contains a listing of RFCs and Internet Drafts that you may find useful in your research.

Table A.5 **Official Documents You Might Find Useful**

Document Defines	Location
Assigned Network Numbers	`http://www.landfield.com/rfcs/rfc770.html`
Border Gateway Protocol (BGP)	`http://www.faqs.org/rfcs/rfc1105.html`
Border Gateway Protocol 4 (BGP-4)	`http://www.faqs.org/rfcs/rfc1771.html`
Distance Vector Multicast Routing Protocol (DVMRP)	`http://search.ietf.org/internet-drafts/` `draft-ietf-idmr-dvmrp-v3-10.txt`
Exterior Gateway Protocol (EGP)	`http://www.faqs.org/rfcs/rfc904.html`
Internet Protocol (IP) version 4	`http://www.faqs.org/rfcs/rfc760.html`
Internet Protocol (IP) version 6	`http://www.faqs.org/rfcs/rfc2373.html`
Open Shortest Path First version 2 (OSPF-2)	`http://www.faqs.org/rfcs/rfc1247.html`
Protocol Independent Multicast Sparse Mode (PIM-SM)	`http://www.faqs.org/rfcs/rfc2362.html`
Routing Information Protocol (RIP)	`http://www.faqs.org/rfcs/rfc1058.html`
RIP version 2 (RIP-2)	`http://www.faqs.org/rfcs/rfc1723.html`
Simple Network Management	`http://www.faqs.org/rfcs/rfc1157.html`
Transmission Control Protocol (TCP)	`http://www.faqs.org/rfcs/rfc761.html`

Many of the locations given here are not the only places to view the documents. This is especially true of the RFCs, which are stored in many places throughout the Internet.

B

Linux Hardware Routing Solutions

Not everyone has time to implement a custom routing solution—nor should you have to. This appendix is dedicated to commercial Linux routing solutions. Sure, there are lots of things out there that don't run under Linux, but we're assuming that if you bought this book you want to specifically look at penguin power first. We provide a list of standalone Linux routing solutions, which is followed by a list of cards that can be used in implementing routing.

Inclusion in this chapter does not represent an endorsement by the authors or New Riders Publishing.

Standalone Linux Routers

Instead of commenting on product line items that might come and go, what we've built here is a set of pointers to the companies that currently offer Linux routers-in-a-box. Not all of these companies are in North America as you might notice. Linux is a wonderfully cross-continent phenomenon; please note, however, that we probably missed some companies that didn't have their web sites in languages we could read or at least skim.

These companies offer either Linux-based or Linux-compatible routing hardware:

- `http://www.rocksolidbox.de/`
- `http://www.cyclades.com/`
- `http://www.imagestream-is.com/`
- `http://www.wholelinux.com/`
- `http://www.datapro.net/`
- `http://www.digi.com/`
- `http://www.equinox.com/`
- `http://www.stallion.com/`
- `http://www.eicon.com/`
- `http://www.emacinc.com/`

Routing Cards That Work With Linux

Another area of interest is that of cards you can plug into a Linux box to provide WAN interfaces and, in some cases, provide routing processing. If you have to have a server with multiple functions, this is one way to reduce the load. The routing card could carry its own workload and let the main motherboard handle firewalling and any other tasks that you have that particular box handling.

Vendors that offer routing cards that work with Linux are:

- `http://www.sangoma.com/`
- `http://www.cyclades.com/`
- `http://www.eicon.com/`
- `http://www.stallion.com/`
- `http://www.LanMedia.com/`
- `http://www.gcom.com/`
- `http://www.imagestream-is.com/`
- `http://www.etinc.com/`

Index

N

T

HOW TO CONTACT US

VISIT OUR WEB SITE

W W W . N E W R I D E R S . C O M

On our web site, you'll find information about our other books, authors, tables of contents, and book errata. You will also find information about book registration and how to purchase our books, both domestically and internationally.

EMAIL US

Contact us at: **nrfeedback@newriders.com**

- If you have comments or questions about this book
- To report errors that you have found in this book
- If you have a book proposal to submit or are interested in writing for New Riders
- If you are an expert in a computer topic or technology and are interested in being a technical editor who reviews manuscripts for technical accuracy

Contact us at: **nreducation@newriders.com**

- If you are an instructor from an educational institution who wants to preview New Riders books for classroom use. Email should include your name, title, school, department, address, phone number, office days/hours, text in use, and enrollment, along with your request for desk/examination copies and/or additional information.

Contact us at: **nrmedia@newriders.com**

- If you are a member of the media who is interested in reviewing copies of New Riders books. Send your name, mailing address, and email address, along with the name of the publication or web site you work for.

BULK PURCHASES/CORPORATE SALES

If you are interested in buying 10 or more copies of a title or want to set up an account for your company to purchase directly from the publisher at a substantial discount, contact us at 800-382-3419 or email your contact information to corpsales@pearsontechgroup.com. A sales representative will contact you with more information.

WRITE TO US

New Riders Publishing
201 W. 103rd St.
Indianapolis, IN 46290-1097

CALL/FAX US

Toll-free (800) 571-5840
If outside U.S. (317) 581-3500
Ask for New Riders
FAX: (317) 581-4663

New Riders

W W W . N E W R I D E R S . C O M

VOICES THAT MATTER

ISBN: 0735709408
800 pages
US$39.99

Inside Linux

Michael Tobler

With in-depth coverage of the installation process, editing and typesetting, graphical user interfaces, programming system administration, and managing Internet sites, *Inside Linux* is the only book "smart users" new to Linux will need. This book guides users to a high level of proficiency with all the flavors of Linux, and helps them with crucial system administration tasks.

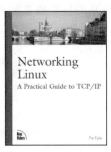

ISBN: 0735710317
400 pages
US$39.99

Networking Linux: A Practical Guide to TCP/IP

Pat Eyler

This book goes beyond the conceptual and shows step-by-step the necessary know-how to Linux TCP/IP implementation. Ideal for programmers and networking administrators in need of a platform-specific guide in order to increase their knowledge and overall efficiency.

ISBN: 073570998X
200 pages
US$34.99

Embedded Linux

John Lombardo

Embedded Linux provides the reader the information needed to design, develop, and debug an embedded Linux appliance. It explores why Linux is a great choice for an embedded application and what to look for when choosing hardware.

ISBN: 0735710430
400 pages
US$45.00

Advanced Linux Programming

CodeSourcery, LLC

An in-depth guide to programming Linux from the most recognized leaders in the Open Source community. This book is the ideal reference for Linux programmers who are reasonably skilled in the C programming language and who are in need of a book that covers the Linux C library (glibc).

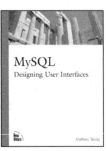

ISBN: 073571049X
656 pages
US$49.99

Linux Firewalls

Robert Ziegler

An Internet-connected Linux machine is in a high-risk situation. This book details security steps that a home or small-to-mid-size, non-enterprise business might take to protect itself from potential remote attackers. As with the first edition, this book will provide a description of the need for security measures and solutions built upon the most up-to-date technology available.

ISBN: 0735710996
640 pages
US$49.99

MySQL: Building User Interfaces

Matthew Stucky

A companion to *MySQL*, this book teaches you to make decisions on how to provide a robust and efficient database solution for any enterprise. The author presents valuable insight from his experience with different companies with varying needs and sizes. This is the only book available that covers GTK+ and database accessibility.

Solutions from experts you know and trust.

www.informit.com

- OPERATING SYSTEMS
- WEB DEVELOPMENT
- PROGRAMMING
- NETWORKING
- CERTIFICATION
- AND MORE...

Expert Access. Free Content.

New Riders has partnered with **InformIT.com** to bring technical information to your desktop. Drawing on New Riders authors and reviewers to provide additional information on topics you're interested in, **InformIT.com** has free, in-depth information you won't find anywhere else.

- **Master the skills you need, when you need them**
- **Call on resources from some of the best minds in the industry**
- **Get answers when you need them, using InformIT's comprehensive library or live experts online**
- **Go above and beyond what you find in New Riders books, extending your knowledge**

As an **InformIT** partner, **New Riders** has shared the wisdom and knowledge of our authors with you online. Visit **InformIT.com** to see what you're missing.

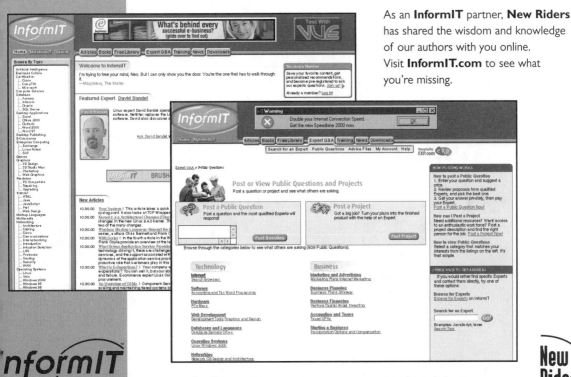

www.informit.com ∎ www.newriders.com

Colophon

The image on the cover of this book is of Snake River, the largest tributary of the Columbia River and one of the most important streams in the Pacific Northwest section of the United States. Snake River rises in the mountains of the Continental Divide near the southeastern corner of Yellowstone National Park in Wyoming and flows south through Jackson Lake along the eastern base of the Teton Range in Grand Teton National Park. Swinging northwest near the mouth of Greys River, it enters Idaho through the Palisades Reservoir. Near Heise the river leaves the mountains and crosses the broad Snake River Plain of southern Idaho, an area covered by lava beds. On the western edge of the state, it is joined by the Boise River. Turning north, it forms the Oregon–Idaho boundary for 216 miles (348 km). From the northeastern corner of Oregon it forms the Washington-Idaho boundary to Lewiston, Idaho, and then turns west to join the Columbia just south of Pasco, Washington, after a course of 1,040 miles (1,670 km). Runoff from the states of Wyoming, Utah, Nevada, Idaho, Oregon, and Washington combines in the Snake, which has a drainage basin of 109,000 square miles (282,000 square km). From elevations of 10,000 feet (3,000 m), the river descends to 300 feet (90 m). Information taken from www.britannica.com.

This book was written and edited in both Microsoft Word and XML/DocBook. The XML from DocBook was exported to Rich Text Format using the Jade style sheet and then imported into Word. It was laid out in QuarkXpress. The fonts used in the body text are Bembo and MCPdigital. It was printed on 50# Husky Offset Smooth paper VonHoffmann Graphics in Owensville, MO. Prepress consisted of PostScript computer-to-plate technology (filmless process). The cover was printed at Moore Langen Printing in Terre Haute, Indiana, on 12pt, coated on one side.